*The Sex Slave in Cinema*

# *The Sex Slave in Cinema*

## An Inegalitarian Spectacle

*Aga Skrodzka*

EDINBURGH
University Press

Edinburgh University Press is one of the leading university presses in the UK. We publish academic books and journals in our selected subject areas across the humanities and social sciences, combining cutting-edge scholarship with high editorial and production values to produce academic works of lasting importance. For more information visit our website: edinburghuniversitypress.com



Grateful acknowledgement is made to the sources listed in the List of Illustrations for permission to reproduce material previously published elsewhere. Every effort has been made to trace the copyright holders, but if any have been inadvertently overlooked, the publisher will be pleased to make the necessary arrangements at the first opportunity.

Edinburgh University Press Ltd
13 Infirmary Street
Edinburgh EH1 1LT

First published in hardback by Edinburgh University Press 2024

Typeset in Garamond MT Pro by
Cheshire Typesetting Ltd, Cuddington, Cheshire
and printed and bound by CPI Group (UK) Ltd,
Croydon, CR0 4YY

A CIP record for this book is available from the British Library

ISBN 978 1 3995 0824 7 (hardback)
ISBN 978 1 3995 0825 4 (paperback)
ISBN 978 1 3995 0826 1 (webready PDF)
ISBN 978 1 3995 0827 8 (epub)

# *Contents*

# *Figures*

# *Acknowledgments*

This book owes its life to a community whose energy sustained me in the solitary task of writing.

First, I would like to thank the anonymous reviewers for their generous suggestions, which motivated me to expand my research, refine my ideas and revise my arguments. Their thoughtful critique has made this work immeasurably better.

My deep gratitude goes to the colleagues who, in various ways and at different stages of development, have engaged with my project: Kasia Marciniak, Kette Thomas, Terri Ginsberg, Kati Beck, Gabi Stoicea, Áine O'Healy, Dave Blakesley, Kim Manganelli, Joe Mai, James Burns, Sarah Cooper, Kaifa Roland, Luca Barattoni, John Smith, Cynthia Haynes, Keri Crist-Wagner, Arelis Moore, April Ayers Lawson, Emily Boyter Hager and Maziyar Faridi. The interim chair of the Department of Interdisciplinary Studies, Cameron Fae Bushnell, and the exceptional dean of the College of Arts and Humanities, Nicholas Vazsonyi, have provided a wonderful working environment.

The project benefited from the kind friendship of philosopher and artist Christopher Grau, who also provided me with access to rare texts and media, critical to the completion of this book. The intrepid librarian Camille Cooper was always there to open the real and symbolic archival gates, so that I could obtain the research materials essential to my progress. I extend much gratitude to my friend Shelly Rae Congdon for her expert help with preparing my illustrations for publication in this book and all my other published work.

At various stages of the book's gestation, I benefited from vital institutional support provided by Clemson University in the form of the Clemson University SEED Grant and the Faculty Research Development Program sponsored by the College of Arts and Humanities. A Fulbright Scholar Fellowship allowed me to travel to Poland in 2019 to carry out contextual field research. While hosted by the Institute of Polish Culture at the University of Warsaw, I met Iwona Kurz, Paulina Kwiatkowska, Magda Szcześniak, Wojciech Michera and Łukasz Zaremba, whose vibrant collegiality will never be forgotten.

Over the many years that it took to develop this book, I learned with my students whose honest and always enthusiastic feedback shaped the direction of my research. Students enrolled in the 2011 graduate seminar titled 'Bodies in Transit: Transnational Theory and Practice' provided me with early critique and taught me the importance of listening closely to conspiracy theories and social media debates. Graduate students Sophia Basaldua-Sun, Aparna Shastri, John David Hunter, Ashlyn Walden, Jessie Reynolds-Clay, Galen Faison and Holland Turner have been there for the ups and downs of this journey. The amazing focus and perseverance in their own intellectual endeavors have inspired me at those times when I most needed inspiration. I also extend my thanks to Cal Schaafsma, my research assistant, who organized my research findings into a scrupulously annotated bibliography.

During the laborious process of composing the manuscript, my friends Joanna Borchert-Kopczuk, Janetta Sidoruk, Julie Meredith, Andreea Mihalache, Tomasz Basiuk, Marcin Lakomski, Anna Banaszkiewicz and Renata Wilczek Sawyer sustained my intellectual work with conversation, emotional support and much good humor. Adriana Isaza kept my world organized and Tim Walker, my infusion nurse, made sure that it did not fall apart. A special thanks goes to poet, performance artist and sister-in-wigs Cyborg Jillian Weise, whose creative force continues to enrich my life and work.

I owe sincere thanks to Jaimie Johansson, who has been my most discerning reader and kindest editor. Jaimie, without your intellectual comradery and our Friday afternoon companionship this book might never have been finished. You are the nurse and the doctor.

I am also indebted to my editors at Edinburgh University Press, Gillian Leslie, Kelly O'Brien and Sam Johnson, who offered continuous words of encouragement and careful editorial and professional guidance. I am enormously grateful for your patience and trust in my work.

My family, especially Jeff and Oskar, have carried me (sometimes literally) through the most trying parts of writing this book. You both rock my world and you do it with so much style!

Portions of Chapters 2 and 4 as well as the Epilogue have previously appeared as parts of the following publications: 'Disempowering Knowledge: How to Teach Not to Help' (in *Teaching Transnational Cinema: Politics and Pedagogy*, eds. Katarzyna Marciniak and Bruce Bennett, New York and London: Routledge, 2016, pp. 236–54); 'Xenophilic Spectacle in Recent Films About Sex Slavery' (in *Transnational Cinemas*, 9:1, 2018, pp. 85–103); and 'Dubai-Gate and the Libidinal Operations of Nation-Making in *Girls from Dubai*' (in *Journal of Contemporary Iraq and the Arab World*, Special Issue: 'Interventions in Film Studies', 18:1, 2024, pp. 47–58).

# *Preface*

When the film *Sound of Freedom* (Dir. Alejandro Gómez Monteverde) hit the theaters in the summer of 2023, I had been researching the recrudescent popularity of the sex slave narrative in cinema for twelve years. Monteverde's film amassed an astonishing $250 million at the box office in record time. The success of yet another anti-trafficking film that pitched the idea of the escalating global sex slavery crisis, this time with much righteous indignation, in many ways confirmed my sense that the story was not fading away. Audiences were still hooked, despite the post-millennium saturation of popular culture with exposés, books, films, art exhibits, documentaries and TV series on the subject. Since the early 2000s, a wave of scholarship has challenged the dominant sex slavery discourse (and the attendant new abolitionist movement) as a gross over-simplification of the complex reality of labor and crisis migration in the era of late capitalism.[1] This academic critique has had little impact on the film industry's long-standing investment driven by continued market demand. The audiences' viral (and zealous) enthusiasm for *Sound of Freedom* validated my suspicion that the over-determined sex slavery narrative still serves a role in our collective psychic life. My impulse to describe and understand this role is at the heart of this book.

Its visual excess, prurient tropes and hyper-inflammatory rhetoric notwithstanding, the sex slavery story touches on – so as not to critically engage – some of the most daunting challenges of our time, many of them related to cross-border mobility, migration, precarious labor and perpetual war. Importantly, this rhetoric also proposes a relatively easy solution to those challenges. It is a story of rescue, return and reparation. It kindles our benevolent impulses as it spins a yarn of selfless humans sacrificing themselves to save the weak and the vulnerable, thus contributing to what Jo Littler has recognized as our milieu's 'sanctified, quasi-religious realm of altruism and charity'.[2] In this story, powerful heroes defend forlorn women and children from nasty criminals. Expediently, the criminals prove to be poorly organized and easy to outwit. They are hyper-visible in their ethnic appearance and foreign inflection, thus easy to track down and defuse. As such, they are comforting phantasms that act as substitutes for the actual villains of our time – the kleptocratic economic and political forces that are responsible for the displacement and degradation of human life on a massive scale.[3] The sex slavery story delivers its salutary promise of setting things right, precisely by filtering out the real villains. A technology that has the ability to insidiously embed sanctioned fantasies into our psychic worlds and ratify those fantasies as real, cinema has participated in constructing and sustaining the hopeful, yet hopelessly naïve, vision of sex trafficking and trade. Films that stage the spectacle of sex slavery offer up simulacra of both 'distant suffering' and 'altruistic action', which Luc Boltanski has identified as instrumental to the (neo)liberal subject's search for authenticity.[4] This volume gathers my research on cinema's lucrative contribution to the audiences' continued seduction by the sex slavery narrative.

The archive for my analysis spans the life of cinema as a medium. However, it is by no means exhaustive. Indeed, my specialized academic training and limited language expertise have greatly restricted the research scope to films produced largely in the West. I begin by looking at early cinema (Austrian, Danish and US) and its silent spectacles of Oriental slave markets and 'white slavery' dens to draw the reader's attention to the fact that the sex slavery narrative was one of the first stories that cinema proffered. Its undue influence on the new medium has imprinted our modern ways of seeing with a set of gendered, classed and racialized conventions. On the pages of *The Sex Slave in Cinema: An Inegalitarian Spectacle*, I consider an assortment of genres and subgenres that, to various degrees of explicitness, have manufactured the sex slave figure, including stag films, pornography, 'slavers', slavesploitation, blaxploitation and the recent outpouring of the social problem films that address sex trafficking and trade. My inquiry into cinema's deployment of the sex slavery narrative brings into dialogue films from different countries, various historical periods and disparate stylistic and rhetorical registers. Together, I read this archive as a constellation of the Western imaginary that underpins and nourishes the (neo)colonial, disciplinary border of the nation-state. An institution whose power to protect the subjects within its borders has been compromised by the transnational agencies protecting the rapid and unimpeded flow of capital, the nation-state has been recruited to control, and often to block, the flow of people in the interest of the global financial order. Various and frequently changing logics of gatekeeping have been implemented to moderate the flow. According to these logics, the security of the border is always already threatened by some form of 'illegal' mobility of the foreign Other. The sex slave is one of the most emblematic figures to embody and center, often in convoluted and continually displacing ways, the collective anxiety about the real and imagined transgressions that threaten the wished-for integrity and coherence of the nation-state, a concept whose enduring and largely unquestioned rationale has long structured the modern social contract. Arguably, this contract has now been contested by a number of actors and social formations who question its racist and gendered foundations, steeped in the Eurocentric ideals of the Enlightenment and largely funded by the colonial exploitation of non-European peoples and their lands.[5]

Because of its role in upholding another fabled and affectively charged concept – the sovereign, (neo)liberal, patriarchal subject – the sex slave projection deserves our scrupulous attention. The hyperbolic, often graphic, and always melodramatic strokes with which the sex slave narrative is cinematically rendered speak of the urgency and fear that permeates the public sense of the impending paradigm shift as new waves of mass migrations and rapid changes to the global world order quickly unsettle the cozy system of white supremacy that the Global North/West secured and solidified for its populations during the eras of Old and New Imperialism. As a cipher of illiberal and inegalitarian impulses, atavistic and horrifying in its constitution, yet somehow also quaint, the sex slave figure discloses the limits and simplifications involved in the (neo)liberal definition of freedom. By imagining the sex slave as the legible exemplar of unfreedom in today's society and by proposing to 'rescue', thus eliminate, the sex slave, the new abolitionist movement (along with the neoliberal state and its administrative and security systems) perpetuates the antiquated belief in a universal 'nobility' and 'moral goodness' of men. At the same time, this movement occludes the fact that 'men' have not been created equal during the rise of modern society as defined by the capitalist land, wealth and resource accumulation in the hands of the few, leading the dispossessed (the vagabonds, the migrants, the refugees and other subaltern classes) to wander in search of safety and sustenance, substantially curtailing their access to such rights *cum* privileges as self-determination and civil liberties. Notably, the liberal ideals of freedom and equality, still at the center of most constitutions of modern nation-states, have been formulated as critique of a select few institutions of dispossession, such as serfdom and chattel slavery. While those forms of dispossession and physical containment are extreme states of unfreedom and in obvious ways diminish the sovereignty of the human – indeed, they produce humans as commodities and tools – they do not describe very well the conditions of the contemporary dispossessed. The outdated definitions of freedom that undergird (neo) liberalism, thus, fail to consider the masses of the displaced whose freedom is restrained despite their apparent (yet, always already deeply compromised) ability to move and to issue consent.

While chattel-like slavery still occurs despite the now universal ban on all forms of slavery across the globe, the millions of what the new abolitionists call the 'modern-day slaves' are not chattel slaves. As Julia O'Connell Davidson has accounted, today about 1.6 million people (in countries such as Niger, Sudan and Mauritania) live within a socially (and illegally) constructed state that strongly resembles chattel slavery. The remaining 34 million or so people that the new abolitionists (working through NGOs such as Walk Free or Anti-Slavery International) identify as 'modern-day slaves', so O'Connell Davidson has argued, are people subjected to various forms of bonded, forced, coerced and semi-coerced exploitation (such as child labor, sex trafficking, forced labor, forced marriage and the like) enabled by various phenomena, economically, culturally, politically and socially determined. These states of exploitation may resemble chattel slavery in certain respects but are not identical to it, and if they are to be alleviated, they require acts of structural reform and not acts of heroic altruism. In fact, O'Connell Davidson has warned against collapsing the difference between the historical experience of chattel slaves and the contemporary experiences of exploitation as this rhetorical gesture discloses 'the staggering disregard for the history of race as a system of domination, and for the afterlife of racial slavery'.[6] This rhetorical conflation also forecloses any future structural solutions by misconstruing the nature and root causes of modern forms of exploitation.

The numbers of so-called 'modern slaves' continue to rise as different NGOs adjust their preferred estimation algorithms by adding new categories of precarity to their definitions of modern slavery. Walk Free uses its own metric called the Global Slavery Index and cites an estimated 50 million people living in slavery in 2024, a substantial increase from the number of 36 million counted by the same agency in 2014.[7] While these numbers are quickly climbing, showing the capaciousness of the humanitarian 'modern-day slavery' rubric, in cinema's production of modern slavery discourse it is persistently one category of slave that continues to dominate the screen: the sex slave. The sex slave has become the 'face' of modern slavery as its most affectively charged and most rhetorically usable construct. The symbolic distillation that cinema performs around the foregrounded sex slave figure stands in stark contrast to the elastic definition of modern slavery and begs the question why this trope of extreme sexual exploitation has become the emblematic unfreedom of the modern age. Is it that the question of sexual and reproductive freedom has somehow become central to our modern conceptualization of personhood and citizenship? Or is it simply that the sex slave figure is supremely spectacular and thus commercially viable as it yields itself to cinematic exploitation (and all forms of mediation) more than all those other, more mundane, forms of labor/resource exploitation ever could?

*The Sex Slave in Cinema: An Inegalitarian Spectacle* attempts to follow these two lines of inquiry, paying attention to cinema's unique participation in the capitalist enterprise and its capacity to mold discursive surfaces and affective infrastructures. While the answers that the book offers are nowhere near conclusive, I do wish to propose that we understand the sex slave figure as both means of producing capital – as cinema's perennial, commercially attractive spectacle – and as a mechanism of the symbolic production of the (neo)liberal subject, whose privileged existence provides the continued rationale for maintaining the social system where accumulation of capital in the hands of specifically gendered and racialized elites becomes the existential goal. One might say that the (neo)liberal subject, imagined as supremely free and utterly emancipated from any and all forms of regulation and dependency, is articulated primarily as one who is *not* a slave. But, in an era of unprecedented demographic transformation of the world – caused by new patterns of migration, mortality and fertility, all of which impact the structure and distribution of various populations across space and, thus, threaten the existing world order – it would be more appropriate to see the (neo)liberal subject as arising from a more specific distinction, a distinction that defines this subject as one who possesses a set of unchallenged reproductive and sexual rights, and maybe even hegemony over the distribution of those rights for others. In our biopolitical moment, the sexual is political. The biopolitical warfare has become a symptom of the demographically challenged nation-state. In this landscape, the (neo)liberal subject comes into being most emphatically as the obverse of not just a slave, but as the obverse of the sex slave – an entity whose reproductive and sexual freedoms have been revoked and whose potential presents itself as pure bio-resource. Arguably, today, the neoliberal subject manufactures his subjectivity as a form of biopolitical self-determination, but also as a form of biopower that guides his humanitarian concern and control over the lives of others and, more generally, over the instrumentalized life itself. Giorgio Agamben has famously defined this usable life as 'bare life',[8] and Anca Parvulescu has linked it to migrant women as reproductive, affective and sexual resource.[9]

As an instrument that consistently generates capital within the media industry while simultaneously producing the symbolic value that justifies capital accumulation as a facet of the (neo)liberal conception of freedom, the sex slave figure offers the kind of 'usability' that Katarzyna Marciniak has theorized in her work on cinema's discursive colonization of the foreign and the migrant.[10] The sex slave figure is used in the visual commons to articulate and consolidate a highly idealized self-projection of the late capitalist society. In the process of such consolidation, this figure serves a focalizing function in defining the (neo)liberal subject through key human rights concepts: liberty, equality, freedom, justice, mobility, charity, love, life and death, among others. Tracing cinema's history of this instrumentalization (its mediation of sexual enslavement and emancipation), through its various generic and stylistic iterations, may help us understand the visual construction of the (neo)liberal subject as embedded in, and arising from, the processes of capital production and accumulation, especially within the increasingly ascendant realms of information technologies and media industries.

Here, I would like to emphasize that my critique of the sex slave figure as a cinematic trope is in no way a denial of various forms of deeply ingrained, always intensely gendered, sexual violence experienced by vulnerable populations including the members of the LGBTQ+ communities, people of color, migrants, refugees, persons with disabilities, war prisoners, prison and detention center inmates, sex workers, children under all forms of foster care, and more. While these instances of sexual violence are sometimes taken up by filmmakers, they hardly ever generate much box office revenue, and they are mainly explored in independent documentary and activist productions that carefully avoid spectacularization.[11] The sex slavery films, by contrast, are produced as narrative features for commercial mass distribution. Because of their heavy reliance on spectacle, recurring iconography and a populist message, all of which drive up their commercial value and popular appeal, we can hardly find in them a transparent and direct exploration of the causes and consequences of systemic sexual violence. This is further complicated by the fact that these films often reproduce sexual violence on affective and epistemic levels, potentially manufacturing sexually violent ways of looking. The analytical work undertaken in this book is based on my conviction that there is much to be gained from investigating sex slavery films as a mediated, symbolic refraction of actual socio-economic phenomena. I hope that by carefully unpacking this refraction, or what Judith Butler has theorized as the 'interpretive maneuver' of visual framing, my study may help us to understand how the sex slavery narrative effectively occludes what it proposes to reveal: the horror of sexual exploitation of women and children.[12]

Indeed, it was the occluded story of the migrant children and adults who, every day, make the perilous journey across the US-Mexico border that I kept thinking about when watching *Sound of Freedom*, a film focused on a saint-like protagonist, a US Homeland Security agent, who embarks on an action-packed mission across South America to find two sex-trafficked children and bring them back to the safety of their original home in Honduras. The trajectory of cross-border movement depicted in the film proceeds in the opposite direction of the migrant routes that have recently led masses of refugees from South America (including Honduras) to North America. By emphasizing this trajectory, *Sound of Freedom* manufactures an ostensibly emancipatory narrative where the border-crossing children are rescued by an employee of the US government from the state of precarious mobility, which, so the film implies, can only lead to the sexual enslavement of minors, and then returned to their country of origin. The Honduran parent is taught a lesson about the dire consequences of aspiring for economic mobility, the US rescuer is extolled as an effective agent of global security and moral justice, and the audiences are offered a heartening tale where good prevails over evil.

Most importantly, the trafficked children can play again. The titular sound of freedom is the sound of children playing. This sound is championed by the film as the only appropriate sound of a child's activity – an implied critique of the sounds that underprivileged children may emit as they work, struggle, or migrate. The plot of the film is motivated by the sex traffickers' violent disruption of a child's play, enabled by the negligent care of the single parent and his or her economic deficiency. The diegetic action is then mobilized around restoring the Honduran child's right to play. This right, as the film suggests, is something that can only be secured by the impassioned and utterly selfless agent of US paternalism, who is aided by God ('God's children are not for sale', declares the protagonist) and global capital (the elaborate sting operation is funded by a private international entrepreneur after the Department of Homeland Security withdraws its support for what becomes the agent's 'passion project'). Importantly, the protagonist can cross all international borders unconstrained and brazenly penetrate the remote FARC militia stronghold, hidden in the thick of the Colombian Amazonía region, dressed as a *Médecins Sans Frontières* doctor. The swift and effortless execution of his rescue mission speaks of cinema's ability to occlude labor, both the labor of cinema's own apparatus and the labor of the showman. Writing about cinema's origins in stage magic, Tom Gunning has observed how, in their pursuit of 'the pure play of sensation,' both magic tricks and cinema operate 'like commodity capitalism through an occluding of labor'.[13] In addition to the standard occlusions of labor made possible by continuity editing (also known as 'invisible editing'), films like *Sound of Freedom* use the sex slavery frame to occlude the labor of migrant sex workers by summoning a gruesome, yet spectacular vision of commercial sex that entails total subjugation and violence. When 'work' is occluded and 'slavery' is used in its place, those who perform sex work are not only epistemically voided, but also criminalized as victims who are to be eliminated by rescue. For undocumented migrant sex workers, the rescue often means deportation or detention.

Since I first viewed *Sound of Freedom*, a film advertised by its producers as a Christian thriller, my reception of the film's deeply troubling politics has become even more attuned to contemporary US politics as I learned about the source material for the story and the real-life inspiration behind the film's protagonist. Based on the life and work of Tim Ballard, the founder of Operation Underground Railroad (OUR), a large anti-sex trafficking non-profit organization and a key player in the US new abolitionist movement, the film has gotten mired in numerous controversies.[14] A quick overview of the news headlines discloses OUR's, Ballard's and Jim Caviezel's (Caviezel plays Ballard in *Sound of Freedom*) associations with QAnon, a far-right American conspiracy movement, which spawned online in 2017 with claims describing organized groups of high-profile US Democrats as members of an international Satanic child sex-trafficking cabal.[15] There is also a growing controversy stemming from Ballard's own sexual misconduct scandals that erupted since the film's release and precipitated Ballard's subsequent resignation from his leadership role at OUR.[16] The scandals involve a series of lawsuits filed by women who have worked with Ballard within OUR, and who claim to have been sexually abused by him during the training sessions and the 'rescue' missions carried out throughout South America. Additionally, Kely Johana Suárez Moya, a Columbian woman who inspired one of the film's supporting characters, has filed a lawsuit against the film's producers, citing misrepresentation of her character in the film, attesting also to the confabulated nature of the child-trafficking situation featured in the film's sting operation scene, which takes place during a 'pedophile party' on Isla de Barú, Colombia.[17] While the judgments in some of the trials are still pending, Ballard's non-profit organization has emphatically distanced itself from its original founder. In the aftermath of Ballard's public fall from grace, which revealed an NGO with a history of dubious 'rescue' practices that apparently routinely exposed minors abroad to re-traumatization and further abuse, Monteverde's film, which takes a heavily hagiographic approach to its portrait of Ballard, cannot be taken seriously as a report from the field. Yet, I propose that we take the film seriously as a means of the kind of dangerous evangelism that consecrates certain lives while instrumentalizing others.

The evangelism of *Sound of Freedom* is indisputably apparent. It is fueled by phobic beliefs and a self-aggrandizing mythology of American exceptionalism that champions the United States as a nation playing a 'special role' in human history.[18] The Honduran children, Miguel and Rocio, become useful tools in Ballard's missionary intervention in South America, where the practice of child sexual enslavement, the film suggests, continues to be carried out because the Honduran parents, the government and society at large are complicit in the exploitation of children. Marciniak has recognized this instrumentalization as the 'selective approval of certain foreign bodies' that some anti-immigrant and anti-refugee movements implement in their otherwise xenophobic initiatives. The 'approved' foreign bodies of the sex slaves are used to consolidate the divine interventionist mandate of the white heteronormative patriarchal subject – the new abolitionist warrior, while other foreign bodies are allowed to undergo what Marciniak has dubbed 'selective dumping', which can be best understood as an epistemic dismissal that leads to institutional neglect, and in extreme cases to social death.[19] A good example of the latter are the thousands of undocumented child migrants languishing in the US-Mexico border detention centers, where all forms of abuse, including sexual abuse, affect them on a daily basis, without much attention paid by organizations such as OUR. While proclaiming the prevention of child endangerment as their *cause célèbre*, many organizations use the rhetoric of modern slavery to draw a distinct line between 'slaves' (also referred to as 'trafficked victims') and 'illegal migrants' in their decisions to afford humanitarian assistance to those who pass the elusive test of victimhood.[20] Within the US commons, the much publicized and frequently applauded efforts to return child 'sex slaves' to their parents abroad, with the expressed intention of reuniting their families, co-exist, side by side, with the government's enforcement of the 'zero tolerance' policy, issued by the US Department of Homeland Security in April 2018, which led to the separation of thousands of migrant children from their parents at the US-Mexico border.[21] In this context, *Sound of Freedom* reads like a compensatory tale that produces the visual 'evidence' for the existence of the category 'sex slave', which epistemically undermines and empties out the endangerment of the person categorized as 'migrant', leading to a myopic and heavily displaced vision of cross-border mobility. Along with other films discussed in this book, Monteverde's film contributes to cinema's depository of iterative and recursive re-enactments of the sex slavery story that over time build an affective infrastructure, which props up a world where modern injustices that arise from migrant mobility may only be seen within a very narrow spectrum, optically and rhetorically circumscribed to the phantom of the sex slave.

## OVERVIEW

*The Sex Slave in Cinema: An Inegalitarian Spectacle* presents cinema as a cultural venue that constructs and disseminates the sex slave figure on a visual plane. The book explores how narrative cinema – a medium steeped in a long tradition of erotic commodification – contributes to the promulgation of the simplified vision of sex work and sex trade, through the captivating image of the sex slave. Based in formal and cultural analysis, the book defines the key tropes of the sex slave iconography and shows how these tropes, along with the well-established sexploitation strategies, lead to a symbolic containment of female sexual agency. Arguably, this containment carried out on the level of cinematic monstration shapes the realm of the visual commons and, with it, a woman's right to visual citizenship. Consequently, the sex slave figure, materialized on screen in a highly charged spectacle, influences our understanding of a woman's right to sex work and agency over her body. This book's analyses of individual films are carried out in the light of cinema's continued investment in the scopophilic exploitation of the female form and cinema's reliance on gendered voyeurism and fetishism, alongside the film industry's recently publicized record of sexual abuse. The affective and libidinal investments activated in the sex slave films are traced back to the medium's birth in the low-brow variety show and the burlesque.

Chapter 1, 'Early Cinema, Erotic Spectacle and Sex Slavery', provides the archaeology of the figure of the sex slave, tracing it to the nineteenth century, where it emerges from the Orientalist fantasies circulating in the public sphere across Europe and the United States. Early cinema is then explored as a medium that contributed to the Orientalist visual discourse, which was first developed in painting and photography. This chapter initiates a key inquiry of the book by examining how early cinema linked sexual monstration with the securitization of the female figure on-screen. The chapter examines how the fetishistic framework established in the early pornographic and 'white slavery' films furnishes the pretense not only for erotic display, but also (and not unrelatedly) for restricting the movement of women and migrants to reinforce the racial dynamics of white supremacy, established during the colonial era. The early history of cinema reviewed in this section is shown to have material and cultural effects that persist to the present day. The following chapters trace early cinema's conventions of looking at and showing the female as sex slave in contemporary cinematic representations of sex trafficking and trade. The extent to which the sex slave figure is spectacularized is determined by the racial and gender politics of the films themselves – this leads into Chapter 2, which observes how the spectacularization of the sex slave is disciplinary.

In Chapter 2, 'Sifting through Images: Sex Slave Iconography', I explore how, when viewed collectively, the films under analysis disclose a shared iconography that contributes a set of shorthand visual cues that shape and affix the sanctioned imaginary of the sex trade and trafficking as a spectacle of sex slavery. A number of arresting and monstrative visual tropes – such as the soiled mattress, the chains and the dungeon – combined with a series of emblematic scenes – including the kidnapping, the rape, the selection, the sale and the rescue – contribute to the hyper-visibility constructed by cinema, which ultimately leads to a narrow and repetitive focalization of the issue of commercial sexual exploitation as a simplistic scenario of abduction and physical captivity, ostensibly carried out by foreign organized crime units, and not a function of labor and income disparities engendered by an oligarchic extractive economy, for which the Global North/West is largely responsible.

Broadly, this chapter triangulates three key elements: commodification, social discipline and securitization.

Chapters 3 and 4 explicitly address the role of race and racialization in films that engage the sex slavery narrative. The figure of the sex slave in commercial cinema is overwhelmingly white, emerging as it did from the encounters between the 'white slavery' panics of the nineteenth century and the cinema of attractions. However, this is not the only cinematic perspective on the sex slave. Chapter 3, 'Converging Slaves: The Case of Blaxploitation', offers an account of the sex slave figure in blaxploitation cinema, a subgenre of the exploitation film that reached the height of its popularity in the 1970s, but which continues to influence contemporary filmmakers such as Quentin Tarantino. I argue that blaxploitation films such as *Django Unchained* (Dir. Quentin Tarantino, 2010), *Slaves* (Dir. Herbert J. Biberman, 1969) and *Mandingo* (Dir. Richard Fleischer, 1975) deliberately reframe the sexual and racial politics of the sex slavery 'plot', often by explicitly addressing the history of sexual exploitation under chattel slavery. While blaxploitation films depict scenes of spectacularized sexual violence and therefore partake in the commodification of the sex slave figure, the politics of these films significantly differs from those that drive narratives of the white sex slave. In these films, the narratives of violence against Black women become narratives of radicalization. Here, women's bodies are mobilized in a different way, toward revenge rather than compliance. The chapter engages with Black feminist thought to explore the problematic aspects of the blaxploitation spectacle, but also to illuminate how this controversial genre invited audiences to draw parallels between the politics of the plantation and the white supremacy that characterized the United States in the 1960s and 1970s.

Chapter 4, 'White Slave: The Commodification and Securitization of Whiteness', opens with a brief discussion of the recent social media sex trafficking panics and proceeds to offer a close reading of a number of commercial mainstream films that engage the sex slavery narrative to manufacture what I call 'imperiled female whiteness' as an instrument of discursive and symbolic securitization closely aligned with the racial politics of the neoliberal nation-state. Here, I draw the reader's attention to a very different pattern of racial motivation that undergirds the white sex slave figure: to re-entrench a chauvinistic understanding of the border, race, female body, gender and sexuality – and, crucially, to maintain white supremacy. In these films, women's proximity to First World whiteness determines the narrative stakes and outcome of the film. Whiteness is both a commodity to be bought, sold and, importantly, reproduced, to maintain the global *status quo*.

This book's epilogue, 'Imagining away Sex Slavery, towards a Counter-Narrative', focuses on a single film, *Bibliothèque Pascal* (Dir. Szabolcs Hajdu,

2010), which offers a counter-narrative to the disciplinary framing that overwhelms the sex slavery film corpus. Hajdu's striking film foregrounds the acts of narrativization and visual representation as integral to the experience of migrant sex work. Indeed, this film can be said to 'untell' the official story (sanctioned by the recognizable icons discussed in Chapter 2) of sex slavery. Engaging in formal experimentation, the film frames its narrative as an interview between a former sex worker and a social worker, a brilliant device that establishes the antagonism between the sex worker's testimony and the social worker's pathologizing conception of sex trafficking. By dramatizing the sex worker's role as the rightful narrator of her own experience of labor exploitation, the film returns agency to her and exposes the power dynamic inherent in the epistemic processing of migrant sex work by the institutions of the neoliberal security state. Through a surprising application of magic realism, Hajdu engages a playful element in an effort to de-pathologize sex work migration and to highlight the paramount value of epistemic justice in the lived migrant experience. The epilogue considers the meta-narrative impetus of *Bibliothèque Pascal* to be an effective confrontation of the phobic and morality policing of sex work. By foregrounding its own representational self-awareness, Hajdu's film comments on cinema's complicity in manufacturing the disciplinary optics used in the operations of policing.

My hope is that this book unveils how cinematic representation sets the parameters and symbolic vocabulary through which the public learns about sex trafficking and trade, and even prescribes the terms of public policy. Throughout my analysis, I explore the stakes involved in the aesthetic and narratorial choices made to illustrate the complex phenomena behind illegal sex commerce as a spectacle of slavery. It is through the process of mediated repetition, quotation and rhetorical co-optation that the cinematic construct helps to materialize the phenomenon of sex slavery as hetero-gender violence and a human rights violation. The spectacularized image of the sex slave, however, has its after-image – an impression that persists beyond the hypervisible spectacle. This after-image is the figure of the migrant claiming a right to citizenship and confronting the national body as defined by the intensely gendered laws of inheritance, property and propriety.

## Notes

1. For examples of such scholarship, see Jo Doezema, *Sex Slaves and Discourse Masters* (London: Zed, 2010); Julia O'Connell Davidson, *Modern Slavery: The Margins of Freedom* (New York: Palgrave Macmillan, 2015); Laura Agustín, *Sex at the Margins* (London: Zed, 2007); Juno Mac and Molly Smith, *Revolting Prostitutes: The Fight for Sex Workers' Rights* (London and New York: Verso, 2018); Julietta Hua, *Trafficking*

*Women's Human Rights* (Minneapolis and London: University of Minnesota Press, 2011); Anna M. Agathangelou, *The Global Political Economy of Sex: Desire, Violence, and Insecurity in Mediterranean Nation States* (New York: Palgrave Macmillan, 2004); Paul Amar, *The Security Archipelago: Human-Security States, Sexuality Politics, and the End of Neoliberalism* (Durham and London: Duke University Press, 2013); Elizabeth Bernstein, 'The Sexual Politics of the "New Abolitionism"', *differences: A Journal of Feminist Cultural Studies*, 18:3, 2007, pp. 144–51.

2. Jo Littler, '"I Feel Your Pain": Cosmopolitan Charity and the Public Fashioning of the Celebrity Soul', *Social Semiotics*, 18:2, 2008, p. 239 (pp. 237–351 inclusive).
3. For a comprehensive analysis of kleptocratic capitalism, see Anne Applebaum's testimony to the US Senate Foreign Relations Committee, excerpted in 'America needs a Better Plan to Fight Autocracy', *The Atlantic,* 15 March 2022, www.theatlantic.com/ideas/archive/2022/03/russia-ukraine-senate-testimony-autocracy-kleptocrats/627061/ (accessed 17 May 2024).
4. Luc Boltanski, *Distant Suffering: Morality, Media and Politics* (Cambridge: Cambridge University Press, 1999), p. xiv.
5. Here I refer to movements like 'No One is Illegal' and the proponents of open borders and free migration as well as border advocacy groups.
6. O'Connell Davidson, *Modern Slavery*, pp. 22–23.
7. Walk Free, 'Global Slavery Index', www.walkfree.org/global-slavery-index/ (accessed 13 May 2024).
8. Giorgio Agamben, *Homo Sacer: Sovereign Power and Bare Life* (Palo Alto: Stanford University Press, 2005).
9. Anca Parvulescu, *The Traffic in Women's Work: East European Migration and the Making of Europe* (Chicago and London: The University of Chicago Press, 2014), pp. 69–93.
10. Katarzyna Marciniak, 'Aporias of Foreignness: Transnational Encounters through Cinema', in Gavin Rae and Emma Ingala (eds), *Subjectivity and the Political: Contemporary Perspectives* (New York: Routledge, 2017), pp. 91–109.
11. For some examples of these filmmaking approaches, see *Calling the Ghosts* (Dirs Mandy Jacobson and Karmen Jelincic, 1996), *Capturing the Friedmans* (Dir. Andrew Jarecki, 2003), *Born into Brothels* (Dirs Zana Briski and Ross Kauffman, 2004), *Finding The Way Home* (Dirs Jon Alpert and Matthew O'Neill), *The Invisible War* (Dir. Kirby Dick, 2012), *Hidden Bruises* (Dir. Refugee Law Project, 2011), *Leave No Trace* (Dir. Irene Taylor Brodsky, 2022), *Chasing Asylum* (Dir. Eva Orner, 2016) and *Turtles Can Fly* (Dir. Bahman Ghobadi, 2004).
12. Judith Butler, *Frames of War: When Is Life Grievable?* (London: Verso, 2009), p. ix.
13. Tom Gunning, 'Flickers: On Cinema's Power for Evil', in Murray Pomerance (ed.), *Bad: Infamy, Darkness, Evil, and Slime on Screen* (Albany: State University of New York Press, 2004), p. 31; p. 29 (pp. 21–37 inclusive).
14. Presumably to repair the damage caused by the recent controversies, the organization has changed its name to 'OUR Rescue.' It continues to use the original acronym 'OUR' as the preferred name in its public communications.

15. For news coverage of this controversy, see David Bixenspan, 'WWE Referee, Wrestler-Turned-Mayor Fundraise for QAnon-Adjacent Charity', *Vice*, 29 September 2020, www.vice.com/en/article/5dzx88/wwe-referee-wrestler-turned-mayor-fundraise-for-qanon-adjacent-charity (accessed 13 May 2024); Anjali Huynh, 'Trump Promotes *Sound of Freedom*, a Conservative Hit about Child Predators', *New York Times*, 19 July 2023, www.nytimes.com/2023/07/19/us/politics/trump-sound-of-freedom.html (accessed 13 May 2024); Herb Scribner and Will Sommer, '*Sound of Freedom* is a Box Office Hit Whose Star Embraces QAnon', *The Washington Post*, 7 July 2023, www.washingtonpost.com/arts-entertainment/2023/07/07/sound-of-freedom-qanon-theories-jim-caviezel/ (accessed 13 May 2024).
16. Molly Olmstead, 'The Damning Details of the Lawsuit Against *Sound of Freedom*'s Hero', *Slate*, 16 October 2023, https://slate.com/news-and-politics/2023/10/tim-ballard-lawsuit-sound-freedom-lds-couples-ruse-trafficking.html (accessed 13 May 2024); Conor Murray, '*Sound of Freedom* Inspiration Tim Ballard and Film Producer Face Allegations of Sexual Impropriety', *Forbes*, 20 September 2023, www.forbes.com/sites/conormurray/2023/09/20/sound-of-freedom-inspiration-tim-ballard-and-film-producer-face-allegations-of-sexual-impropriety/?sh=67bdf830d0f1 (accessed 13 May 2024).
17. Miles Klee, 'God's Children: New Lawsuit against Tim Ballard Also Targets *Sound of Freedom* and Angel Studios', *Rolling Stone*, 23 February 2024, www.rollingstone.com/culture/culture-news/sound-of-freedom-tim-ballard-angel-studios-lawsuit-1234974841/ (accessed 13 May 2024).
18. Leah Payne, '*Sound of Freedom* and the Media Fueling Belief in America's "Special Role" in Human History', *Public Religion Research Institute*, 27 September 2023, www.prri.org/spotlight/sound-of-freedom-and-the-media-fueling-belief-in-americas-special-role-in-human-history/ (accessed 14 May 2024).
19. Marciniak, 'Aporias of Foreignness', p. 92.
20. Matthew Haag, 'Thousands of Immigrant Children Said They were Sexually Abused in U.S. Detention Centers, Report Says', *New York Times*, 27 February 2019, www.nytimes.com/2019/02/27/us/immigrant-children-sexual-abuse.html (accessed 14 May 2024).
21. Nick Miroff, '"Kids in Cages": It's True That Obama Built the Cages at the Border. But Trump's "Zero Tolerance" Immigration Policy Had No Precedent', *The Washington Post*, 23 October 2020, www.washingtonpost.com/immigration/kids-in-cages-debate-trump-obama/2020/10/23/8ff96f3c-1532-11eb-82af-864652063d61_story.html (accessed 15 May 2024).

# CHAPTER ONE

# *Early Cinema, Erotic Spectacle and Sex Slavery*

Early cinema's investment in the erotic spectacle is well documented and analyzed as an aspect of the medium's origins, which are steeped in the traditions of popular entertainment, such as the fairground, the vaudeville, the variety show and the burlesque. Most famously, Tom Gunning has assigned an important role to the early erotic films, with their deliberate and literal exhibitionism, in his theory of the 'cinema of attractions', a designation for early cinema that 'harnessed visibility' and celebrated the 'act of showing and exhibition' at the expense of storytelling.[1] Some of the earliest films ever made, such as *The Kiss* (Dir. William Heise, 1896) or *Bedtime for the Bride* (*Le Coucher de la Mariée*, Dir. Albert Kirchner, 1896), feature scenes that summon erotic titillation through elaborate acts of exposition. While these earliest of films carefully avoid nudity and cannot be considered explicit, they nevertheless strategically utilize spectacle for erotic play, with an 'accent on [the] direct stimulation' of the spectator.[2] In just eighteen seconds, *The Kiss*, produced by Thomas Edison's Black Maria studio, manages to build up suspense toward the enactment of the titular kiss, extending the act's foreplay through the shot's emphasis on physical proximity: the couple (played by the famous stage actors May Irwin and John Rice) flirt and smile as their faces touch, cheek-to-cheek, before they separate, laughing, and finally consummate the kiss. Produced by Eugène Pirou for Pathé, *Bedtime for the Bride* uses the same strategy of escalation to summon its erotic effect. The film stars Louise Willy (a Parisian cabaret performer) in the role of a newlywed wife who undresses for her impatient husband in their nuptial boudoir. As every layer of her elaborate wedding gown falls off, Willy's striptease routine accentuates the progress towards the consummation of the marriage, while slowing it down, using the duration of time to generate suspense. The increasing proximity between the two partners' bodies is highlighted by the husband's excited restlessness as he moves furtively about, wipes his brow, checks his watch and attempts to read a newspaper, repeatedly peeking from behind the folding screen where the wife has asked him to wait. Like the erotic and pornographic photography before the dawn of cinema, early films engaged in and promoted sexual and sensual stimulation with the help of an elaborate spectacle. The new medium of cinema innovated this experience for its viewers, utilizing the public space of exhibition and consumption to enter these displays into our collective social life on an unprecedented scale and with far-reaching cultural consequences.

The importance of erotic display to the cinema of attraction (and of cinema as such) must be attributed to the transformation of something that was once private, often even clandestine and limited to intimate or semi-intimate space, into an act that the modern medium unmetaphorically enlarged, collectivized, commodified and disseminated for unlimited circulation and repeated exposure to mass audiences around the world. While this expansion changed the culture around erotic commerce, it also transformed our private experiences of eroticism and reshaped our sense of erotic fantasy and embodiment. The image of the erotic body was now literally illuminated, animated, magnified and made available for public viewing, almost without restriction – at least in those first few unregulated years following the birth of cinema, before the censors emerged to enforce various regulations and decency codes to control and restrict both the viewer and the screen.[3]

For the purposes of the present study, it is essential to note that some of the earliest films in cinema history showcased scenarios of sexual exploitation, including scenes of abduction, selection, transport, containment, procurement and rescue of women for sex. It is also necessary to observe that the titles of such silent films refer to these scenarios as 'slavery'. The continued archival restoration and preservation of these early films allow us to understand the presence of these scenarios as the foundational images of the medium. No case highlights this history better than the changing narrative of the origins of Austrian filmmaking. Writing in 1998 for the *Journal of Film Preservation*, film historians Michael Achenbach and Paolo Caneppele have made a compelling case for the need to reframe the story of the early Austrian film by considering the existence of the Saturn studio and its prolific output of erotic feature films:

> Asked about early Austrian cinema most film historians will mention *Von Stufe zu Stufe* or *Der Müller und sein Kind*, movies filmed between 1908 and 1911. Not many people know that before them, in 1907, a Viennese studio called Saturn started mass production of feature films. Unfortunately, because of the [studio's] peculiar topics, up until now certain reluctance combined with a large amount of bashfulness caused a distortion in the historical reconstruction of Austrian filmography. The chronology of the real events was falsified and important sources of the birth of Austrian cinematography were kept as a secret.[4]

Achenbach and Caneppele proceeded to sketch the brief history of the Saturn studio and its owner Johann Schwarzer (1880–1914), a photographerchemist-turned-filmmaker whose erotic films are, in fact, the first Austrian films ever made. Schwarzer specialized in child and family portraits, before taking up erotic photography as a more lucrative pursuit. An astute businessman, he was inspired by the success of the French erotic films produced and distributed at the time by Pathé Frères throughout Europe. Schwarzer acquired a film camera and began producing his own erotic films in 1906. In terms of erotic scenarios, his films, as Achenbach and Caneppele have explained, 'were situated between the rather bashful French productions and the pornographic products of his time'.[5]

Under the Hapsburg Empire, both the imported French productions and the local Saturn films were discreetly shown to adult viewers strictly during the so-called '*Herrenabende*' (gentlemen's evenings, for male audiences only) and '*Pariserabende*' (Parisian evenings, for male and female adult audiences).[6] These screenings were scheduled as the final feature of the program, often late in the evening to avoid public scrutiny and potential police intervention. Pointedly distinguishing the Saturn films as erotica rather than pornography, Mary Bergstein has regarded them collectively as a text of great importance, emerging at a time when Europe's visual culture cast a decidedly gendered and exploitative look at the woman and her body. In an interdisciplinary study, Bergstein has examined the Saturn films as the illustration of an erotic culture marked by a 'morbid and intrusive kind of misogyny' and fixated on 'the humiliation of female flesh', exemplifying how gender over-determined the discourses of hypnosis, psychoanalysis, social work, surgery and early cinema, as they intersected in their voyeuristic focus on women's psychology and physiology.[7] According to Bergstein, the Saturn films concentrated and popularized this prying, scopophilic gaze cast upon the female subject, a perspective already present in the research methods of the many pioneers of modern medical sciences, including Sigmund Freud, Jean-Martin Charcot, Eugène-Louis Doyen, Camillo Negro, Gheorghe Marinescu, Hippolyte Bernheim and Georges Gilles de la Tourette, many of whom documented their patients using photography and the emerging medium of film.[8] Bergstein's analysis points to the affinity between early cinema's fascination with the manipulation, domination and control of the female figure and the modern medical discourse's construction of the female patient as a figure in need of surveillance, discipline and specific subduing treatments. Further, Bergstein has pointed out how the early erotic films would often be shown on the same bill with early medical films, both depicting scenarios of the female flesh being in need of male domination, pathologized and humiliated, thus leading to 'a perplexing slippage' between early medical and erotic films.[9]

Achenbach and Caneppele have identified the five most common themes that recur in early erotic cinema, including the Saturn output: Oriental tableaux, dances, scenes of voyeurism, scenes of undressing for bed or bath, and scenes of nude figures posing as art models.[10] In the Saturn productions, the Orientalist films enact highly contrived scenes from the harem, the bathhouse or the slave market, all popular subjects of the Orientalist painting and photography that were in wide commercial circulation in mid-to-late-nineteenth-century Europe (and which continued to circulate well into the twentieth century).[11] Iconography such as this linked sexuality with violence and, according to scholars of post-colonial studies, performed the dual task of projecting the imagined barbaric East with its 'inferior' societies as a tool of legitimizing the civilizing project of colonial domination, on one hand, and constructing a seductive symbolic space where the stifled Western subject found 'an escape from the dictates of the bourgeois morality of the metropolis', on the other hand.[12] The Saturn distribution catalog from 1907 includes five titles in the so-called Oriental tableaux category: *Slave Destiny* (*Sklavenschicksal*), *The Abduction of the Slave Women* (*Sklavenraub*), *The Slave Market* (*Sklavenmarkt*), *In the Harem* (*Im Harem*) and *Slavery in the Orient* (*Die Sklaverei im Orient*).[13] These short films animate the fantasies of erotic practices ascribed by the imperial European imagination to the people of North Africa and the Middle East, which, even by that time, were clichéd scenarios that would have been highly legible to the bourgeois metropolitan public across Europe. This class of audience created an intense market demand for artifacts of the Orientalist visual culture, itself a function of colonial and imperial power relations.[14] In cinema, the nineteenth-century Orientalist topoi found a more modern and more effective medium, thus extending the colonial fantasy of the 'East' well into the twentieth century and imbuing it with movement and the degree of verisimilitude that surpassed that found in the academic-style painting and still photography. The role of early cinema in the processes of transmediation and mass diffusion of Orientalist images, coupled with the commercialization of image production and distribution, has been acknowledged by Neil Macmaster and Tony Lewis as the key factors behind the continued perpetuation of Orientalism well into the twentieth-century post-colonial visual cultures of the West.[15]

Directed in 1906, Johann Schwarzer's silent, black-and-white film *The Slave Market* (Figure 1.1) depicts the emblematic Orientalist genre scene of slave trade, where a handful of captive women are ushered in front of the buyer, their bodies disrobed, exposed and inspected one by one in the process of selection. The buyer, who is coded as a wealthy Oriental man – a stereotypical bearded and turbaned 'sheikh' figure – sits outside of his tent on a rug, smoking shisha. His servant assists him as the slave sellers arrive at the scene. The sheikh sits back leisurely, ready to appraise the human merchandise and make his purchase. He is the diegetic voyeur

***Figure 1.1*** *Slave Market* (*Am Sklavenmarkt*), a film by Johann Schwarzer, 1906.

who models the act of gazing at the erotic spectacle for the film viewer. The gun-wielding sellers manhandle the five female figures, whom they push around and corral as they tear off the women's clothes. This scene thoroughly illustrates and indeed invites the sadistic gaze that Laura Mulvey later identified as quintessential to classic cinema's on-screen portrayal of the female form.[16] The sheikh selects the women by waving them into his tent and sends the undesirable ones away. The last section of the film depicts the actual transaction between the sellers and the buyer, which is focused around gestures of intense price negotiations and money changing hands. The film concludes with an image of the sheikh entering his tent to join his three new sex slaves. The camera lingers for quite some time as the tent flap closes behind the sheikh, leaving the viewer to imagine the action within the tent. The stylistic feel of this tableau, which was shot on location in daylight within a pastoral landscape, is patently kitsch in the proper sense of the term, which was coined in nineteenth-century Germany. First introduced by the Munich art dealers sometime during the 1860s, 'kitsch' referred to a then-distinctly modern phenomenon: commercial art that was cheap, supremely marketable, intended for mass consumption and characterized by 'aesthetic make-believe and self-deception'.[17]

Although astonishing on account of the film medium's novelty in 1906, the scene from Schwarzer's film described above would have been very familiar to its audience. It had been popularized throughout the second half

***Figure 1.2*** *The Slave Market*, an Orientalist painting by Otto Pilny, 1910. From WikiCommons, public domain.

of the nineteenth century in numerous Orientalist paintings, often bearing the same generic title as Schwarzer's film, authored by European academic-style painters, such as Jean-Léon Gérôme, Otto Pilny (Figure 1.2), Gustave Boulanger, Victor Julien Giraud and Edwin Long. Set outdoors and furnished with a pastiche assemblage of Orientalist props – including patterned rugs, tasseled drapes, an ornate Ottoman tent, a shisha and an oud – the two-and-a-half minute film observes all of the conventions of Orientalist fantasy. These images, conjured by white male European painters, embody the tense race and gender relations produced by the colonial project as well as anti-colonial and anti-slavery movements, including abolitionist initiatives and legislation. These relations shaped imperial Europe's knowledge formation and its cultural imagination, especially the newly redefined concepts of 'the West' and 'the East'. The Orientalist painters, who rarely traveled to the Orient (defined then in European discourse as a combination of the Near and Middle East), labored alongside other artifact producers to create representations of the colony (or former colony) as inferior to the West, saturated with unbridled sexuality and violence, and in need of the West's paternalist protection and re-education.[18] In 1978, Edward Said delivered his damning critique of Europe's long-standing tradition of Orientalist representation, placing particular focus on the role of the image in creating the 'visual expression' of the Orient as a realm of 'sensuality, promise, terror, sublimity, idyllic pleasure, intense energy' – a compelling cultural construct that perpetuates the conflation of the Orient with 'not only fecundity but sexual pleasure (and threat), untiring sensuality, unlimited desire, deep generative energies'.[19] In their analysis of European representations of Maghrebi and Middle Eastern women, Neil Macmaster and Toni Lewis have listed child marriage, *purdah* – which included the segregation of women and veiling practices – the harem, polygamy, the subjugation of women, slavery, despotism, sadism and lasciviousness as practices routinely represented and hyper-focalized in the Orientalist iconography, which functioned as colonial signifiers of the region's presumed religious fundamentalism and cultural inferiority.[20] Similarly, in their analysis of Eurocentrism as the 'ideological substratum common to colonialist, imperialist, and racist discourse', Ella Shohat and Robert Stam have identified 'the visual embodiments of gendered and eroticized tropes of "virgin lands" and "dark" continents, of "veiled" territories and imaginary harems, and of fantasies of rape and rescue'.[21] This reiteration of the image of subjugation as an Oriental practice allowed the European audience to displace the responsibility for Europe's own reprehensible record of colonial subjugation as well as gender and race segregation and discrimination.

Although Said's analysis mainly focused on textual representations, he also recognized the essential role that visual representation played in 'the economy that makes Orientalism a coherent subject matter'.[22] Borrowing Michel Foucault's concept of the episteme, Said regarded Orientalism as a network of colonial measures, both discursive and material, that allowed the modern European subject to define and consolidate his (white, heterosexual and male) identity – ostensibly liberal, progressive, emancipated and rational – by creating a systemic and pervasive vision of the Oriental subject as the Other 'with supporting institutions, vocabulary, scholarship, imagery, doctrines, even colonial bureaucracies and colonial styles'.[23] The slave market tableau was one of the most popular images in the late-nineteenth- and early-twentieth-century Orientalist iconography and is best understood in conjunction with Said's claim that, at the time, 'European culture gained in strength and identity by setting itself off against the Orient as a sort of surrogate and even underground self'.[24] Concentrating and hyperbolizing inegalitarian gender relations, the tableaux of sex slavery (variously depicted as an Ottoman, Arab, African, Islamic or Barbary practice) – spectacularized via diverse media technologies of drawing, painting, photography and later film – performed complex cultural and political work in defense of the bourgeois, patriarchal European *status quo*. This endeavor occurred at the very moment when issues of labor rights, women's rights and human rights became publicized through national and international campaigns for equality and emancipation, promoted by the socialist, suffragist and abolitionist movements. The tableau's staging of women and children as sex commodities enslaved and traded by non-Europeans redirected the internal national, gender and class tensions rising among the European bourgeoisie outward and projected them onto the Orient. The scenario worked as a displacement tactic, delaying, or in some cases suspending, the efforts to fully and transparently acknowledge and address the reprehensible legacy of imperial domination, labor exploitation and resource extraction, which heavily relied on the enslavement of colonized people.

Aside from its political performative function, the inegalitarian spectacle of the slave market also functioned as an erotic object that channeled unorthodox practices and queer desires prohibited by Christian puritanism and Victorian prudery, including homosexuality, polygamy and sex commerce. The high market demand for such taboo-breaking images stemmed precisely from their dual erotic and political function – the erotic contemplation of scenarios considered inappropriate in Victorian Europe was ideologically laundered by the 'progressive' politics of the so-called enlightened West, whose colonial intervention was to 'civilize' the Orient by infiltrating and exposing its 'savage' mores. As such, the images provided erotic stimulation while serving as symbolic sites where the redemption fantasy operated as a mechanism for the displacement of local conflicts and the repression of the history of sexual exploitation in the colonies. While Orientalist paintings of slave markets carried a degree of high-brow decorum, and thus hid their erotic function to a certain degree, the Oriental photographs, often sold as the so-called 'boudoir cards' (or 'French postcards') did not. Among the colonial photographers, the Austrian Rudolf Franz Lehnert and his German partner Ernst Heinrich Landrock were among the commercially most successful.

Active during the first few decades of the twentieth century, their studio, Lehnert & Landrock, first located in Tunisia and later in Egypt, was known for producing highly staged images of the North African people and landscapes for the European market (Figure 1.3). A large part of Lehnert & Landrock's portfolio consisted of erotic postcards that depicted women and children posing in different stages of undress, in scenarios that frequently emphasized bondage, ownership, seclusion and the disciplining of bodies within the spaces of the harem, the *hammam* and the slave market. Along with Orientalist paintings and early cinema, these photographs not only eroticized and feminized the Orient, but they also eroticized the 'infamous' cultural practices that the colonial powers ostensibly set out to civilize away. The body spectacle, ubiquitous in the staged images of sex slavery and harem captivity, activates specific patriarchal, colonial, racial and gendered ways of looking that, in turn, engender a variety of erotic attractions. Complex dynamics of desire, power and pleasure, combined with fluid axes of identification, charge

***Figure 1.3*** *Marché d'esclave, Tunisie.* A boudoir card by Lehnert & Landrock, *circa* 1910. From WikiCommons, public domain.

these images with erotic potential that exceeds the literal, even if explicit, content.

Produced for a heteronormative bourgeois European audience, the Orientalist image activated contradictory fantasies of rescue, liberation and empowerment alongside domination, possession and enslavement, while allowing the viewer to navigate freely and inconspicuously between what Julia

Kristeva has called the 'consecration' and 'defilement' of the female body on display.[25] The imagined Oriental slave, whose vulnerability is dramatized in the slave market tableau as it spotlights the materiality of the body as commodity, is offered to be consumed as an erotic object to be doubly defiled – both by the Oriental slave master within the world of the tableau, who acquires the slave for his use, and the European consumer, for whose viewing pleasure the tableau was produced. However, as I try to demonstrate throughout this study, the slave can also be consumed via an elaborate mechanism of sublimation as a consecrated figure, a radical victim with no agency, a prized object who must be rescued.[26] In this way, the framework of consecration informs and directs all Orientalist iconography, which arrogantly portrays 'the Orient' as in need of continued Western protection and intervention, thus sublimating the colonized. This protectionism has also an erotic dimension. It enforces a subject-object relation of power that organizes the encounter libidinally, foreclosing any agency on the part of the totally instrumentalized colonized subject. The performative rescue of the slave masquerades as a gesture of liberation from the abject inhumanity of the Oriental slave master, or what Kristeva would call his non-assimilable alienhood.[27] Produced at a time when anti-slavery movements secured mass support for abolitionist legislation, which led to the slow but systematic eradication of slavery in most modern states by the end of the nineteenth century, the sex slavery spectacle mediated through the novel medium of cinema offered a nostalgic excursion into the realm of colonial sexual conquests, which Doris Garraway has theorized as 'colonial libertinage', a system of colonial domination where racial segregation co-existed and was, in fact, reinforced by interracial sexual and intimate, coerced and consensual relations between the colonizers and the colonized.[28] Importantly, in her analysis of the libidinal economy of the colony, Garraway has framed the colonizer's sexual and erotic relationships with the colonized as constitutive of, and central to, the exploitative relations of power within the system of white supremacy, the ideology that fueled the European colonial project. Furthermore, Garraway has drawn attention to the body of research linking the discourse of Western sexuality, especially the eighteenth-century libertine tradition defined by the rituals of submission and domination, to the exploitative social relations of colonialism and, more specifically, to the logic of subjugation embedded in the institution of slavery.[29]

Within an older analytical frame that reaches back to the Greek Golden Age, Michel Foucault has also found a connection between the Western discourse on sexuality and the social relations predicated upon the practice of slavery. Curiously, he has attributed this connection to a moral concern, with which the ancient Greeks approached sexuality, as a domain of individual freedom. In *The Use of Pleasure: The History of Sexuality, Volume 2*, Foucault has traced the discourse of Western sexuality back to the sexual ethics of early Greece (the fourth century BCE), where the ideal sexual conduct was defined against the state of slavery and closely related to one's ability to perform 'self-mastery', which was identical in type to the Greek citizen's mastery over his slaves.[30] Seen as an aspect of the 'practice of the self', sexual behavior, or *aphrodisia*, as the early Greeks called it, was to be practiced in moderation and with careful control, so as not to succumb to the 'bondage' of desire. Foucault has argued that *aphrodisia* was a discourse of power, very much informed and shaped by the institution of slavery in ancient Greece and closely connected to the agonistic technology of the self. In practicing sexual restraint, the Greek citizen attained his freedom from enslavement by exerting his dominion over his desire through the power of subjugation already enforced upon others:

> But this freedom was more than a nonenslavement, more than an emancipation that would make the individual independent of any exterior or interior constraint; in its full, positive form, it was a power that one brought to bear on oneself in the power that one exercised over others.[31]

The ancient Greeks, Foucault has explained, constructed sexual pleasure as a 'relationship of domination, a relation of mastery' with the self, modeled after their relations of 'domination-submission', 'command-obedience' and 'mastery-docility' with the subordinates, including slaves, within their intensely hierarchical society.[32] Throughout his four-volume study of the history of Western sexual discourse, Foucault has found this early Greek emphasis on the mechanisms of discipline and subjugation to be recurring and active over time, leading up to the modern paradigm of sexuality, which is understood to be governed by a sophisticated network of institutions and systems of discipline and self-discipline. As such, Western sexual discourse, along with the visual representations that often shape lived sexual practice, may be understood as a material culture invested in the logic of enslavement, whereby the desiring subject and the desired object are always defined through relations of power and property. Foucault's and Garraway's projects not only provide accounts of historic incidents where the Western institutions of slavery enabled sexual exploitation and oppression, but they also crucially illustrate how slavery has informed the Western sexual imaginary whose logic has been ingrained in the most intimate operations of the self. The figure of the sex slave found in early cinema, a medium considered by many to be formative in training modern erotic sensibility, embodies and concentrates the inegalitarian fantasy of subjugation and transports it into the realm of mediated desire.[33]

The figure of the sex slave is also prominently situated in the history of early Danish cinema. Denmark's film production started relatively late, in 1906, but it quickly moved its film output from single-reel films to longer productions, pioneering the multi-reel narrative film before nearly every other contemporary film industry. In April of 1910, a small independent film studio, Fotorama, produced a forty-minute, multi-reel film, titled *The White Slave Trade* (*Den hvide Slavehandel*), directed by Alfred Cohn. This was not the first Danish film on the topic of sex slavery. A single-reel, eight-minute film, *The White Slave Girl* (*Den hvide Slavinde*), directed by Viggo Larsen, was released in 1907. This short film, according to Julie K. Allen, a scholar of Danish modernity, did not achieve 'the runaway success' of Fotorama's longer multi-reel film that 'allowed audiences to identify more with the characters'.[34] Indeed, Fotorama's film was so popular upon its release that the police force had to moderate the crowd. The more established studio, Nordisk Films Kompagni, made their own heavily plagiarized copy of Fotorama's hit the very same year, which Nordisk, a company with a wide international distribution network, sold worldwide. Nordisk's version, directed by August Blom, retained the same title as Fotorama's original.

In these early Danish feature films, the sex slave enters the screen not as an Orientalist trope, as was the case in the Austrian example, but as the figure of the so-called 'white slave', constructed as a rhetorical tool in the service of various social welfare reformers, including the anti-regulation prostitution abolitionists, who sought the complete eradication of sex trade, and those activists who fought for state regulation and protection measures to be extended to everyone employed in the sex industry.

Initially, 'white slavery' was a term used by nineteenth-century labor rights activists in Britain and America, who coined it as an emphatic metaphor to describe the abject political and economic disempowerment of workers in the early capitalist industrial economy. The low wages, interminable hours and harsh working conditions that characterized the plight of the modern worker were thus compared to the situation of a person living under the bondage of race-based chattel slavery. This metaphor was first used in the context of sex trade by Victor Hugo, the French novelist often engaged in social justice campaigns, in a letter dated 20 March 1870 and addressed to Josephine Elizabeth Butler, a British suffragist famous for her fight against the state regulation of prostitution and her role in establishing the International Abolitionist Federation, an organization founded to eliminate prostitution and the international traffic in women and children. Writing about the state regulation of prostitution, Hugo has argued that 'the slavery of black women is abolished in America; but the slavery of white women continues in Europe and laws are still made by men in order to tyrannize over women'.[35] Eventually 'white slavery' lost its broader, labor-rights currency as 'the systemic metaphor representing unequal power in the capitalist state' and became a term used by anti-vice reformers to refer specifically to 'involuntary brothel prostitution' engendered by private enterprise, which often was imagined to be organized by a racialized or classed 'Other'.[36] As a result, the white slavery polemics shifted its focus away from the structural problems of industrial capitalism (such as mass migration, employment exploitation and violations of workers' rights) to issues of moral degeneracy and organized crime, often producing sensationalist narratives about the abduction of innocent girls by foreign sex traffickers.

As historians of sexuality have commented, these stories provided the members of the white bourgeois society (in the Anglo-American and the European contexts) with a voyeuristic access to the world of paid sex and triggered waves of moral panic surrounding rapidly changing sexual mores, gender roles and the public behavior of women.[37] In the words of historian Keely Stauter-Halsted, '[f]ears about trafficking reached "epidemic proportions" in the early years of the twentieth century, prompting the rise of rescue societies, international conferences, and multilateral agreements devoted to curtailing the traffic in innocent women and children'.[38] Stauter-Halsted has also commented on the disparity between the 'overblown media coverage' of the perceived white slavery epidemic and the data reported by the record-keeping agencies and 'contemporary experts on domestic and international vice' that monitored sex migration and prostitution.[39] With rare exceptions, the qualitative and quantitative reports failed to provide evidence of entrapment and/or abduction, instead furnishing evidence for increased voluntary sex migration and prostitution, especially among peasant and working-class women.[40]

Prevalent in the late-nineteenth- and early-twentieth-century debates on prostitution as a pressing social problem, the 'white slavery' metaphor writes the white body into the center of the discourse, thus re-entrenching racialization and further establishing a racial hierarchy of victimhood. The language normalizes epistemic whitewashing, which had already been present in the Orientalist images of sex slavery, which, as art historians have observed, compulsively placed fair-skinned women in the role of the slave, often revising the historical truth and displacing the facts surrounding the ongoing practice of colonial subjugation of non-white peoples. Reina Lewis has famously analyzed the racial dynamics of the sex slave figure in Orientalist visual representations as follows:

> Black female figures often appear in Orientalist paintings, but are not marked as the overt object of desire; usually the pairing of a light- and dark-skinned

> woman prioritizes a reading in which the white woman is the object of desire (like Jean-Jules Antoine Lecomte du Nouy's *The White Slave Girl*, 1888 . . .) Whilst the pale Circassians and Georgians could easily be registered as objects of desire, they could also be seen as objects of pity. Imagined as unwilling victims of Oriental despotism (as typified by the pale nude female slave in Gérôme's *Slave Market* . . .) they could be conceptualized as potentially asexual and, therefore, more moral than Black women who were stereotyped as actively sexual and, consequently, immoral. The pale harem women oscillate between being like and not like European women, i.e. as both the permitted and the forbidden object. Part of the frisson of the white odalisque comes from the projection of the white wife (the licit object) into what amounts to a brothel situation (an illicit site): she is pitied but desired as the fantasy combination of Europe's splitting of female sexuality. This is why the desire to save as well as to savour the harem woman is so significant – it allows the West to view her within a lofty Christian and abolitionist rationale, saves her from taints of the harem, but does not prohibit voyeuristic pleasure in her image.[41]

Early white slavery films similarly invest the body of the abducted white woman with the status of the desired object that can be both saved and savored, in ways that combine licit and illicit desires. Originating at a time when European colonial projects (including their foundational reliance on the institution of slavery) were being scrutinized, the metaphor of 'white slavery' leads to a discursive slippage in a gesture where the conditions of colonial-era slavery that almost exclusively affected people of color are equated with the conditions of coerced prostitution and presented as a plight that affected only white bodies. As a result of this slippage, the female white suffering and the symbolic worth of the female white body displace and diminish the long history of race-based slavery founded on the colonial plunder of Africa that was still a lived memory among scores of Black people in the late nineteenth and early twentieth century, particularly in the United States. The social, moral and indeed visual focus on the 'white slave' simultaneously evacuated Black suffering into the past, which, since it was now regarded as history, could be regarded as less reprehensible. As a designation, 'white slavery' relied on whiteness as a necessary modifier that demonstrated whiteness as an exceptional, aberrant and, in the case of the films and images described above, even exotic racial category of the slave. As such, 'white slavery' reinforced the racial hierarchy of empire and the body politic of the newly conceptualized nation-state. The discursive and visual rhetoric of white slavery can thus be understood as a strategy to repress, or at least delay, the urgency of recognizing the crimes of colonial slavery that informed the early local and global struggles of decolonization. By disseminating a vision of slavery where whites enslaved other whites, the practice of enslavement became an abstract and universal practice of humanity, rather than one spurred by the logic of racism or colonial extractivism.

Except for a few fragments, the Fotorama version of *The White Slave Trade* has been lost. Fortunately, the 33-minute Nordisk version has been preserved, having been painstakingly restored in 1991.[42] Combining elements of melodrama and crime thriller, the film offers a fast-paced narrative, filled with car chases, fight scenes, disguises, moments of physical violence and erotic innuendo. The opening scene occurs in the living room of a Danish working-class family, where a mother and her daughter, Anna (Ellen Diedrich), are shown in a two-shot, working diligently on mending and sewing garments. The father returns home, bearing a newspaper with an ad for what seems to be a lucrative employment opportunity for his daughter. An agency is looking for an educated young woman to work abroad as hostess in a mansion. The position comes with a 'large honorarium'. While the father and the daughter become very excited about the prospect of employment, her fiancé, Georg, and her mother, are skeptical: The job involves international travel and the young woman's separation from the family. However, father and daughter manage to assuage their doubts and, after a quick interview with a female recruiter, the daughter finds herself *en route* to London. Unfortunately, Anna quickly discovers that her mother's suspicion was warranted: the mansion turns out to be a brothel managed by a ruthless madam, the same woman who earlier had posed as recruitment agent. After fighting off the advances of her first client and the physical abuse by the madam of the brothel, Anna persuades a chambermaid to smuggle out a letter to her parents, in which she alerts them to her desperate circumstances. An intertitle informs the viewer that, upon learning of his daughter's abduction, '[t]he father makes a report to The Association for Combatting the White Slave Trade'. Hastily, Georg travels to London and enlists the help of a private detective. Soon, the two men are able to locate the brothel where Anna is being held captive. Posing as clients, they infiltrate it and orchestrate Anna's escape. However, the unrelenting traffickers engage in a hot pursuit and manage to intercept her. In the film's spectacular grand finale, Georg and the detective, now aided by the police, manage to board a ship and rescue Anna just moments before her slavers dispatch her as 'human cargo' to another country. The film ends with a scene of Anna's happy reunion with her parents and her return to the familial domestic space in Denmark.

Directed by August Blom – an actor, prolific director and successful Nordisk producer who later was recognized as the lead pioneer and innovator of Danish silent film – *The White Slave Trade* established the narrative and aesthetic conventions of the 'white slavery film' that would be replicated by subsequent Danish films of the same genre. A total of at least six films were produced on this topic between 1907 and 1912, in addition to American white slavery films, which form a larger cycle that roughly spans the period between 1913 and 1917. The recurring narrative elements include an innocent young woman, usually of modest class and economic background, who is lured into captivity by white slavers acting as agents of legitimate employment; a man who rescues her (and also happens to be her love interest); the distraught family of the abducted woman; depictions of clandestine brothel life, often showcasing the honest woman's unflinching resistance to the sexual advances of the brothel customers; and action-packed chase scenes that typically culminate in the arrest of the slavers, the liberation of the young woman and her return to the familial home. In terms of *mise-en-scène*, the films contrast the domestic interiors with the outdoor urban spaces. Much effort is invested in featuring diverse means of transportation and communication to signal the modern time-space contraction, the increase in mobility and migration, as well as the shifting dynamics of commerce and industry in relation to social bonds and family life.

Blom experiments with the film medium to signal the experience of modernity through an elaborately crafted split-screen scene, using an innovative film technique to link modern means of transportation with new technologies of communication, information and mediation within a single frame (Figure 1.4). The composite image consisting of three panels that show simultaneous action in three different locations accentuates the contrast between old and new ways of life. The central panel shows Anna and her father standing in a busy street, right after they leave the hotel, where they have just signed her fraudulent employment contract with the slave traders. In this frame, the viewer witnesses father and daughter face each other in profile as they celebrate what they believe to be a great opportunity for their family's economic advancement. Anna is holding the contract. The two carry on a lively conversation, looking into each other's eyes and smiling, while their bodies remain still in the foreground. In the background, street traffic moves vertically and horizontally, showcasing not only cars and electric trolleys, but also horse-drawn carriages and push carts. The urban pedestrians rush along and across the street. In the other two panels, which bracket the central panel on both sides, the viewer witnesses the two slave traders (one male and one female) in their respective interior spaces, communicating with each other over the telephone as they discuss Anna's impending abduction. Their long-distance, technologically enhanced and transactional communication stands in contrast to the central panel's intimate and unmediated exchange between the father and his daughter, visually piercing and permeating it. The viewer suspects, and soon finds out, that the

***Figure 1.4*** Modern means of communication in the service of 'white slavery' in *The White Slave Trade* (*Den hvide Slavehandel*), a film by August Blom, 1910.

phone conversation between the slave traders will impact Anna's life in ways that she – and her father – have not foreseen. Structurally, the scene builds up a conflict in the knowledge transfers carried out in these overlapping conversations and comments on the primacy of the technologically mediated knowledge, because of its smooth transition through time and space, as well as its collusion with clandestine crime operations. More importantly, the viewer is implicated in the criminal transfer of knowledge in a gesture, where cinema – yet another modern technology – stands on the side of the slave traders in terms of the epistemic dynamics of this shot. The viewer, the film and the slave traders all have privileged insight into the truth of Anna's situation, through their access to technology long before Anna finds out. In Blom's film, and in other white slavery films, new technologies of material and symbolic transfer are often visualized as resources that exacerbate the ills of the modern life and challenge the established moral norms and customs.[43] Whether intentionally or not, the scene under analysis, by drawing the viewer's attention to the manipulation of the film form through the split-screen technique, produces a meta-cinematic comment on the medium's own role in the networks of commercial trafficking as a technology of information and representation.

The Danish white slavery films, much like the Austrian films just discussed, employ an erotic gaze.[44] However, they are less explicit in spectacularizing the female form and do not include scenes of nudity. Rather, they generate their erotic frisson by staging the spectacle of violence, manipulating the female body against the will of the woman, or during a temporary loss of her consciousness. The process of erasing her agency focalizes the spectacle. The sadism deployed in these scenes showcases the operation of objectification, or more specifically of reification, to use a term developed by neo-Marxist Georg Lukács to describe the effects of commodification on the human subject under capitalism.[45] In white slavery films, the woman becomes a commodity in the marketplace as her body is transported, pushed around, beaten, drugged, starved, bound and packaged. Such scenes use the female body as resistant but ultimately malleable material capable of being controlled, disciplined, possessed and in some cases dis/appeared. The manipulation of the female form is also a spectacle of the male agent's mastery and as such it champions his agency, while the female becomes the prop, the matter that is being worked on. Before such scenes appeared in films about white slavery, they had already emerged in the early medical films mentioned earlier in this chapter, as well as in the trick films made by the pioneers of cinema, the magician filmmakers – most prominently Georges Méliès, who saw the new medium as the greatest resource in advancing the art of the magic show. In his 1896 film *The Vanishing Lady* (*Escamotage d'une dame chez Robert-Houdin*), a magician, played by Méliès himself, vanishes a woman, transforms her into a skeleton and finally returns her to her original form. Lucy Fischer, who has analyzed the treatment of the female body in the hands of the magician in the films by Méliès and Thomas A. Edison, has argued that 'the act of conjuring and "vanishing" ladies tends to dematerialize and decorporealize the female sex – to relegate woman to the level of "spirit"'.[46] While I agree with Fischer's general feminist critique of the gendered dynamics of these early trick films, I see the spectacle of the vanishing as a scene of reification more than of dematerialization. While not explicit, such scenes are imbued with a libidinal charge, whereupon the erotic pleasure – according to the then-dominant Freudian paradigm of sexual drives, informed by the nineteenth-century economic discourse – is concentrated in the act of the manipulation of the female form. The radical control exercised over the female body, including its disappearance and reappearance, accentuates the body's material worth, its entry into the market and discourse as a consumable object. Consequently, the female figure's divestment of her human subjectivity is on display while she is being 'produced' into a commodity in the hands of the magician and the filmmaker.

In August Blom's second white slavery film, *In the Hands of Imposters* (*Den hvide Slavehandels sidste Offer*, 1911), there are many more scenes where the protagonist Edith (Clara Wieth) is being physically handled by the slavers in ways that are elaborate, protracted and more spectacularized than in his *The White Slave Trade*. Longer by about fifteen minutes, the plot of the 1911 film follows the general storyline of the earlier film. A vulnerable young woman, who is traveling alone internationally, is abducted by slavers and taken to a brothel, where she resists sexual coercion. Once again, a housemaid helps the entrapped woman, and eventually she is rescued by a man who falls in love with her. The police assist in the final rescue mission. However, *In the Hands of Imposters* offers both a more menacing and a more salacious scenario than Blom's earlier film. There are two gangs of slavers fighting to take ownership of Edith, an orphan unprotected by the nuclear family. The slavers are more numerous, more organized, more brutal in their handling of Edith and her helpers, more effective in avoiding detection and more skilled at eluding the forces of law and order. The first two attempts to rescue Edith fail. The rescue itself depends on the intelligence, good will and perseverance of a stranger, Mr Faith, whom Edith meets on the boat, while traveling to her aunt who is to assume custody over her recently orphaned niece. After rescuing Edith, Mr Faith imposes himself on her, romantically and physically, which the film presents as the desired 'happy' ending.

The viewer arrives at this ending only after seeing an accelerated series of action scenes stacked in the last ten minutes of the film. The scenes focus on the violent disciplining of Edith as she continues to resist. The demands on her body begin soon upon Edith's arrival at a brothel, where her captors try to persuade her to change from her demure black dress to a more seductive outfit. She refuses for a while and preserves her dignity, only to be transferred to a harsher situation where her resolve is violently tested. In quick succession, the viewer sees Edith being groped, pushed down to the floor, shoved into a car, tossed onto a bed, whipped, bound, gagged and stuffed into a wardrobe. Edith loses her consciousness a few times during this ordeal. While she is fully dressed in these scenes, she is only wearing a dressing gown, and her appearance becomes increasingly disheveled as her body sustains different kinds of physical aggression and manipulation (Figure 1.5). In the climax of this abusive sequence, she is disappeared into a small piece of furniture, which is used to hide her from the police inspection and, moments later, to carry her into another hideout. These scenes not only carry an obvious narrative meaning that signals the alleged dangers of white slavery, but they also – and, as I argue, foremost – function as a riveting and highly eroticized cinematic spectacle, inviting the viewer to participate in Edith's increasing reification and her ultimate conversion into a sexual commodity packaged into a wooden box and carried away.

***Figure 1.5*** The white slavers bind, gag and stash Edith in the wardrobe in August Blom's *In the Hands of Imposters* (*Den hvide Slavehandels sidste Offer*, 1911).

As theorists of early cinema, Tom Gunning and André Gaudreault have famously distinguished the two discursive modes within early filmmaking practice – the mode of 'monstration', which offers a display of individual, often unrelated, visual 'attractions', and the mode of 'narrative integration', which uses the filmic discourse to visualize a continuous story – a sequence of related actions unfolding in time and space.[47] With the advent of full-length narrative film around 1915, the mode of narrative integration, so they have argued, became institutionalized and dominant. The mode of monstration, which reigned supreme in the first fifteen years of cinema's history, so closely linked to fairground attractions, would from then on be activated more sparingly, within the scenes of visual excess punctuating the narrative, or more liberally in experimental film, art film and pornography.

The concept of monstration, with its emphasis on the self-contained and autonomous visual pleasure delivered within a singular shot, is rather useful in understanding the dual currency of the early sex slavery film as a source of sanctioned erotic spectacle couched in the framework of a social problem rescue narrative, which 'integrates' the erotic spectacle (attraction) within a noble story of female victimhood and male chivalry. All of the scenes in *In the Hands of the Imposters* that focus on the manipulation of Edith's body are fundamentally monstrative and can be consumed individually, outside of the narrative sequence. Their content and energy, their excess and repetition, as well as their focus on the materiality and pneumatics of the female body far exceed the narrative need of constructing the cautionary tale of the evils of white slavery. Arguably, these scenes are filmed to attract and entertain the voyeuristic gaze. Yet, because they are not explicit, and because they effectively substitute violence for sex, they are also eminently excusable as narrative detail, if the viewer, the filmmaker, or the censor needed to explain away the salacious energy of these images.

The balance between the mode of monstration *vis-à-vis* the mode of narration, as Gaudreault has argued, shifted between 1908 and 1914, as single-reel films were gradually replaced by multi-reel films and as 'the various components of cinematic expression were thus mobilized around, and subjected to, strict narrative ends'.[48] The new, longer film format invited the narrative integration of images into increasingly more complex stories; thus, monstrative exhibition became secondary, often marginalized as the decorative or comic element within the narrative proper, or relegated to genres that functionally relied on monstration, for example, the musical or the pornographic film. This shift is evident when the Orientalist sex slavery films of Johann Schwarzer are compared to Danish white slavery films. The much shorter Austrian films are more explicit, use nudity and revolve around the erotic spectacle. The narrative arc is only summarily suggested, as the impetus of the film resides in the monstrative act, typically the disrobing of the female figure and the showcasing of her body. This act is often protracted in time, or even multiplied within the same film as a couple of female figures are exhibited in the same manner. Unlike the Austrian films, which were shown predominantly at stag parties and private screenings, the Danish films targeted the mainstream audiences of commercial theaters. Their longer format allowed for more elaborate storytelling. The proportions of narrative integration and monstration changed – the erotic spectacle, sublimated through violence, was now less central and delimited to a few climactic scenes. The story world was constructed with more nuance, employing a complex characterization of protagonists, as well as highly realistic set and location design.

The fact that the Danish filmmakers traded the explicit erotic spectacle for a more subdued product, whose social problem framing attracted a mixed-gender mass audience, was key in securing unprecedented commercial success for the films. Nordisk sold *In the Hands of Imposters* internationally, finding local distributors throughout Europe, the United States and Australia. A quick search in the British Newspaper Archive (an online database of historic Irish and British newspapers) yields a large number of enthusiastic reviews for *In the Hands of Imposters*, published in local newspapers throughout

1911, the year of the film's release. In its section titled 'The Picture Halls', the *Sheffield Daily Telegraph* reported the screening of the film at the Picture Palace to 'two large audiences', who were 'thrilled with delight' by a picture 'full of exciting and absorbing interest' with an 'admirably presented' story that 'deals with the dangers besetting the young and inexperienced female traveling alone in great cities'.[49]

*Nelson Leader*, a newspaper from Lancashire, England, remarked on the apparent publicity stunt used to attract an audience for *In the Hands of Imposters*, in which 'a bill appeared on the boardings of the town', alerting street crowds to the 'abduction of Miss Edith Hope' and offering a reward of one-hundred pounds for anyone with information that could assist the police. The film reviewer then explained that the bill served as an advertisement for the Nordisk film, screened at The New Electric Theatre, and commented on the film's 'many very exciting and thrilling scenes, including the abduction of a girl'.[50] The Scottish newspaper *Motherwell Times*, in a section titled 'New Century Theatre', referred to Blom's film as 'a specially attractive picture' that is 'proving a good draw' to a large audience, who followed the film's 'dramatic and farcical incidents' with 'intense interest'.[51] Finally, *The Bioscope* reported how the New Century Film Service secured the 'exclusive rights' to distribute Blom's film, which turned out to be 'a great success' and was received 'with unstinted applause' as it 'made the top-liner' at two new screening halls at Cleator Moor and Workington in Cumbria.[52]

Much like the Danish cycle, the early Hollywood films on the subject of white slavery – the so-called 'slavers' or 'white slave pictures' – justified erotic content through an avowed educational agenda of critiquing forced prostitution. This strategy thus appealed to radically different audience groups, from those interested in erotic entertainment to those expecting a didactic lesson on social pathologies. Among these pre-Hays Code productions, the best-known is still *Traffic in Souls* (Dir. George Loane Tucker), which premiered in New York City in November 1913. According to scholars of early cinema, Tucker's film is the first American multi-reel film with an original story.[53] Therefore, as was the case in Denmark, the transition from the single-reel to the multi-reel format happened in the United States while narrating the cautionary tale of the dangers of white slavery. More numerous than the Danish output and extending well into the late 1910s, the American 'slavers' expressed collective anxieties regarding female migration; the heyday of their popularity overlapped with the latter part of the American Progressive Era (1896–1917), a period of social, political and economic reform in the United States. Concerns about women's mobility and its potential impact on class, race and gender relations underpinned the progressive anti-white slavery discourse, which resulted in a widespread moral panic about female migration (both inter- and intra-national). Following in the footsteps of the Danish film producers, Hollywood (and Broadway) capitalized on the public outcry. Commenting on the common narratives found in American films about white slavery, Shelley Stamp, a scholar of early cinema in the United States, has described 'slavers' as tales that 'stress the vulnerability of women in America's cities, particularly immigrants new to the country, rural women emigrating to urban centers for the first time, and young working women eagerly participating in a new commercial dating culture'.[54] A survey of the titles of these commercially successful films reveals not only their alignment with the climate of paranoia surrounding the then unprecedented and socially transgressive phenomenon of female mobility and agency, but also their sensationalistic tone: *The Inside of the White Slave Traffic* (Dir. Frank Beal, 1913), *Smashing the Vice Trust* (Dir. John Melville, 1914), *The House of Bondage* (Dirs Pierce Kingsley and Raymond West, 1914), *A Soul in Peril* (1914), *The Traffic in Girls* (Dir. unknown, 1914), *Is Any Girl Safe?* (Dir. Jacques Jaccard, 1916), *The Little Girl Next Door* (Dirs Richard Foster Baker and M. Blair Coan, 1916), *The Lure* (Dir. Alice Guy, 1914) and *Little Lost Sister* (Dir. Alfred E. Green, 1917).

As Stamp has explained, white slave pictures have historically indexed a displaced national phobia of the explosion of female mobility and immigration rather than an existing sex-trafficking epidemic. By and large, the anti-white-slavery discourse relied on fabricated statistics, forged police records and exaggerated, often 'histrionic' journalism.[55] Women's vulnerability, as well as the vulnerability of immigrants and children, were given specific representational figurations within the heavily tendentious moralistic framework of concerned critique, which superseded any labor and immigrant rights discussion in the mainstream public consciousness and imaginary. The increasingly complex issues surrounding commercial sex in the modern urban space received an alarmist tenor in the American progressives' paternalistic rhetoric that sought to emancipate all women, but especially those of the lower social classes, from selling sex.

The American early white slavery films have received thorough scholarly consideration and have been credited with an important role in the systematization and institutionalization of narrative cinema nationally and globally. Stamp has tied those films to the modern standards of exhibition and reception that led to the establishment of female cinematic spectatorship. She has argued that the films allowed women a look into the urban space, including the forbidden vice districts, thus leading to the formulation of the critical spectatorial gaze, even if the female patrons of the early movie exhibition halls were sometimes subjected to uninvited sexual attention and the erotic gaze from other patrons.[56] Tom Gunning has analyzed *Traffic in Souls* against the tradition of *flâneurie*, arguing that the film expressed the pernicious nature of the new 'vast network' of the 'invisible paths of power' that characterized the modern urban milieu, while also observing that cinema became an organ of the panoptic surveillance of women's conduct outside of the home. In a gesture toward Marxist critique, Gunning has also noted that the early white slavery films, with their emphasis on both the clandestine operations of traffickers and police operations of detection and discovery, denote an affinity between cinematic vision and the critical scrutiny required for the modern spectator to break through the bedazzlement of the early capitalist commodity spectacle.[57] As such, the white slavery films, although not a reliable source of information about the complexities of commercial sex trade in the early twentieth century, may be a source of subtle commentary on the role of public vision in modern life, especially in the lives of working women as they entered the public sphere *en masse* as new labor markets emerged in the first few decades of the twentieth century. In her book on the role that American silent cinema played in shaping modern patterns and methods of mobility (along with the attendant mechanisms of regimentation and standardization), Kristin Whissel has noted that traffic 'had become the primary emblem of modern life', in conjunction with the rise of cinema as a medium. According to Whissel, traffic 'was a fungible concept used to elaborate fantasies and anxieties about the experience of technological modernity in the United States'. Cinema was therefore uniquely placed, formally and historically, to process these fantasies and anxieties at the same time as it produced them. Whissel has understood the early white slavery film cycle as a collection of narratives that explored the possibility of the human beings' absorption into the circulation of goods. In her analysis, the films 'suggest that the mass mobilization of bodies, commodities, and capital by transportation technologies allow these separate types of cargo to become mixed and even dangerously confused'.[58] Whissel's analysis rightly returns the matter of white slavery to the realm of political economy.

Studying the social history of the transatlantic migration of the late nineteenth and early twentieth centuries, Michael G. Esch has suggested another productive course of interpretation. Interested in the operations of 'whitening' that shaped the immigration policies in the North and South Americas, Esch has investigated the role of race construction in the discourse generated by the modern nation-state's institutions of biopower, including the brand-new institution of cinema. Supported by archival research, Esch has asserted a direct connection between the key figures of the eugenics movement and the campaigners against white slavery: 'South American, North American, and European physicians and eugenicists linked the campaign against trafficking of women to their own considerations on how to ensure the biological optimization of desired populations'.[59] Esch's perspective invites one to view early white slavery films as instruments of mass indoctrination, driven by the proto-Aryan ideals of reproductive purity. For example, as Esch has pointed out, the campaigns, journalism and films that addressed the perceived white slavery epidemic often assigned Jewish identity to the traffickers, contributing to the inflammatory antisemitic discourse already directed against Eastern European immigrants, many of whom were Jewish. It is not coincidental, as Esch has suggested, that in the context of the United States the anti-white slavery discourse (including its cinematic representation) corresponded with the onset of race-informed migration legislation, including the Mann Act, also known as the White Slave Traffic Act of 1910. Although originally written to protect women against trafficking across state lines, the Mann Act quickly became a mechanism for homophobic and racist litigation against homosexual and mixed-race couples. It also criminalized a range of consensual sexual practices outside of marriage and, as such, further enabled various moral purity movements of early-twentieth-century America.[60] Esch's interdisciplinary research on social history and the history of cinema brings to the forefront the natural affinity between the ideologues of modern social engineering and the forces of white supremacy as they colluded in creating the symbolically capacious and rhetorically exacting metaphor of white slavery, which early film materialized on screen with much sensationalism. In the process of such materialization, the metaphor concretized the relationship between whiteness and slavery, leading to the dangerous displacement, if not the complete repression, of the record of sexual exploitation of non-white subjects, whose lives had been forced into circulation as commodities, either through the only recently abolished institution of chattel slavery and, later, Jim Crow laws, or through the criminalized sex trade industry.

The above review of early cinema reveals that the medium has, since its inception, engaged in the trafficking of the spectacularized female body, providing, among its many attractions, the popular erotic entertainment for private and public consumption. Images of female nudity in the context of scenes of the examination, manipulation and discipline of the female body were central to the construction of 'monstrative attractions' from the very earliest period of film history, which Gaudreault has argued dominated the medium until 1908.[61] The gradual narrative integration that led to the development and eventual dominance of narrative cinema by 1913 was made possible by the invention of the multi-reel film technology. In an attempt to sell a longer, more costly product, the early film industry had to attract a wealthier and more educated customer – the middle-to-upper-class audience. This precipitated the process of folding the soft-core erotic spectacle into palatable stories that suited bourgeois sensibilities and prevailing moral standards. The slavery scenario provided a didactic and morally acceptable narratorial platform for the continued trafficking of the spectacularized female body within the increasingly institutionalized medium that was quickly entering the mainstream public space. It is no coincidence that, around the same time, hard-core pornographic content was pushed underground and relegated to a separate genre, the stag film. The first stag films were produced approximately between 1907 and 1917. The Kinsey Institute of Social Research in Sex, Gender and Reproduction has identified three films as the earliest hard-core pornographic feature films: the German *In the Evening* (*Am Abend*, 1910), the Argentinian *El Satario* (c. 1907–15) and the American *A Free Ride* (c. 1915–17). Often, the production and distribution of the early pornographic films relied on the film industry's collaboration with the sex trade industry; for example, brothels were among the most common spaces to screen the hard-core pornographic films to their patrons, and filmmakers sourced women working in brothels to perform in their films.[62]

## Notes

1. Tom Gunning, 'The Cinema of Attractions: Early Film, Its Spectator and the Avant-Garde', in Thomas Elsaesser and Adam Barker (eds), *Early Cinema: Space, Frame, Narrative* (London: BFI Publishing, 1990), p. 56 (pp. 56–62 inclusive).
2. Ibid. p. 59.
3. For superb historical analyses of these early censorship efforts in the US context, see Lee Grieveson, *Policing Cinema: Movies and Censorship in Early-Twentieth-Century America* (Berkeley: University of California Press, 2004); Jennifer Fronc, *Monitoring the Movies: The Fight over Film Censorship in Early-Twentieth-Century Urban America* (Austin: University of Texas Press, 2017).
4. Michael Achenbach and Paolo Caneppele, 'Saturn: The Erotic Beginnings of Austrian Cinematography', *Journal of Film Preservation*, 57, December 1998, p. 13 (pp. 126–39 inclusive).
5. Ibid. 13.
6. See Willy Riemer, 'The Cultural Status of Early Austrian Cinema and Film', *Modern Austrian Literature*, 37:3–4, 2004, pp. 1–12.
7. Mary Bergstein, 'Freud, Saturn, and the Power of Hypnosis', in Shawn Michelle Smith and Sharon Sliwinski (eds), *Photography and the Optical Unconscious* (Durham: Duke University Press, 2017), pp. 104–33.
8. Ibid. p. 106. For further discussion, see Georges Didi-Huberman, *Invention of Hysteria: Charcot and the Photographic Iconography of the Salpêtrière*, trans. Alisa Hartz (Cambridge and London: The MIT Press, 2003).
9. Bergstein, 'Freud, Saturn, and the Power of Hypnosis', p. 130.
10. Michael Achenbach and Paolo Caneppele, 'Born under the Sign of Saturn: The Erotic Origins of Cinema in the Austro-Hungarian Empire', *Griffithiana: Journal of Film History*, 65, 1999, p. 129 (pp. 126–39 inclusive).

11. See Isra Ali, 'The Harem Fantasy in Nineteenth Century Orientalist Paintings', *Dialectical Anthropology*, 39:1, 2015, pp. 33–46; Ana Hoffner ex-Prvulovic, 'Non-Aligned Extinctions: Slavery, Neo-Orientalism, and Queerness', *e-flux journal*, 97, February 2019, www.e-flux.com/journal/97/252398/non-aligned-extinctions-slavery-neo-orientalism-and-queerness/ (accessed 15 June 2023); Malek Alloula, *The Colonial Harem*, trans. Myrna Godzich and Vlad Godzich (Minneapolis: University of Minnesota Press, 1986).
12. Rana Kabbani, *Imperial Fictions: Europe's Myths of Orient* (London: Al Saqi Books, 2008), p. 112.
13. Achenbach and Caneppele, 'Born under the Sign of Saturn', p. 138.
14. See Jill Beaulieu and Mary Roberts (eds), *Orientalism's Interlocutors: Painting, Architecture, Photography* (Durham: Duke University Press, 2002).
15. Neil Macmaster and Toni Lewis, 'Orientalism: From Unveiling to Hyperveiling', in Haideh Moghissi (ed.), *Women and Islam: Images and Realities, Volume I* (London and New York: Routledge, 2005), p. 147 (pp. 147–62 inclusive).
16. Laura Mulvey, 'Visual Pleasure and Narrative Cinema', *Screen*, 16:3, 1975, pp. 6–18.
17. Matei Calinescu, *Five Faces of Modernity: Modernism, Avant-Garde, Decadence, Kitsch, Postmodernism* (Durham: Duke University Press, 1987), p. 262.
18. Ali, 'The Harem Fantasy in Nineteenth Century Orientalist Paintings', pp. 39–42.
19. Edward Said, *Orientalism* (New York: Vintage Books, 1978), p. 119; p. 188.
20. Macmaster and Lewis, 'Orientalism: From Unveiling to Hyperveiling', p. 147; p. 151.
21. Ella Shohat and Robert Stam, *Unthinking Eurocentrism: Multiculturalism and the Media* (London and New York: Routledge, 2014), p. 9.
22. Ibid. p. 202.
23. Ibid. p. 2.
24. Ibid. p. 3.
25. Julia Kristeva, *Powers of Horror: An Essay on Abjection* (New York: Columbia University Press, 1982).
26. On the role of the rescue fantasy in colonial discourse, see Ella Shohat and Robert Stam, 'Tropes of Empire', in *Unthinking Eurocentrism: Multiculturalism and the Media* (London and New York: Routledge, 2014), pp. 137–77.
27. Kristeva, *Powers of Horror*, p. 11.
28. Doris Garraway, *The Libertine Colony: Creolization in the Early French Caribbean* (Durham: Duke University Press, 2005), pp. 24–34.
29. Ibid. p. 26. Garraway here referred to Peter Brooks, writing on Laclos' *Dangerous Liaisons*, Joan Dayan, analyzing the Marquis de Sade's erotic imaginary, and Marcel Hénaff's Marxist reading of de Sade's *The 120 Days of Sodom*.
30. Michel Foucault, *The Use of Pleasure: History of Sexuality, Volume 2*, trans. Robert Hurley (New York: Vintage Books, 1990), pp. 75–76.
31. Ibid. p. 80.
32. Ibid. p. 70.

33. This argument is central to Miriam Hansen's much-cited article, 'The Mass Production of the Senses: Classical Cinema as Vernacular Modernism', *Modernism/Modernity*, 6:2, 1999, pp. 59–77.
34. Julie K. Allen, 'The White Slave Trade Gets Religion in *A Victim of the Mormons*', *Kosmorama*, 31 May 2013, www.kosmorama.org/en/kosmorama/artikler/white-slave-trade-gets-religion-victim-mormons (accessed 15 August 2023).
35. Cited in Mara L. Keire, *For Business and Pleasure: Red-Light Districts and the Regulation of Vice in the United States, 1890–1933* (Baltimore: The Johns Hopkins University Press, 2010), p. 71.
36. Ibid. p. 71.
37. For examples of this scholarship, see Petra de Vries, '"White Slaves" in a Colonial Nation: The Dutch Campaign against Traffic in Women in the early Twentieth Century', *Social and Legal Studies*, 14:1, 2005, pp. 39–60; Mary Ann Irwin, '"White Slavery" as Metaphor: Anatomy of a Moral Panic', *Ex Post Facto: The History Journal*, 5, 1996, pp. 1–22; Mara L. Keire, 'The Vice Trust: A Reinterpretation of the White Slavery Scare in the United States, 1907–1917', *Journal of Social History*, 35:1, 2001, pp. 5–41; Alain Corbin, *Women for Hire: Prostitution and Sexuality in France after 1850*, trans. Alan Sheridan (Cambridge, MA: Harvard University Press, 1990).
38. Keely Stauter-Halsted, *The Devil's Chains: Prostitution and Social Control in Partitioned Poland* (Ithaca and London: Cornell University Press, 2015), p. 120.
39. Ibid. p. 120.
40. Ibid. pp. 121–22.
41. Reina Lewis, *Gendering Orientalism: Race, Femininity and Representation* (Abingdon and New York: Routledge, 1996), p. 172.
42. This film has since been digitized and can be viewed in its entirety via a platform supported by the Danish Film Institute.
43. In his study of the white slavery theme in early American cinema, Alex Bordino has made a similar point, arguing that white slave narratives in film often not only rely on new technologies for the trafficking of women, but also on the detection and prevention of trafficking. Alex W. Bordino, 'Modernity, Parallel Editing, and the Flâneuse: Examining the White Slave Narrative in Early and Contemporary American Cinema' (Master's thesis, City University of New York, 2015).
44. Marguerite Engberg has explored the importance of the genre of erotic melodrama in the rise of the Danish film industry. She has included the white slavery films within this dominant silent film genre and identified the genre's strong erotic focus as the key factor in popularizing the new medium in Denmark and abroad. Marguerite Engberg, 'The Erotic Melodrama in Danish Silent Films, 1910–1918', *Film History*, 5, 1993, pp. 63–67.
45. Georg Lukács, 'Reification and the Consciousness of the Proletariat', in *History and Class Consciousness*, trans. Rodney Livingstone (Cambridge, MA: MIT Press, 1971 [1923]), pp. 83–222.
46. Lucy Fischer, 'The Lady Vanishes: Women, Magic, and the Movies', in John L. Fell (ed.), *Film Before Griffith* (Berkeley and Los Angeles: University of California Press, 1983), p. 341 (pp. 339–54 inclusive).

47. In his 2008 book *Film and Attraction*, André Gaudreault has recounted his early collaborative project with Tom Gunning, from 1989, when they first theorized the cinema of attractions as distinct from the institutionalized narrative cinema. Their paradigm-shifting theory of early cinema has proposed the dual concepts of 'monstrative attractions' and 'narrative integration', which in turn has inspired the rise of the so-called 'new film history' movement. André Gaudreault, *Film and Attraction: From Kinematography to Cinema*, trans. Timothy Barnard (Urbana, Chicago and Springfield: University of Illinois Press, 2011), pp. 52–55.
48. Ibid. p. 54.
49. 'The Picture Halls', *Sheffield Daily Telegraph*, 11 April 1911, p. 11.
50. 'The New Electric', *Nelson Leader*, 7 April 1911, p. 11.
51. 'New Century Theater', *Motherwell Times*, 19 May 1911, p. 7.
52. 'We Are Informed That the Nordisk. . .', *The Bioscope*, 6 April 1911, p. 33
53. See Bordino, 'Modernity, Parallel Editing, and the Flâneuse', p. 24; Kristin Whissel, *Picturing American Modernity: Traffic, Technology, and the Silent Cinema* (Durham: Duke University Press, 2008), p. 165. Bordino's research has showcased the fact that the cinematic technique of parallel editing was 'intimately linked with the white slave narratives' and pioneered by D. W. Griffith in a series of single-reel films on the topic of women's enslavement, comprising *The Fatal Hour* (1908), *The Miser's Heart* (1911) and *The Musketeers of Pig Alley* (1911). See Bordino, p. 4.
54. Shelley Stamp, 'Moral Coercion, or the National Board of Censorship Ponders the Vice Films', in Matthew Bernstein (ed.), *Controlling Hollywood: Censorship and Regulation in the Studio Era* (London: The Athlone Press, 1999), p. 43.
55. Shelley Stamp, *Movie-Struck Girls: Women and Motion-Picture Culture After the Nickelodeon* (Princeton: Princeton University Press, 2000), pp. 42–44.
56. Ibid. p. 48.
57. Tom Gunning, 'From the Kaleidoscope to the X-Ray: Urban Spectatorship, Poe, Benjamin, and *Traffic in Souls* (1913)', *White Angle*, 19:4, 1997, p. 40; p. 45 (pp. 25–61 inclusive).
58. Whissel, *Picturing American Modernity*, p. 173; p. 215.
59. Michael G. Esch, 'Migrants from East-Central Europe in South America: Discourses and Structures between Mission, Pogrom, Escape, Human Trafficking, and "Whitening"', in Katja Castryck-Naumann (ed.), *Transregional Connections in the History of East-Central Europe* (Berlin and Boston: De Gruyter, 2021), p. 287 (pp. 259–90 inclusive).
60. In his PBS documentary on the life of Jack Johnson, the first African American heavy-weight boxing champion, Ken Burns has shed light on the specific ways in which the Mann Act was used in the systemic persecution of Black citizens during the Jim Crow era. In 2018, Jack Johnson was posthumously pardoned for allegedly violating the Mann Act in 1913, by engaging romantically and travelling with a white woman. See also Lorelei Lee, 'The Roots of "Modern Day Slavery": The Page Act and the Mann Act', *Columbia Human Rights Law Review*, 52:3, Spring

2021, www.hrlr.law.columbia.edu/hrlr/the-roots-of-modern-day-slavery-the-page-act-and-the-mann-act/ (accessed 13 September 2023).

61. Gaudreault, *Film and Attraction*, p. 53.
62. Michael G. Esch has mentioned *El Satario* and suggested that its female characters were played by women who worked in the brothels of Buenos Aires. See Esch, 'Migrants from East-Central Europe in South America', p. 287. For more information about the role of brothels in the production and circulation of early pornographic film, see Dan Erdman, *Let's Go Stag! A History of Pornographic Film from the Invention of Cinema to 1970* (New York, London, Oxford, New Delhi and Sydney: Bloomsbury Academic, 2021).

# CHAPTER TWO

# *Sifting Through Images: Sex Slave Iconography*

In the spring of 2019, large posters of Jean-Léon Gérôme's famous painting *The Slave Market* began to appear on billboards around Berlin. The key text of nineteenth-century Orientalist imaginary, the 1866 painting focuses on a naked, light-skinned female slave whose body is being inspected by four darker-skinned men, whose robes and turbans code them as Middle Eastern or North African. A man on the left, the potential buyer, places a finger in the slave's mouth to check her teeth while the man behind her holds a white cloth in his arms – possibly her own dress, removed to allow potential buyers to inspect the human merchandise more easily. Across the poster, a foreboding message read: 'Damit aus Europa kein "Eurabien" wird!' or, 'So that Europe won't become "Eurabia"!' This was the campaign slogan for Germany's far-right party, Alternative für Deutschland (AfD, Alternative for Germany), who defended their use of Gérôme's painting, now in the public domain, in a statement: 'The German public has the right to find out the truth about the possible consequences of illegal mass immigration'.[1] Like many other extreme-right political parties across Europe, AfD has been steadily gaining support for its xenophobic policy proposals, which include closing the EU borders, introducing regular identity checks and establishing holding camps abroad to prevent the influx of refugees into Germany and Europe.

Although the original Gérôme painting is held thousands of miles away from Berlin at the Sterling and Francine Clark Institute in Massachusetts, the iconographic message of AfD's propaganda copy was not dissimilar to that of the 'real' painting. Indeed, the poster recapitulated many of the anxieties – and ideological functions – of the nineteenth-century context from which the painting first emerged. As Bergstein has written, this painting and other nineteenth-century Orientalist images offered . . .

> . . . [a] phantasy that undermined the bourgeois husband-wife relationship that prevailed as an ideal in newly industrialized Europe. The non-European women who were sexualized in exotic scenarios provided a reactionary phantasm for men whose wives, daughters, and even mistresses were evolving in a rapidly changing European society.[2]

In this sense, the woman in the painting holds a dual significance that indexes both the exoticized, sexualized, non-European woman and the white Western woman imperiled by her newfound mobility. Here, we can identify a thread that runs through nineteenth-century genre painting, the 'white slavery' panics in Europe and in the Progressive-era United States, as well as the AfD's recent promotion of the 'Eurabia' conspiracy – the phobic notion circulating widely among the right-wing extremists that the growth of Muslim populations in Europe and North America will lead to the 'Islamization' of the Western world.[3] Like the genre paintings, the 'Eurabia' paranoia is a transparent projection of the European and, later, American-led imperial adventures in the Middle East whose ideological rationale has always been the delivery of Western values to supposedly barbaric and uncivilized lands. A continuation of the 'white slavery' panic of the late nineteenth and early twentieth centuries, the AfD's redeployment of *The Slave Market* articulates a reactionary fantasy in which white women's sexuality (or rather, sexual innocence) is negatively linked to immigration, which is presented as a threat to the nation-state. In this fantasy, the crossing of national borders inheres the crossing of the sexual boundaries and so-called racial purity established by colonial morality. It is for this reason, for example, that the Mann Act in the United States was quickly employed to prosecute interracial relationships after the abolition of slavery. Gérôme's image applies to the fantasy of Fortress Europe in the same way, although the symbolic slippage between woman, nation and border is announced even more explicitly in its iteration as far-right icon.[4]

*The Slave Market* and similar Orientalist images feature the figure of the sex slave – the foundation for an iconography that has persisted into early cinema and beyond, its iterations detectable in contemporary sex trafficking and sex slavery films. As discussed in Chapter 1, the nineteenth-century Orientalist narrative in many ways initiated the colonial era's 'sex slave' discourse, in which prurience masqueraded as progressivism. Today, the very same images continue to be evoked as powerful tools in hegemonic operations of global biopolitics and the gendered construction of the nation-state in the developed West. Gérôme's painting centers one of the emblematic 'icons' of the sex slave narrative: the 'selection scene' – that is, the inspection of human goods that precedes the scene of purchase and is an essential part of the whole transaction process. This is a version of the ubiquitous 'auction block scene', borrowed from the visual inventory of the transatlantic slave trade, one instance of the contemporary sex slave narrative's parasitic extraction of content from the visual archive of chattel slavery.

When viewed collectively, sex slave films disclose a shared iconography that contributes a set of shorthand visual cues that shape and affix the imaginary of the sex trade and trafficking as a sanctioned spectacle of sex slavery. A number of visual tropes – such as the soiled mattress, the chains and the dungeon – combined with a series of emblematic scenes – including the abduction, transport, rape, rescue and sale of the 'sex slave' – contribute to the hyper-visibility of the figure constructed by cinema. The resulting narrative precipitates a narrow focalization of the issue of commercial sexual exploitation as a simplified scenario of abduction and captivity, not a problematic function of the oligarchic extractive economy – a complex transnational network of relations shaped by the financial, political and security mechanisms designed and maintained by the institutions of the Global North. The characteristic icons of sex slavery films construct a realm of barbaric, primitive and perverse sexuality, where the sexual 'Other' still mythically resides. This illiberal realm both repels and attracts Western liberal sensibility. The 'foreign body', unmoored from the protective rhetoric of family and national unity and caught up in endless traffic, is appropriated as a site of numerous projections of psychic and social fantasies. Indeed, it is at this very juncture that cinema itself, as a medium that creates and stokes fantasy, is revealed as implicated in this traffic.

In their ubiquitous recurrence, the iconic images that the sex slavery films produce are long-lasting, evocative and often charged with strong affect, as they intersect the lines between sensory perception and cognitive configuration. The icons work to produce the sex slave as an object of knowledge, visually inscribing this object as representational fact. In both its analog and digital forms, film as a photography-based medium produces icons that imbue fantasy with a strong sense of verisimilitude. In film theory, this effect is known as the reference principle. The icons are used to create shorthand semblances of reality or what Jean Baudrillard has called the *simulacra* – hyper-real copies whose symbolic impact far outstrips the impact of the real, whose actual complexity and messiness always resist mediation and lag behind the image.[5] In Baudrillard's view, the cinematic image forecloses the faithful rendering of reality so successfully precisely because its form broadcasts referential authenticity as its constitutive feature. In other words, the cinematic image convinces before it informs. Its perceived sincerity announces exposure as it simultaneously occludes. For Baudrillard, the danger of the cinematic image is its implementation of the 'logic of the extermination of its referent, a logic of the implosion of meaning in which the message disappears on the horizon of the medium'.[6] Yet, the embedded sense of verisimilitude in the cinematic image, so Baudrillard has explained, makes us want to trust it:

> [W]e all remain incredibly naïve: we always look for a good usage of the image, that is to say a moral, meaningful, pedagogic or informational usage,

> without seeing that the image in a sense revolts against this good usage, that it is the conductor neither of meaning nor good intentions, but on the contrary of an implosion, a denegation of meaning (of events, history, memory, etc.).[7]

The referential relationship between the cinematic construct and the antecedent experiential reality of sexual exploitation is grossly simplified in sex slavery films, through the emphatic image that persuades about the presumed dialectical connection – the primacy of reality that is then simply recuperated (and untransformed) in the image. Cinema does this much more effectively than non-photographic forms of representation ever could (including realist painting). The moral use that, so Baudrillard has argued, we eagerly apply to all cinematic images, including the image of the sex slave, is responsible for its lasting attraction and endless potential for political and ethical deployment. Arguably, the image of the sex slave, much like that of the religious icon, operates as a concentrated field of psychic, affective and spiritual intensities that respond to one's need to believe, markedly more so than one's need to know. Cinematic icons activate our 'belief' and 'trust', subordinating the social reality to the spectatorial experience that binds the cinematic spectator to a specific (imaged) world.

In what follows, I shall compile an inventory of sex slavery iconography, using the term 'icon' to invoke *both* the Christian pictorial tradition of devotional art, where the icon is constructed as a sacred object used in religious practice, and Charles Sanders Peirce's theory of the sign, where the term 'icon' refers to a sign that gains its meaning from its mimetic relationship to the referent (referent being the aspect of reality to which the sign refers). It is important to note here that Peirce's 'icon' is distinct from the 'index', which retains its contiguous relationship to the referent – the material and organic link to reality, as in the smoke that indexes fire.[8] In a sense, the index is part of reality, while the icon can only ever gesture toward it, a mere imitation. In spite of the indexical presumption invited by cinema's impression of verisimilitude and famously championed by André Bazin, cinematic signs, including images of sex slavery, are imitative constructs at best.[9] This claim to a contiguous relationship to reality, while often convincing, is an illusion, albeit a powerful one; cinema's showing, its act of monstration, is a self-referential spectacle first and foremost. As such, icons of sex slavery are the film industry's trafficked commodities, fashioned to meet the commercial demand for explicit content, particularly images of sexual violence. This chapter explores some of the most frequent, and therefore iconic, images in sex slavery films – images that challenge and seduce the liberal and egalitarian sensibility across the developed world today. My use of the term iconic throughout this chapter is conscious of the Christian concept of the icon and its connotation, which allows me to emphasize the emotion, specifically the moral feelings, that sex slavery icons elicit in the viewer. The devotional association with the Christian icon that I am inviting here echoes Patrick Maynard's claim that the photographic image is the secular icon of the modern West and, as such, it functions to manifest a certain presence.[10] It is a ritual image used to consecrate certain ideas and their corresponding figurations, including the figure of the sex slave, who serves an important function in the sexual theology of the patriarchal nation-state.

Further, the devotional association allows me to reflect on how the sex slavery discourse, including its powerful iconography, has been coopted by various evangelical movements whose philanthropic activism has increasingly focused on fighting the so-called 'modern-day slavery' – ostensibly a form of contemporary sexual enslavement of women and children practiced in what is described as the 'global brothel system' – by organizations such as the International Justice Mission, a large Christian non-governmental organization committed to seeking 'Biblical justice' by implementing 'God's plan to end slavery'.[11] Writing on the faith-based abolitionism in the evangelical church, sociologist Elizabeth Bernstein has outlined its alignment with the capitalist state and its avoidance of a confrontation with the structural economic exploitation that often undergirds the involvement of undocumented migrants in sex trade:

> For modern-day abolitionists, the dichotomy between slavery and freedom poses a way of addressing the ravages of neoliberalism that effectively locates all social harm outside of the institutions of corporate capitalism and the state apparatus. In this way, the masculinist institutions of big business, the state, and the police are reconfigured as allies and saviors, rather than enemies, of unskilled migrant workers, and the responsibility for slavery is shifted from structural factors and dominant institutions onto individual, deviant men: foreign brown men (as in the White Slave trade of centuries past) or even more remarkably, African American men living in the inner city. What is perhaps most ironic and surprising about the sexual politics of the 'new abolitionism' is that it has emerged not only from the simultaneous rightward migration of feminists and other secular liberals toward the politics of incarceration but also from a leftward sweep of some evangelical Christians away from the isolationist issues of abortion and gay marriage and toward a 'new internationalist', social justice-oriented theology.[12]

Advocates for the new abolitionism envision sex slaves in terms of 'the stock colonialist tropes of the backward traditionalism of third world women' who are prone to self-objectification and servitude. The sex slave is depicted both in cinema and the wider public discourse as ignorant, oblivious to liberal ideals of freedom and enterprise. As Jasbir K. Puar has written, these 'forms of US gender and (hetero) sexual exceptionalism from purportedly progressive spaces have surfaced through feminist constructions of "other" women, especially via the composite of the "third world woman"'.[13] The normative framework of human rights, particularly women's rights, allows for an apparent embrace of stigmatized figures – among them undocumented migrants, religious Others such as visibly Muslim women and sex workers, who are prone to self-objectification and servitude – as counterposed to the assumed autonomy of Western women who, precisely because of their self-proclaimed emancipation, feel entitled to, even called upon, to undertake the rescue of the enslaved.[14] In this sense, nominally secular progressive feminism and Christian conservatism are not at all at odds: both situate the Global North as the moral arbiter of the world, justifying military, legal and police intervention. In my critique, the sex slave emerges as a figure of disciplinary, spectacularized violence that warns against the free movement of women across economic, national and sexual borders. By understanding the iconography of the sex slavery film, it is possible to understand the dialectic of punishment and rescue that traverses the cinematic sex slave. Each icon demands and maintains what Paul Amar has dubbed the 'sexual-security regime' of the modern nation-state and its attendant global security industry, which includes the police, the penal system, the military-industrial complex, the rescue NGOs, as well as various (often international) religious organizations.[15] Amar's vision of the modern security state provides a helpful theoretical frame for my analysis of sex slavery iconography because it foregrounds how the contemporary oppression and resistance movements need to be considered *vis-à-vis* the increasing sexualization of politics and 'the new discourse of sexual terrorism' developed by the global security apparatus.[16] Within this weaponized discourse, Amar has found two key sets of figures: the 'hyperpassive agents' who are the working-class women often configured as sex slaves – 'duped, victimized, and trafficked across borders' and thus in need of being 'rescued, contained and localized' – and the 'hyperaggressive agents' who are the queer men identified as the perverse minority – the 'despised traitors' who invade or infect the country (by queering normative masculinity) and thus threaten national security, while ostensibly operating in the transnational, inter-urban global brothel community.[17] These figures arise from and enact the hyper-visibility of the 'sexual-security' logic deployed by the hegemonic powers of the security state. The hyper-visibility, in turn, racializes, sexualizes and stigmatizes the female and queer bodies exposed to precarity, through a host of volatile factors, often combinations of the economic instability of carnivorous capitalism, environmental emergencies, political or religious suppression, sexual or ethnic marginalization, and warfare. The icons constructed in sex slavery films directly contribute to the hyper-visibility of the migrant and working-class subjects who trade sex, thus disarticulating those subjects' potential for parity, equality and citizenship. The hyper-visible register in which these icons circulate exists to manage social subjects who elude the sanctioned categories of social hierarchy. Once contained within redacted icons, the subordinate subjects begin to accrue value within the security regime as *objects* whose hyper-articulation increases their manipulability within the repressive operations of sexual disciplining and social cleansing.

Cinema, I argue, is a technology uniquely equipped to manufacture the hyper-visibility of the subjects on which the security state relies to legitimize the 'state of exception' and its interventions. It is a medium that trains a heightened sense of vision, relying on asymmetrical, enhanced and vicarious structures of looking. Cinema produces hyper-visible figures through its deployment of spectacle, which enchants, attracts and shocks the viewer away from careful reflection, political consciousness, economic analysis, or ethical action. The following is a preliminary inventory of the sex slavery icons: monstrative visuals that cinema circulates within the long-form narrative, both as the evidentiary footage of the alleged sexual crimes committed within the global economy of sex trafficking and as its own cinematic commodity, the lucrative spectacle in a desire industry. Presented in an intentionally randomized sequence, this inventory is intended to demystify the sex slavery narrative by showcasing its compulsive return to the same set of flat, one-dimensional illustrations that the medium of cinema imbues with iconic manifestation thanks to its enhanced power of exposition. In the process of bringing these illustrations to the forefront of my analysis, I wish to suggest that these illustrations are, indeed, the main content being proffered in the visual marketplace that generates profit by rendering certain human subjects as hyper-visible and others as completely invisible. The imaged story of sex slavery provides the rationale for the visual articulation of some bodies as illegal and in need of immediate regimentation, and other bodies as sovereign and engaged in self-determination and determination of others. As one of the key information technologies that shapes the twenty-first century's culture industry, cinema must be considered as a tool of the economic and political operations that the neoliberal state employs to stigmatize (that is, visually and physically arrest) and utilize, both economically and symbolically, the boundary- and border-crossing subject as a racialized, gendered and sexualized object.

## Auction/Selection

The production of the sexual Other relies on the use of the xenophilic/ xenophobic spectacle. The figure of a foreign captive in an international slavery ring is frequently at the center of this spectacle. The sequences that showcase this figure are some of the most emblematic scenes of the contemporary sex slavery film cycle, which includes such notable examples as *Lilya 4-ever* (Dir. Lukas Moodysson, 2000), *La vie nouvelle* (Dir. Philippe Grandrieux, 2002), *Eastern Promises* (Dir. David Cronenberg, 2007), *La sconosciuta* (Dir. Giuseppe Tornatore, 2006), *Holly* (Dir. Guy Moshe, 2006), *Trade* (Dir. Marco Kreuzpaintner, 2007), *Little Soldier* (Dir. Annette K. Olesen, 2008), *Taken* (Dir. Pierre Morel, 2008; plus two *Taken* sequels), *The Whistleblower* (Dir. Larysa Kondracki, 2010), *Bibliothèque Pascal* (Dir. Szabolcs Hajdu, 2010), *Trade of Innocents* (Dir. Christopher Bessette, 2012), *Hope Lost* (Dir. David Petrucci, 2015), *Òlòtūré* (Dir. Kenneth Gyang, 2019) and *Sound of Freedom* (Dir. Alejandro Monteverde, 2023).

In this section, I will explore the icon of the auction-selection scene. Paradigmatic examples here include scenes of women dancing for male audiences in a nightclub setting, or scenes where the client selects their preferred woman from a line-up of different women. I see this latter scene as a variant of the iconic 'auction block' scene, whose visual charge rests on a quotation from the much older discourse of the transatlantic slave trade. In the films under discussion, spectacle is the operative visual mode. Its impact is intensified by the *mise-en-abyme* structure: the use of diegetic spectacle, viewed by the diegetic audience (pimp or client), then doubled in the extra-diegetic spectacle, viewed by the spectator. The presence of the patently compromised diegetic surrogate (he is either a criminal or a pervert) provides a vantage point for the film viewer to engage in voyeuristic pleasure without the threat of direct implication, as the surrogate's moral bankruptcy so obviously prevents identification, especially in a current zeitgeist so acutely attuned to issues of sexual abuse and sexual exploitation. A much quoted and critically appraised example of such a display scene introduces Giuseppe Tornatore's film *La sconosciuta* (*The Unknown Woman*, 2006; Figure 2.1).[18]

Evoking the 1970s' sexploitation genre, which often staged its erotic extravaganzas in antique aristocratic settings (vide the Castle of Balsonaro in Radley Metzger's *The Lickerish Quartet*, 1970), Tornatore's scene is set in a crumbling palazzo with all of the trappings of its former glory on display – old paintings, sculptures and antique furniture included. In the midst of this faded opulence, in a long shot, we see three semi-naked women parade in and out of the camera's field of vision. Soon, another group of three attractive women, dressed only in underwear and high heels, file in, exposing different

***Figure 2.1*** The process of selection in Giuseppe Tornatore's *La sconosciuta* (*The Unknown Woman*, 2006).

angles of their bodies to the camera in obedient response to the orders of a disembodied male voice directing the display. The women wear identical masks that anonymize and regulate their expressions, ensuring that the gaze falls on the nude bodies. Eventually only one woman is asked to remain on display. The voice instructs her to remove the already skimpy garments. She obeys. Now in mid-shot, along with the camera, the viewer inspects her perfectly proportioned, unblemished and otherwise normative white body. However, the viewer is not alone: the camera briefly rests on the impresario figure standing in the wings of this highly eroticized show. He watches and directs the women's stage traffic, choreographing their movements through curt, yet polite instructions. However, he is not the intended audience. The diegetic viewer, for whom this show has been staged, looks through a concealed peephole, also a common trope in the sexploitation genre. In close-up, we see the gazing eye. In fact, we see two different sets of eyes approach the aperture to look. On its own, this proliferation of eyes highlights the hypervisibility, not only of the nude women on the screen, but also of the figure of the sex slave in general, as a consumable object. Subsequent scenes provide an explanation for this elaborate opening sequence: the show is, in fact, a part of the reproductive selection process, wherein wealthy Italians (would-be parents) choose a pregnancy surrogate from a group of immigrant women forced into reproductive and sex slavery by an organized crime network. Tornatore's scene is a great example of the exposition set-up, reminiscent of the display technology of the marketplace or the fair ground.

In the vocabulary of sex slave films, there exists a variant of the selection scene that speaks of the abundance of commodities and modes of consumption, the many choices that the customer may have, depending on his refined desire for specific sexual pleasure, and the space devoted to their display.

In such scenes, which often use tracking shots, the camera takes the viewer on a walk through something akin to a modern shopping arcade: a series of rooms or enclosures, where different bodies are displayed for selection and consumption. These scenes are intriguing for how they distribute movement and stasis to comment on late modernity's tendency to immobilize and confine certain bodies while granting bewildering and unobstructed mobility to others. They visualize the market as a space where the consumer breezes through a structure designed to maximize the display and reach of the goods. Complex examples of such a scene can be found in *Trade*. Directed by German filmmaker Marco Kreuzpaintner and released in 2007, the film focuses on the fate of a thirteen-year-old Mexican girl, Adriana (Paulina Gaitán), who is kidnapped by sex traffickers from her home in Mexico City and smuggled across the Mexico-US border, all the way to New Jersey. Notwithstanding its excessively sentimental plot and clichéd characters, I find the film's emphasis on the construction of the foreign body as a commodity illustrative of the exoticizing spectacle that organizes films about sex slavery. An early scene depicts the traffickers' efforts to catalog and mediate the new 'merchandise', taking profile pictures of their captives for a secret online auction place, a virtual shopping arcade that specializes in peddling under-age bodies. While their physical bodies are captive, the mediated images of the women and children are entered into and circulated on the cybermarket in a swift process of commodification.

But it is a later scene that speaks most directly of the sex market as the modern space of commerce, where merchandise is displayed in an arcade-like structure to a potential customer (and the film viewer) who can visually assay the many options while on the move. After Adriana and a handful of other women and children are smuggled across the border, they stop at a rest area where the traffickers trade with American men from the local town who come to pay for quick sex. While the trafficked are *en route* to large metropolitan areas where they will be traded on a global market, they are also, in the meantime, sold for pennies at the rest stop, where an improvised local market exploits the opportunity of the presence of the many captive bodies waiting for their next dispatch. The rest area is a nexus of global and local trade, of early and late capitalist commerce, a hybrid space where the foreign body is both mobile and seized. It is at this rest stop that Adriana is sold for the first time. While no explicit content is shown in the ensuing images, the scene is perhaps the most disturbing in the film as it strategically reveals and conceals a space where foreign children are forced to trade sex. The man who pays for Adriana pulls her down a well-trodden path in a thick field of tall brush adjacent to the rest stop. Littered with trash, the natural area has been adapted into a makeshift bathroom and brothel. As the characters walk deeper into the maze of pathways, the camera sutures the viewer to Adriana's point of view, which is distinctly claustrophobic and frightened. As we reluctantly move along with her (she cries and tries to resist the force of the man who is walking right behind her and pushing her ahead), we see a succession of small clearings in the field. Each clearing displays new human merchandise. We get glimpses of other children, some of them dressed in communion white, some of them clutching their dolls; there are boys and girls of different ages. The camera's gaze is furtive. We see fragments and are invited to fill in the missing parts of the scene, which communicates the horror of pedophilic sexual abuse. Kitchen timers are set by each clearing to keep time.[19] The soundtrack is a mix of somber guitar music, kitchen timers ticking and buzzing, children whimpering and men coaxing compliance in hushed voices. A superimposition shot of money changing hands is edited into the scene to spell out Adriana's transformation into a commodity product for exchange.

Significantly, throughout this disturbing scene, the camera, walking us through the make-shift brothel, constructs the mobile vision characteristic of the modern spaces of commodification, discovery and exhibition – shopping centers, museums, galleries, zoological gardens, fairs and other similar spaces – which, in his *Arcades Project*, Benjamin has famously recognized as defining our modern experience. These spaces, which arguably cinema has always worked to replicate, orchestrate mobile vision as the perceptual cathexis of the subject-as-spectator-on-the-move engaging with the spectacularized object.[20] In the scene under analysis, the suture effect complicates, although it does not prevent, the potential for gratification and consumption inscribed in the mobile vision centered here on the child's body as an object of erotic pleasure. Kreuzpaintner draws the viewer's attention to the privilege and power inherent in the mobile vision. In the scene at the rest stop, Adriana begins as the traveling subject, discovering and surveying the exhibition of other bodies as sex objects, only to be refused the privileged position of agential vision and forced into the object position herself. The scene is focused on the moment of her divestment of visual subjectivity. Indeed, the scene breaks off at the moment when no doubt remains as to Adriana's loss of agency and her transformation into a sex object. In that sense, like many other sex slavery films, Kreuzpaintner's film resorts to a punitive framing when it comes to representing the foreign subject's potential mobility. The foreigner (a stand-in for the undocumented migrant) gains her dramatic entry only upon losing her status as subject. Ultimately, Adriana is punished for her desire to access mobile vision, a formative and fundamental function of modern subjectivity. It is important to note that Adriana is kidnapped as she rides her newly acquired bicycle, which, in an earlier scene, her mother expressly forbade her from doing. As such, the girl's exit from the domestic sphere, her newfound (and forbidden) mobility, her surveying vision and her technology-enhanced entry into public space each have severe consequences.

As the final example of the selection scene, I wish to discuss the audition as an exposition set-up common in the film industry and often repurposed in sex slavery plots. David Petrucci's *Hope Lost* uses this trope in ways that help us understand the prurient aesthetics that link cinema and sex commerce. Petrucci's film tells the story of a young Romanian woman, Sophia (Francesca Agostini), who meets Gabriel (Andrey Chernyshov), a man posing as a film director at a nightclub in Romania. Gabriel convinces Sophia to travel with him to Italy to take part in a casting audition. Once in Rome, Sophia is quickly passed on to a pair of pimps, Manol and Marius (played by B-movie actors Michael Madsen and Danny Trejo), who ensnare her in a prostitution racket. Much of the film follows the typical sex slavery film conventions: the girl is duped into traveling abroad, her passport is taken away from her, she is confined in an abandoned, dilapidated warehouse, verbally intimidated into compliance, raped by the traffickers to 'break her in' and forced to sell sex to 'buy' her way back to freedom. The story veers from the established sex slavery film script in the final portion of the film, when the traffickers decide to pivot their operations by taking Sophia and her fellow captive, Alina (Mischa Barton), off the streets to use them in the making of a snuff film instead. Here, the sex traffickers become film producers, the sex slaves are forced to act on an improvised film set, and the coerced sex services that the women had to perform in the streets are replaced with acting in an extreme sexploitation film.

Most of Petrucci's film is tendentious and rather predictable, almost grotesquely so, to a degree where the viewer wonders if the filmmaker is not, in fact, poking fun at the sex slavery tropes, compiling them into a self-reflexive graphic catalog. The unabashed meta-cinematic framing of Petrucci's film, however, offers an original addendum to the sex slavery film cycle that draws the viewer's attention to the collusion of the film industry with the sex trade, while also posing questions about the cinematic conventions of the sex slavery film. *Hope Lost* begins with a sort of sonic epigraph in the form of an audio quotation from a scene that plays out much later in the film. While the opening credits roll, the viewer hears a distressed female voice begging 'No, no!' The sounds of clanking metal, the whoosh of a blade and the crack of a whip are also audible. The calm and forceful male voice responds to the female cries with a cryptic statement: 'It's one of the golden rules of cinema. Before inevitable doom, there must always be a scene of hope'. Snippets of a disturbing torture scene quickly flash by on the screen, where the viewer can barely discern two female figures gagged and chained to the cement floor. After this disquieting prelude, the film turns to realism, opening with a scene at a garment factory, where its female staff, including the protagonist Sophia, engage in tedious manual labor, sewing, ironing and folding, toiling late into the night.

This sharp turn foreshadows the unsettled duality of Petrucci's film, which oscillates between torture porn and social problem film. Through this tension, the film meaningfully illuminates the contradictions of the sex slavery film as a genre characterized by a constant negotiation between sexual spectacle and didactic lesson. The film's final act sharpens these strains. The sequence begins when Alina and Sophia are roused from their sleep by 'the Professor' (Francesco Acquaroli), one of Manol's associates, who announces his intention to save them. The desperate women agree, only to find themselves in a new, even more exploitative predicament. They are transported to a villa and forced to perform another kind of sexual labor, this time in show business. Torture porn and social realism grotesquely merge as the film becomes a meta-cinematic snuff film with lights, cameras, props and actors. The improvised film set is now in focus, revealing the cinematic mode of production, specifically of sexploitation filmmaking. In a strange compositional conceit, the initial ploy of the audition that was used to recruit Sophia and the snuff film project that concludes *Hope Lost* bracket the sex slavery film on both ends with a meta-cinematic commentary, where Petrucci, perhaps quite intentionally, charts out important parallels between the use of the female figure in the sex slave film and the snuff film. Both genres, Petrucci seems to be saying, use conventions – 'golden rules' – to attract viewers and ensure successful commercial return. Both genres exploit images of extreme female suffering, eroticizing the violated female body and traumatizing the female actors in the process.

In the end, Petrucci's film tellingly fails to deliver what the viewers of these two genres would expect, deconstructing them instead. The rescue mission that has been methodically built up in the sex slavery portion of *Hope Lost* is aborted at the moment when the rescue figure dies on the set of the snuff film. Ultimately, the rescue, a requisite element of the sex slavery narrative (discussed later in this chapter), turns out to be unnecessary, as the sex slaves prove to be women strong enough to liberate themselves. The snuff film is also never fully completed: its makers have to stop the production because the female actors whose lives are to be 'snuffed out' on camera successfully fight back, sabotaging the production and ending their exploitation on the screen. Sophia and Alina will neither be rescued nor snuffed out. The director/cameraman is stabbed to death on the set of his own film. In a somewhat anti-climactic and rather comic gesture, Manol, the producer of the snuff film, admits defeat and walks away from the set, seemingly fed up with his criminal life. Perhaps unsurprisingly, Petrucci's film – a film that broke the conventions with which it was toying – was not successful at the box office. It received no critical attention. Yet, its twofold contribution to the canon of sex slavery film is significant. *Hope Lost* stands out as a piece of self-aware cinema that is not afraid to equate the sex slavery film with sexploitation cinema, by constructing a narrative where the social problem film morphs into an explicit and potentially titillating scenario. Both genres, so the film suggests, cater to specific audience expectations, which are mostly centered around narrative and visual pleasure. Petrucci's film also draws parallels between the sex industry and the film industry, both of which capitalize by coercing women into positions of subjection. Here, film acting and sex work overlap under the same category of performance, as women's bodies are forced to perform for and fulfill the expectations of specific customers/audiences. The film's ruse, a casting audition which the traffickers use as a ploy to recruit women for sexual exploitation, raises, albeit indirectly, the systemic sexual exploitation of female actors in the film industry, which frequently occurs during the cast selection process, an issue that has gained widespread public visibility following the #MeToo movement and the numerous exposés of the 'casting couch' and audition abuses.[21]

## Commodification: Branding and the Stripping Pole

Scenes of commodification are one of the most common conventions of sex slavery cinema. Such scenes illustrate the process of producing goods that are circulated in the sex industry, one of many desire industries that capitalize on the commodification of women's flesh and labor. These scenes are not merely didactic tableaux or public awareness vehicles; they are themselves products, each a unit of consumption. Together, these commodities are produced for profit within the film industry, in response to the economic demands of the marketplace. Scenes of commodified appearance, which often take the form of showcasing the sex slave's body to the diegetic audience, are apt contemporary examples of how cinema implements monstration, theorized by Tom Gunning and André Gaudreault as a spectacle of exhibition, to attract the viewer and ensure their investment in the film's narrative. These scenes are important icons to analyze and understand as they disclose the affinity between cinema and sex trade as industries that respond to, and ultimately produce, our late capitalist exhibition culture and arrogate profit by exhibiting racialized and sexualized flesh. While sex slavery films are certainly works of long-form narrative cinema, their consistent reliance on sexual monstration challenges their legitimacy as social critique. There is a complex dialectical relationship between narration and monstration in these films, whereby the continuous, linear ethical narrative is validated by and perhaps even requires the monstrative spectacle; together, they perpetuate the process of the commodification under the pretense of a humanitarian narrative.

The scenes of commodification are doubly monstrative: the diegetic spectacle that is consumed by the diegetic viewer(s) is mediated and delivered on screen as a scene of monstration directed at the film viewer, who consumes the female flesh as commodity at two degrees of separation from within the cinematic apparatus. The fact that the films' viewers are invited to derive pleasure from the eroticized spectacle similar to that of the diegetic viewer is, of course, obscured by the film's manifest ethical mission to disclose the revolting criminal act of sex slavery. The righteous horror is there to disguise the not-so-coincidental pleasures of the sex spectacle. Both the sex slavery film's own commodification spectacle and its avowed moralizing narrative that cautions against the evils of sex slavery commodification – two sources of the genre's continued appeal – prove lucrative alone and become all the more so in combination. The seeming paradox between these two registers, one that deploys commodification and one that warns against it, is quickly resolved when one considers the connection between the processes of commodification and the processes of security control in the neoliberal state – both approach the undocumented migrants instrumentally as objects of manipulation and control. Both also rely on exhibition and enhanced visibility. Finally, racialized and sexualized, whether as sex commodities to be consumed or as sex slaves to be rescued, the undocumented migrants are re-articulated in the films under discussion as tools of constructing and consolidating the empowered patriarchal neoliberal subject.

Petrucci's *Hope Lost* addresses the violence of bodily commodification, which the film reproduces in a horrifying scene of human branding – a method, associated with the history of slavery, of marking the ownership of an enslaved person by searing or cutting the enslaver's insignia into the flesh of the enslaved. In the scene, Manol punishes Sophia for refusing to have sex with a client who does not wish to wear a condom. Manol asks Sophia to look at Alina's back where he has cut his initials into her skin as punishment for past disobedience. In a series of quick shots, Alina's body comes into a close-up, her robe is violently torn off her shoulder, and the camera zooms in on the mutilated surface of her skin, revealing a raised, white scar in the shape of an 'M'. In extreme close-up, we witness the extent of Alina's dispossession of her body and its objectification by Manol's brand. Manol comments that branding, in his business, is a way to discipline the women, but also a way to show them who their boss is. It is crucial to note that Fabian (Diego Pagotto), the handler who caught Sophia in her act of resistance, is paradoxically reprimanded by Manol for slapping and bruising her face, thus 'spoiling' the merchandise. The need to physically discipline without defacing is a common motif in slavery films and underscores the fact that both the sex trade and cinema are industries of appearance wherein female flesh must remain attractive even as it is punished. Manol then breaks a wine bottle and, handing Sophia one of the shards, tells her that she has two 'choices': either brand herself by carving his initial 'M' into her skin, or be raped by Fabian. Sophia attempts to but is unable to self-mutilate and is instead brutally raped.

A scene of such visceral and unmetaphorical human commodification naturally invites associations with chattel slavery and its characteristic biometric practices, which notoriously employed human branding to track, code, mark and market the bodies of enslaved Africans and their descendants.[22] Petrucci's image of branding invites a not unproblematic analogy between the biometric strategies of the transatlantic slave trade and contemporary sex traffickers operating in Europe today – departing rather liberally from the reality of contemporary bonded sex labor practices and commercial strategies, which rely on digital technologies to track and manage sex workers. Rhetorically, this over-determined analogy occludes the women's status as undocumented migrant workers who, when they are exploited, lack any legal recourse or protection from their traffickers. As Anna M. Agathangelou has written, 'while the organization of the desire industries and the trafficking trade is not the same as the slave system in the antebellum South, it still draws upon understandings and practices of slavery, recolonization, exploitation, and racism in its everyday constitution and reproduction'.[23] By equating the contemporary sex trade with historic chattel slavery, the film obscures these complexities; instead, it presents a highly-mediated, elaborate spectacle of women's abjection that displaces the political economy of present-day sex trafficking. The brutal image of branding is meant to shock and frighten the contemporary viewer; the act's association with chattel slavery positions present-day trafficking as an incursion from a barbaric and widely condemned past, rather than a current struggle for labor rights that could be negotiated and bargained for.

Visual commodification organizes another quintessential scene often found in sex slavery films: the stripping pole scene. With its emphasis on choreographed display and the performing body, the scene offers what Laura Mulvey has famously called 'woman as image' – the female figure transformed into a fetish, a thing.[24] Mulvey has also observed how the female object's 'alien presence' tends to 'freeze the flow of action in moments of erotic contemplation'.[25] When one considers the spectacularized female object in the context of sex slavery films, there emerges a compounded effect of alienness, whereby the female figure provokes anxiety due to both her gender and her foreignness. While the selection scene discussed earlier in this chapter constructs the female figure as a commodity exhibited and circulated in the global sex trade market, the stripping pole scene builds an area of textual engagement for the film viewer that is less concerned, at least on the surface, with the socio-economic and/or ethical quandaries of the sex trade, which otherwise determine the plot. If we agree with Mulvey, the scene suspends such concerns in the interest of visual pleasure. But how exactly is the sex-slave-as-object constructed to evoke pleasure? What kind of pleasure is the object designed to elicit? The stripping pole scene 'performs' for the diegetic audience, occupying a role similar to that of the showgirl in classic Hollywood cinema; both are used to integrate the eroticized spectacle into the diegesis.

Whether such scenes depict drugged, under-age Ukrainian girls forced to perform at a stripping pole in a suburban brothel on the outskirts of London, as in David Cronenberg's *Eastern Promises* (2007), or Balkan women made to perform in an illegal night club in post-war Sarajevo, as in Philippe Grandrieux's *La vie nouvelle* (2002), they operate according to a rigid convention. The 'exotic' dancers perform as the camera zooms in on their bodies, focusing on their undulating breasts and buttocks moving to the diegetic music. These bodies are hardly the flat 'cut-outs' of Mulvey's theory.[26] The iconicity of classic Hollywood cinema that Mulvey has theorized only partially elucidates the stripping pole performance and what it might communicate. Indeed, the scene constructs a female object through the use of the pornographic lens. In its repetitive movement, rhythmic choreography and close-up framing, the object manifests a certain athleticism, plenitude and inexhaustible stamina. As such, the pornographic object that emerges becomes a commentary on the commodification of the foreign body in the sex trade market and its controlled mobility. The stripping pole scene deploys the xenophilic spectacle to attract consuming desire to a consumer object whose desirability is determined by its imported provenance. Unlike other scenes in sex slavery films, which connote the precarity and fragility of the trafficked women and children (through specific narrative tropes, composition, lighting, props and make-up), the stripping pole spectacle presents the human commodity as athletic and renewable. Inexhaustible, phallic and opulent, the foreign object as fetish loses its human aspect in the act of being consumed and circulated.

The spectacle focused on this object halts the ethically charged narrative and invites the consuming gaze of the diegetic and extra-diegetic viewer. Guilt is displaced, as the erotic spectacle frames off the foreign female body and delegates it to what Mulvey has called the 'no man's land' of sexual pleasure – the space where time stops and plot ceases.[27] Arguably, much of the pleasure has to do with the power to manipulate the human object (the female object, the foreign object), to control its movement. In the stripping pole scene (or any of its variants), the sex slave obeys the choreography of erotic exhibition; such scenes illustrate the abdication of control that is so

***Figure 2.2*** Boyan choreographs Melania's movement in Philippe Grandrieux's *La vie nouvelle* (*A New Life*, 2002).

central to the process of objectification. Alongside the diegetic audience member, the film viewer contemplates a mobile object, which on a very basic level presents as animated matter (pliable material) that is choreographed by the viewing subject's desire.

Grandrieux's *La vie nouvelle* features a rare and controversial scene that vividly dramatizes this process of animation (Figure 2.2). In this scene, which is found toward the end of the film, Melania (Anna Mouglalis), one of the women exploited by trafficker Boyan (Zsolt Nagy), is transformed into a human spinning top by her handler. In a series of experimental and technically virtuosic shots, Grandrieux stages a spectacle wherein Boyan choreographs Melania's movements, literally causing her to spin out of control and into physical collapse. The sequence focuses on Boyan's hands, whose movement in the air appears to 'conduct' Melania's dancing body. Remotely, without touch, the hands manipulate and control to a disconcerting degree. The sound effects throughout the sequence imbue Melania's body with the inertia and weight of an object spun by an external force; we witness the loss of Melania's own bodily agency and her conversion into a thing. Although critic Adrian Martin has extolled the scene as a performance of 'magical and lyrical transport', where '*the metteur en scène*' directs the female form into some kind of liberating abstraction 'detached from time and space', I find the scene grotesque in its blatant and unapologetic display of the heterosexual male subject's desire to possess and control the exhibition of the female form.[28] But I also agree with Martin that the scene can be read as a meta-cinematic reflection on male directorial agency; specifically, how such agency is exercised over the female form (including Grandrieux's manipulation of Mouglalis' form throughout his film), indicating intriguing parallels between trafficking and visual mediation.

Following Bachmann-Medick's work on the connection between mediation and alterity, which argues that media is a conduit between Self and Other, I propose an examination of sex slavery films as spectacles of the Other that imagine for us those paths of desire for the embodied foreign object where that object is mediated for erotic use and consumption. As Bachmann-Medick has argued, '"alterity" itself unfolds as a projection screen for imaginations, fantasies, wishes, national anxieties, and self-exaggerations – visions of the unknown as well as projections onto the alienized, exoticized, or stereotyped Other'.[29] Here, the erotic field becomes the site for the production of the modern subject who is summoned into identity and contoured out through a complex operation of mediation and phallic spectacularization of the Other-as-sex-slave. The desire for the pliable Other, its coming into sight, gives rise to the subject of global modernity. The consumption of this Other as a sex commodity, which the sex slavery film narrative ostentatiously decries (yet furtively promotes), and the rescue of this Other from such consumption, which the humanitarian anti-slavery narrative ostentatiously promotes (yet furtively decries), appear to depend on xenophilia deployed as an appropriative impulse that brackets the Other off as foreign body spectacularized – an object of desire to be used, manipulated, arranged, cataloged, animated, de-animated, and always mediated. The xenophilic desire that undergirds both the cinematic spectacles of sex slavery and the philanthropic rescue industry that seeks to save women and children from the plight of sex slavery may also play a role in displacing the xenophobic sentiments directed against undocumented migrants, who often enter the global job market through voluntary sex work. One may argue that it is easier to muster empathy for those bodies that were forcefully smuggled across the borders by criminals than to find paths of identification with women and children who have elected to cross borders illegally to perform sex work as their rite of passage into the global marketplace. The victim of slavery functions as a desirable Other that occludes the undocumented migrant Other, the latter functioning as a participant in, and witness to, a rather banal social contract that tolerates all forms of exploitation and utilization of humans as commodity. The naïve discourse of sex slavery ostensibly decries the desire for the utilizable human object – casually ubiquitous degradation assigned to the undocumented migrant who labors in the shadow economy of sex trade. In an idealistic way, this grand gesture may contain a silent but unpotentiated critique of late capitalism's exploitation of undocumented migrant labor.

## VIOLATION

Scenes of physical and sexual abuse are *de rigueur* in sex slavery films. They have the dual function of delivering a cautionary message about the dangers of female mobility (and as such these scenes enact the disciplinary regime of the state security apparatus) and of providing the kind of sadistic spectatorial pleasure that Laura Mulvey has defined in her theory of the voyeuristic look in narrative cinema. Writing about images of bodily trauma in films about trafficking and the position of the viewer as witness, Yana Hashamova has diagnosed the tension between these two functions and defined the relationship between them as 'a fragile line between seeking to create an empathetic viewer and titillating the spectator with the objectification of female bodies'.[30] Her comparative analysis of images of bodily violations – including the beating, stripping, binding, humiliating, insulting, threatening and raping – in films produced in the West (the region of demand in the economy of trafficking) versus those produced in the East (the region of supply) suggests no significant difference in how the films construct the uneasy and 'elusive balance' between empathetic witnessing and spectatorial pleasure.[31] The representational ambiguity – the tension between depicting the sexual and bodily violence as evidence of trauma that provokes spectatorial indignation, on one hand, and as the voyeuristic spectacle that entertains and amuses the spectator, on the other – is found 'across national and regional cinemas'.[32]

The motivation behind the two impulses, however, may be quite related. Despite the aesthetic, affective and libidinal differences, there may be a connection between creating and consuming the images of objectified women on screen, specifically as objects of sadistic violence (and as such, the objects of voyeuristic spectatorial pleasure), and creating the cinematic narrative of sex slavery, where such images would provide the rationale for the neoliberal security discourse that seeks to control women, especially if they are presenting as transgressive, in order to integrate them into the heteropatriarchal system of power relations. The economic interests of the film industry that has a long and well-documented history of objectifying women, both on and off screen, are very much the interests of the capitalist hegemony. Hashamova's reading of the trafficking feature film as a site of awareness-raising and social activism is restricted to a carceral feminist approach. To arrive at a less limited understanding of the trafficking film's social function, I believe it is crucial to consider its place within the political economy. Such films are at once a product of the capitalist economy, which the neoliberal security state is mobilized to protect, and a form of governmental control. As vehicles of securitization carried out in the register of media culture, sex slavery films *sell* images of women's violated bodies; both titillating and lucrative, this spectacle also happens to bolster the patriarchal relations of power that continue to underpin and maintain the capitalist economy and the neoliberal security state. Despite the many cultural emancipatory movements that unfolded during the twentieth and the twenty-first centuries, the capitalist economy continues to subordinate and oppress women (including trans women), whose primary role in this economy continues to be as agents of support for the male workers (and the patriarchal family structure) through providing housework, childcare, reproductive, affective and sex labor. By showcasing the scenes of violating the female body, sex slavery films speak of the material ways in which oppression and subordination will be exacted, especially onto the bodies of women who defy the mandate of domestic docility by aspiring to physical and economic mobility.

The violation icons proffered by sex slavery films are best understood as Foucault's 'hundreds of tiny theaters of punishment', where women are disciplined on screen, their bodily torment infinitely re-enacted as a mechanism within the corrective discourse of the modern security state and the ultimate technology of panoptical biopower. Foucault has presented his vision of the modern security state as a theater of discipline in the dystopic tableau of 'the punitive city' wherein every punishment is a 'visible punishment', often strategically choreographed by 'scenery, perspectives, optical effects, *trompe l'œil*' that convince the public of 'the existence of certain cruelties which, in fact, do not take place'.[33] The mere visual 'fable' of punishment – 'this serious theater, with its multifarious and persuasive scenes' – will be sufficient to discipline the citizens of the punitive city.[34] Foucault's explicitly dramaturgical framing of the security state is particularly apt and conceptually rich when considered in dialogue with the sex slavery film, with its punishing spectacles of violation. At its most self-reflexive, the sex slavery film can act as a comment on the integration of discipline and spectacle, as well as the conditions for both. At its most disturbing, it re-enacts that discipline, revealing the biometric ability of cinema itself – uniquely equipped to stigmatize certain bodies through spectacularization – to facilitate the discursive, institutional and state surveillance of those bodies. Within the corpus of sex slavery films, the most extreme example of this Foucauldian theater of discipline may well be the brutal rape scene featured in Larysa Kondracki's *The Whistleblower*, a film whose trafficking narrative occurs within the context of the Balkan Wars. Set in the late 1990s in Bosnia and Herzegovina, the film explores the collusion of the United Nations peace-keeping forces with local criminals in the administration of a large-scale sex slavery ring that trafficks women to and from the war-torn (and therefore unsecured) region. The film follows two protagonists, Kathryn Bolkovac (Rachel Weisz), a Nebraskan police officer hired by the fictional American military contractor Democra International

***Figure 2.3*** The diegetic audience in the scene of disciplining the slave in *The Whistleblower* (Dir. Larysa Kondracki, 2010).

to work with a United Nations task force in the country; and Raya (Roxana Condurache), a young Ukrainian woman who escapes her trafficker-captors. Raya finds refuge at a women's shelter, where Kathryn convinces her to testify against her traffickers and the corrupt peace-keepers. Because they are collaborating with the authorities, the traffickers eventually recapture Raya, whom they sexually torture in front of other trafficked women to terrorize them into compliance and silence.

The torture scene is composed as a fast cut and chaotic series of shots that show the traffickers bringing Raya back to the holding space (configured as the sex slavery 'dungeon' to be discussed below). Immediately upon arrival, Raya is rushed into the space where the other women are confined. A table is moved to the center of the room. Two men drag Raya inside and strip her to her bra and jeans. In the meantime, other men rouse the rest of the young women captives, who are forced to stand up and look at Raya. The men explicitly frame Raya's imminent assault as a punishment for her disobedience, an example of what will happen if anyone thinks of reporting the traffickers. The men go so far as to hold up the women's heads, forcing them to take in the intimidating spectacle that is quickly unfolding in front of them (Figure 2.3). Raya is thrown onto the table; her pants and underwear ripped off; she is turned face down, beaten over the head and then raped with a metal pipe. While Raya cries out in pain, the traffickers ensure that every woman bears witness to Raya's punishment. The position of the hand-held camera, combined with the film's rapid editing, suture the viewer into the scene: the viewer not only watches alongside the captive women, but also watches the women watching. Close-ups and extreme close-ups are frequently deployed throughout this scene to construct a very uncomfortable, furtive gaze. Hashamova has identified this shock-saturated viewing perspective as possessing 'the sickening effect' and argued that such a perspective may border on inciting in the viewer a certain kind of voyeuristic pleasure derived from the vicarious exploitation of the victimized subject, rather than producing the reflective witnessing spectator.[35] Hashamova's theory may be the reason why the viewer does not actually see the rape itself: the insertion of the pipe into Raya's body happens off screen. Instead, the viewer sees Raya's face contorted in physical agony before a bloodied pipe is thrown onto the floor. The occlusion of the most disturbing act of the violation may allow for the vicarious gaze to persist, as Hashamova has suggested. But the viewer also sees the facial expressions and hears the screams of the women forced to witness the punishment of one of their own. This set-up can interpellate the viewer as a witness, a perpetrator, or a victim, in the 'fable' of punishment defined by Foucault as the dominant form of disciplining the modern subject. More likely than not, the potential female viewer is disciplined through the *mise-en-abyme* structure of looking that is so cleverly set up within this monstrative scene.

Sex slavery films arguably deliver scenes of punitive violation as a way of disciplining the female subject through a discursive (cinematic) form of social control – a way to enforce specific gender relations that invite the colonization and submission of the laboring female body. Here patriarchal power operates predominantly through the spectacle of corporal punishment; the female subject is disciplined via the 'uninterrupted play of calculated gazes' into an object position.[36] The spectacle of the violation of the female body, an icon in sex slavery films, subtly rationalizes the phobic logic of the neoliberal security state that relegates the female to specific spaces, simultaneously reinforcing the gendered, sexed and racialized power relations that shape the capitalist economy in which the female circulates in commodified forms.

The sexual violation of a child is also a common icon in sex slavery films. However, this violation is always implied or carried out off-screen, in order to protect the film from charges of producing child pornography. The interesting aspect of this variant of the violation icon is the racialization of the child who is subjected to violence. White Western children are rarely depicted as the victims of sexual exploitation. When they are featured, they are presented as an adolescent who is typically saved from the impending violation by their powerful white protector/savior, as is the case in *Taken*. Generally, the young child victims that do feature in films about sex slavery tend to be depicted as non-Western. In their didactic mode, rather than examining the political economy of the sex trade, such films make an Orientalizing gesture towards the local culture and its attendant poverty and corruption to explain the root causes of, and institutional apathy towards, the violent exploitation of children. In films such as *Holly*, *Trade* and *Trade of Innocents*, parental complicity or neglect precipitate the trafficking of the racialized child sex slave, reproducing a long-standing colonial construction of non-Western cultures, which regards non-Western kinship structures and social contracts as primitive and often aberrant; in this way, it legitimizes and affirms the supremacy of Western values, which are understood to constitute 'civilization'. As a result, when sex slavery films depict the physical or sexual assault of young girls (and, less commonly, boys), these violations register as crimes enacted by foreign criminal networks that have been enabled, if not encouraged by, the erosion of the traditional family structure. In the films under analysis, when Western (often American) white men witness and react to violence against children of color, it is often as protectors of human rights, borders and democracy in general. Whether it is Ray Sheridan (Kevin Kline) in *Trade*, a border patrol agent who rescues the Mexican girl Adriana (Paulina Gaitán), or Patrick (Ron Livingston), the would-be savior of the Vietnamese girl Holly (Jacquie Nguyen) in *Holly*, or the American couple Alex (Dermot Mulroney) and Claire Becker (Mira Sorvino) who protect Amy, a Vietnamese-American girl (Thawanrat Tantituvanont), white protectors appear to engage in their rescue missions to right the wrongs carried out by foreign criminals (including undemocratic and corrupt foreign governments). In these scenarios of the trafficking and abuse of foreign children of color, xenophilia and empathy are affective performances that occlude the xenophobia that in truth pervades the discursive overlap between immigration and trafficking in the United States and Europe. In a rhetorical gambit, the violations of the trafficked foreign children broadcast the many dysfunctions of their families and societies of origin (those dysfunctions are in turn responsible for the children's displacement, exploitation and even death), thus supplying the Western protectors with a rationale to enforce their conceptions of law and order. In their capacity as xenophilic narratives of child protection, sex slavery films often displace and silence xenophobic narratives about migrants while addressing the very same anxieties about foreign invasion, racial mixing and border security. Guy Moshe's *Holly* is a potent example of a film where the violation of the child sex slave acts as a wholesale indictment of Southeast Asian culture. The film's plot revolves around Patrick, a jaded American who moves to Cambodia to escape his troubled past as a stolen artifacts dealer and gambler. When Patrick's motorcycle breaks down in Phnom Penh's notorious red-light village Svay Pak, or K11, he runs into Holly, a twelve-year-old girl who has been sold to traffickers by her impoverished Vietnamese parents and subsequently forced to work in a Cambodian brothel. Patrick befriends Holly, who is at first presented as a typical child and still a virgin. Patrick decides to rescue Holly, but the local sex traffickers and corrupt police sabotage his noble mission.

A scene of child rape punctuates the storyline and functions as a symbolic act that dooms not only Holly but the entire local society to the position of wretched exploitation and moral decrepitude. The scene where Holly is raped occludes the moment of sexual violation, which happens off screen. Yet, it communicates much more than what it conceals. In the scene, a corrupt government official enters the brothel where Holly is kept. The official has been encouraged to visit the brothel on the recommendation of the local police officer, who promises the official an opportunity to have sex with a virgin. The first shot in this sequence shows Holly in a bed with the sheets pulled up over her shoulders, completely concealing her body. She sits up when the official enters the room. He offers her candy, and she accepts it. The camera cuts to the exterior of the brothel, where men sit outside of their cars, smoke and tell jokes, seemingly undisturbed by what is happening inside. The scene moves back to the room, where the man is shown buttoning up his shirt. Behind him, Holly lies flat, almost like a corpse. He offers her another piece of candy, but she does not respond. When he leaves, the camera closes up on her feet, which twitch slightly. A shot of her hand balled up into a fist follows. Then, from above, the camera focuses on her face, her eyes full of tears. These shots offer after-images of the assault; they also act as synecdoche for the assault, making it explicit by way of reference rather than showing it. The way in which the camera fragments the child's body, visually disassembling it into parts, speaks of Holly's reification as a sex commodity.

There are a few important factors that set this scene apart from the rape scene constructed in *The Whistleblower*. First, in *Holly* the whole scene is occluded. The viewer has no access to the victim's experience of violation, neither directly nor via witness reactions, as is the case in Kondracki's film. As a result, Holly's assault is presented as systematic and normalized, a part of everyday life. Featuring the local official as the perpetrator places the responsibility for child exploitation on the racialized local populace and away from the neocolonial Western expats that populate the background of the film. I would argue that this effect is produced intentionally to communicate that the sexual exploitation of minors is normalized in Southeast Asian cultures (*Holly* takes place in Cambodia and Vietnam). It is telling that the rape marks a change in Holly's characterization. From this point on, she no longer acts as a child. Instead, she compulsively solicits Patrick for sex, seemingly unable to understand a relationship with an adult man that is not a sexual transaction. While the first half of the film showcases Holly's resolve to escape her plight (indeed, she manages to escape twice) alongside Patrick's determination to save her, the post-rape half of the film takes on a bleak, capitalist realism, where there is no reasonable alternative to the *status quo*. This realism is focalized through Marie (Virginie Ledoyen), a French NGO worker who disabuses Patrick of his rescue fantasy – a fantasy worth disabusing, but whose rejection is delivered as a wholesale rejection of any imaginable alternative to the *status quo*. Marie, another Western outsider, explains to Patrick that neither Holly nor any of the thousands of other children who are sex-trafficked in Cambodia can be rescued. Reciting a list of sobering statistics, Marie voices the 'different values, different morals' assessment telegraphed throughout the film. In this conversation between a French woman and an American man, the film neither identifies nor critiques France's long history of colonial exploitation in the region; neither does it explore the impact of United States' twenty-year-long war on Vietnam, Cambodia and Laos. The film does not connect these histories to the systemic poverty of local communities, which drives women and children to take up sex work. The film also fails to address the dubious role of some NGOs in the rescue industry, including the controversy around AFESIP Cambodia (an NGO that apparently employs Marie) and its founder Somaly Mam.[37]

## Rescue

The icons of the rescue mission and the figure of the rescuer are so integral to the sex slavery film that the films may well be grouped together as 'rescue cinema'. The rescue operations span from efforts undertaken by concerned citizens (*Holly*, *Trade of Innocents*, *Òlòtūré*, *Little Soldier* and *Eastern Promises*), over those by distraught family members of the abducted woman or child (*Taken*, *Trade*), and active or retired agents of law enforcement who act out of some sense of professional ethics (*The Whistleblower*, *Taken*, *Trade*, *Sound of Freedom*, *Hope Lost*, *Little Soldier*), to clients who fall in love with the sex slave after buying their services (*Hope Lost*, *La Vie Nouvelle*). Sometimes the rescuer may have multiple motivations, as do the rescue figures in *Little Soldier*, *Taken* and *Hope Lost*, where the rescuer is both emotionally invested in the sex slave and happens to be an agent (or former agent) of law enforcement. In films such as *Trade* and *Trade of Innocents*, the law enforcement rescue figures are also motivated to rescue a child sex slave in an effort to symbolically recuperate the loss of their biological child, who either had died tragically or has gone missing.

Gender and race greatly inform the production of these rescue tropes. The rescue can be carried out by male or female rescuers, with a pronounced tendency to showcase the powerlessness and impotence of the female rescuers, as is the case in *Hope Lost*, *Òlòtūré*, *Little Soldier* and even *The Whistleblower*.

The films whose rescue missions are not only successful but also spectacular are typically carried out by white male (former) law enforcement agents such as Bryan Mills in *Taken* or Tim Ballard in *Sound of Freedom.* Race further inflects the construction of the rescue figure and the success potential of the rescue mission. In the corpus of sex slavery films, films that feature a person of color in the role of the sex slave are rare; and when they do depict a sex slave as a person of color, there is often a white proxy figure who actually motivates the rescue of the person of color that is, in turn, carried out by the white rescue figure. *Trade* illustrates this complex work of racial substitution and displacement well – the white rescuer Ray Sheridan (Kevin Kline) embarks on the mission to rescue the Mexican girl Adriana because she reminds him of his estranged daughter who has recently gone missing. Additionally, Adriana – whose story drives the plot of the film, which is bracketed by her abduction and eventual rescue – for much of the film is paired with a white Polish woman, Victoria (Alicja Bachleda), who has also been trafficked. Similarly, in *Trade of Innocents*, the white American couple Alex and Claire Becker rescue young Cambodian and Vietnamese girls from the plight of sex slavery, in an attempt to displace the guilt and grief they feel after their own daughter was kidnapped and murdered. In both films, the rescue missions – sites of displaced grief, atonement and possible closure – become instrumentalized as therapeutic adventures that enable the white rescuers to process their original traumas and thus articulate a racially-informed hierarchy of suffering. Further, in the overwhelming majority of these films, the sex traffickers are coded as foreign and non-white. These tendencies of racialized character construction disclose a very specific racial politics of the genre, which I will discuss in detail in Chapter 4.

The 2019 Nollywood film *Òlòtūré*, however, stands in sharp contrast to films that present the rescue of the sex slave as a spectacle of white Western agency and First World moral superiority, bringing into relief the tendentiousness of the sex slavery narrative and its neocolonial discursive work. *Òlòtūré* emphatically does not deliver the conventional rescue action adventure, proffered by the popular *Taken* franchise, that has been so embraced by audiences in the developed West. Directed by Nigerian filmmaker Kenneth Gyang and financed by Netflix and Mo Abudu's production company EbonyLife, this film in many ways undermines the phobic white fantasy embodied by Morel's blockbuster. Precisely because it does not rely on or reinforce the cultural coordinates of successive 'white slavery' panics, the film offers a vital and more complex, if still spectacularized, perspective on the sex trade. Like the other films I have discussed in this chapter, *Òlòtūré* navigates the tension between social realism and didacticism, on the one hand, and spectacularized violence, on the other. Although fictional, the film's journalist protagonist

***Figure 2.4*** Crossing the border in *Òlòtūré* (Dir. Kenneth Gyang, 2019).

similarly invites a direct relationship between a social reality and its cinematic adaptation. *Òlòtūré* focalizes the 'supply side' of sex trafficking in Lagos, depicting sex workers and traffickers as part of the wider local and global economy. Indeed, local madam Alero (Omoni Oboli) is first introduced at a local marketplace, maintaining a stall that serves as cover for her operation. By posing as sex worker, Òlòtūré gains access to Alero, a local madam who facilitates the movement of migrants from Nigeria to Italy for a flat fee of $1,200. Unwilling to break her cover, Òlòtūré joins a small group of brothel workers managed by Alero and experiences first-hand the dangerous circumstances of unauthorized border-crossings involved in the journey to Europe. When she finally wants out, she calls her male colleague Emeka, but his efforts to secure a police intervention are sabotaged. Emeka's sting operation fails, and the film ends with a brutalized and unconscious Òlòtūré being smuggled out of Nigeria on a missionary bus (Figure 2.4).

*Òlòtūré* is therefore a narrative about illegal migration and sex work rather than sex slavery. As Gyang has explained in an interview, the film withholds the happy ending for a political reason: 'I didn't want a "Hollywood ending" for this film because I want people to talk about the film, and the only way you can really talk about it is to show the reality of these women's lives. Because very few of them are actually saved in real life'.[38]

*Òlòtūré* taps into many of the tropes that circulate in sex slavery films. For example, there is a scene where women's bodies are closely scrutinized and selected by the traffickers who evaluate them as potential commodities. Which women promise the best return on investment? Which bodies meet the expectations of the Western men seeking to buy recreational sex services? Some women are shown to be rejected on the basis of this selection. There are also quite a few gruesome scenes of violation and discipline, where the women are sexually assaulted and physically abused. One of the women, who attempts to make phone contact with her family, is killed on screen with a machete, in a scene staged similarly to the disciplinary rape scene in *The Whistleblower.* She is allowed to bleed to death in front of the terrorized women, whom the traffickers mean to teach a lesson in compliance. However, Gyang's film also differs from other sex slavery films in a few essential aspects. No abduction and no rescue are featured in the film. In fact, the women who are trafficked to Europe have to engage in considerable effort to persuade the traffickers that they are indeed the best candidates for their investment. The women have to pass a humiliating physical inspection, raise enough money to be able to pay the traffickers and ask no questions about their passage. The film shows the women engaging in these requirements willingly, although quite often reluctantly.

The film ends with a scene at the Nigeria-Benin border, which the traffickers intend to cross with their human cargo, paying off guards in exchange for illegal passage. The corrupt immigration officers happily accept the bribes and declare their enthusiasm for the continued 'business' with the traffickers. While Òlòtūré and her journalist colleague attempt to stop the transport of women, their efforts are ignored and overpowered by the collusion between the authorities and the traffickers. Òlòtūré is beaten into submission and shown slumped over in her seat. Emeka, who follows the traffickers to the checkpoint, tries to draw the attention of the border security officers, but they draw their guns and tell Emeka to get in line. In another shot, the viewer sees the smuggled women (including the now unconscious Òlòtūré) and the two traffickers sitting in a minivan, with pensive expressions on their faces, anticipating the next leg of their journey. Compared to most sex slavery films, Gyang's film offers a more realistic portrayal of the conditions of unauthorized migration and the role of the sex industry in facilitating migrant mobility for many African women. By featuring Black women as the victims of trafficking, the film corrects the wider sex slavery narrative by drawing attention to the fact that most women who have been trafficked and work in the illegal sex industry today are in fact persons of color and not white American middle-class teenagers. By aborting the tropes of abduction and rescue, *Òlòtūré* frames sex work migration as a feasible, if dangerous, option for women's economic advancement and upward mobility. Using realism and the careful geographic mapping that underscores the Africa-Europe migration axis, Gyang situates his film within the long-standing tradition of anti-colonial African cinema. In his review of the film, Tambay Obenson has compared it with Ousmane Sembene's *Black Girl* (1966), perhaps the most famous African film to address the legacy of colonial exploitation through the contemporary story of a Senegalese woman imported to France as a domestic servant and abused by her French employers.[39] Although subtle, the anti-colonial subtext is present in *Òlòtūré*, a film where the characters speak Nigerian Pidgin, or Naija, an English-based creole. The sex traffickers use a bus with the word 'missionary' written across its back, a gesture toward the history of the Christian missionary expansion in the country. Before the final credits, a title card appears that makes an explicit connection between the contemporary practice of human trafficking and the transatlantic slave trade. It reads: 'Human trafficking is modern-day slavery in action'.

While comparisons between contemporary sex trafficking and the history of chattel slavery are highly problematic in films (particularly those created by and about white people) that center whiteness and 'white slavery', Gyang's analogy draws attention to the link between colonial history and the neocolonial present. In other words, the fact that Nigerian women today engage in sex work is in itself not a function of colonial domination, but the conditions of their labor, the available levels of compensation and their access to specific sex trade markets and labor rights (all factors that contribute to the more or less coercive nature of migrant sex work) are all determined by a world system that was largely set in place during the period of European colonial expansion. This is to say that 'modern-day slavery' in the contemporary African context is not just a metaphor, as it is in the context of the Western white anti-trafficking discourse; rather, it points in the direction of the colonial provenance of neocolonial patterns of labor mobility and labor exploitation.

While *Òlòtūré* depicts Lagos as the departure point for Nigerian sex workers looking to illicitly migrate to Europe, the Danish director Annette K. Olesen's 2008 film *Little Soldier* depicts the life of the Nigerian sex worker Lily (Lorna Brown) who has already arrived (Figure 2.5). Together, the two films form a continuous, albeit incomplete, picture of one of the major unauthorized migration routes, concentrating on Nigerian women who enter into debt bondage schemes with their traffickers. Much like *Òlòtūré*, Olesen's film takes care to problematize the rescue that it simultaneously stages. However, in the Danish film, the conditions of illegal sex work are observed from the perspective of a white rescue figure, Lotte (played by the renowned Danish actress Trine Dyrholm), a former soldier in Iraq. Addicted to alcohol and traumatized by the war, Lotte asks her estranged father (Finn Nielsen), who owns a shipping company and an illegal brothel, for money. Instead, he offers her a job as driver for Lily, one of his brothel workers. Lily is also his

***Figure 2.5*** White woman as the rescuer in Annette K. Olesen's *Lille Soldat* (*Little Soldier*, 2008).

girlfriend, which adds another layer of tension between Lily and Lotte. As she drives Lily from client to client, Lotte learns more about Lily's life in Nigeria. Like many migrants, Lily sends most of her earnings back home, to support her mother who is raising her daughter. Olesen's film is therefore careful to foreground the issue of consent and coercion to distinguish the difference between the narrative of 'sex slavery' and the reality of bonded labor of unauthorized migrant sex workers. Lily and the other brothel workers operate in confinement and under harsh conditions, receiving only a fraction of the profits that they generate for their traffickers and pimps, but are presented as migrant workers who willingly engage in commercial sex.

As the film progresses, Lily and Lotte's intimacy grows. Soon Lotte develops affection and sexual attraction towards Lily. This, combined with an incident during which Lotte saves Lily from a deranged client, motivates Lotte to intervene in Lily's life. Without consulting Lily, Lotte decides to organize a rescue mission. Stealing money and Lily's passport from her father's safe, Lotte coerces Lily into boarding a plane to Nigeria via London. Lotte's rescue is based on a fantasy of reuniting Lily with her daughter in Nigeria, where they will presumably live off the money from the safe. To realize this fantasy, however, Lotte exploits her power as a white Danish national, threatening to report Lily to the police if she refuses to board the plane. Having no other choice, Lily submits to Lotte's 'rescue' fantasy. Near the end of the film, Lotte's father confronts her naivety, predicting that Lily will never return to Nigeria. Instead, he asserts, she is likely to use his money to set up her own brothel somewhere else in Europe. As Elizabeth Oxfeldt has persuasively argued, *Little Soldier* articulates the rescue mission as a misguided act of white guilt that asserts white female agency and dominance over the Black migrant.[40] As with her father, Lotte's possession of Lily's passport is a sign of control and subordination. Much like border officials and sex traffickers, Lotte uses the passport to constrain and direct Lily's mobility. While her father exploited Lily economically, Lotte exploits her symbolically in her desire to fulfill the role of a successful rescuer (and to compensate for her own past shortcomings while deployed in Iraq). Indeed, *Little Soldier* provides an account of a white woman who colonizes a Black woman's suffering in order to gain a position of power alongside the patriarch. Saidiya Hartman's account of racialized gestures of abolitionist empathy well describes the film's displacement:

> The effort to counteract the commonplace callousness to black suffering requires that the white body be positioned in the place of the black body in order to make this suffering visible and intelligible. Yet if this violence can become palpable and indignation can be fully aroused only through the masochistic fantasy, then it becomes clear that empathy is double-edged, for in making the other's suffering one's own, this suffering is occluded by the other's obliteration.[41]

Afropessimist neo-Marxist thought, including that of Hartman and Frank B. Wilderson, focuses on the impossibility of Black liberation without the eradication of the entire capitalist system (and with it the neoliberal state) that has been shaped and maintained by white supremacy and anti-Black violence. Such a framework helps to understand why films like *Òlòtūré* and *Little Soldier*, which both frame sexual exploitation within the economic reality of capitalist market relations, showcase the impossibility of rescue or its futility with regard to the Black migrant subject within the existing global relations of power defined by white hegemony. Although he never addressed the issue of sex trafficking explicitly, Wilderson's dismissal of the liberal reformism, which includes state, Christian and NGO philanthropy, makes any prospect of rescuing Black subjects from sexual exploitation impossible as, according to Afropessimism's 'negative dialectic', such pandering reformism is designed to only ever sustain the anti-Black status quo.[42]

## Abduction

The abduction scene is one of the major building blocks of the sex slavery narrative. It depicts the physical capture of a woman, the violent taking possession of her, in order to exploit her sexually. Some sex slavery narratives dramatize the abduction scene even further by framing it as the theft of innocence. In films such as *Trade*, *Holly*, or the *Taken* trilogy, the sex slave is a child or young adult, thus activating what Sara Ahmed has described as the protection narrative around the 'figure of vulnerability, the purified body' that focuses the production of the nation space in unique ways.[43] The abduction of a child plays out the imagined 'contaminated desires of strangers' who prey on the purest members of the community and thus threaten its integrity and cohesion. This variant of sex slavery films thus contributes to the work of producing the nation in a very specific way, by imagining the heroic action of protecting the child from the pedophilic predators and in the process enforcing the symbolic boundaries of the healthy – morally cleansed – community. Ahmed has explained the elaborate act of symbolic differentiation as follows:

> The figure of the child comes to perform a certain role within the narrative of crime prevention and stranger danger: the innocence of the child is what is most at risk from the proximity of strangers. The child comes to embody, in a narrative that is both nostalgic (returning to an imagined past) and fearful (projecting an unimaginable future), all that could be stolen or lost by the proximity of strangers. The child's innocence and purity becomes a matter of social and national responsibility.[44]

The cipher-like function of the figure of the child allows it to represent the vulnerability of a nation to contamination from the outside. The imperiled white child holds a special function in the nationalist imaginary. While there are many examples of sex slavery films that feature the abduction of children who are not white (as is the case in *Holly* or *Trade*; Figure 2.6), the narratives that gain most visibility within the Western corpus of sex slavery films are those that center on the white figure of innocence. This race-informed focus is also prevalent in the more general media landscape across North America and Europe, which publicizes disproportionately the stories of abduction and disappearance of white women and children, thus disclosing a racist lens in the symbolic construction of the nation, from colonial 'captivity narratives' to sensationalized headlines about missing white women and girls.[45] In recent decades, a series of abductions and disappearances of white females has gripped the public imagination, including the cases of JonBenét Ramsey, Elisabeth Fritzl, Elizabeth Smart and Madeleine McCann. The collective symbolic investment in such cases has been translated into very successful novels and film adaptations that play out scenarios of abduction and disappearance, such as Gillian Schieber Flynn's *Gone Girl* and Paula Hawkins' *The Girl on the Train*, whose intense popularity attests to the continued role that the figure of the vulnerable white child/woman plays in contemporary biopolitics. Race remains a factor in the neocolonial constructions of the national unity throughout the West. 'The neocolonial regime of global capitalism' is

***Figure 2.6*** The abduction of Adriana (Paulina Gaitán) in *Trade* (Dir. Marco Kreuzpaintner, 2007).

seen by Áine O'Healy as 'a system whose borders are both more ubiquitous and elusive than those of historical colonialism but whose modalities of exclusion and marginalization are no less insistent'.[46]

One of the most commercially successful sex slavery films of the last two decades, Pierre Morel's *Taken* (2008) tells the story of two American girls whose European vacation, telegraphed as a rite of passage and possible sexual adventure, quickly turns into a nightmare when they are abducted by Albanian sex traffickers. The film opens in Los Angeles, where former CIA agent Bryan Mills (Liam Neeson) manages celebrity security detail. His professional vigilantism is curiously gender-pitched: in one of the earliest scenes, Bryan saves the life of a young female pop star from a crazed fan's attack. This riveting scene of rescue is a prelude to the more melodramatic – and violent – rescue of Bryan's seventeen-year-old daughter, Kim (Maggie Grace). In broad strokes, the film establishes Bryan's estrangement from Kim and her mother, his ex-wife Lenore (Famke Jansson), who is now remarried to a wealthy man. Bryan's desire to bond with Kim is thus pitched as the real motivation behind the action of the film; it is also the doubly 'domestic' problem of the film, originating in the 'broken' nuclear family from within the national borders of the United States. In one important scene, Kim and Lenore meet with Bryan to receive his permission for Kim to travel to Europe with her friend Amanda (to follow U2's continental tour). Bryan

***Figure 2.7*** Bryan Mills (Liam Neeson) fights to get his abducted daughter back in *Taken* (Dir. Pierre Morel, 2008).

is worried about the safety of his teenage daughter, but eventually relents. Upon arriving at Charles de Gaulle airport, Kim and Amanda run into Peter, a flirtatious French stranger with whom they agree to share a taxi into the city. Unbeknownst to Kim and Amanda, Peter, who is really a procurer for an Albanian sex trafficking ring, conveniently learns their Paris address after the taxi drops them off. Soon, Bryan's worst fears come true when a group of men invade the apartment and abduct the girls. In the moments preceding Kim's capture, she manages to call her father (not the French authorities, who are later shown to be corrupt) for help. The remainder of the film is focused on Bryan and his spectacular rescue mission, which culminates in a scene at a secret, elite sex slave auction where Kim is sold to Sheikh Raman (Nabil Massad), an Orientalist caricature of a Saudi man. As a former Green Beret and CIA operative, Bryan is ostensibly well-positioned to find and rescue his daughter, and it is no surprise that he does just that in a film that is, in terms of genre, decidedly more of an action thriller, which foregrounds Neeson's Bond-like character (Figure 2.7), rather than a social problem film about sex trafficking.

In Morel's film, the moment of abduction is protracted and imbued with maximum dramatic tension. When Kim and Amanda arrive at their posh apartment in central Paris, Amanda turns on loud rock music to celebrate as they unpack, announcing her intention to sleep with Peter ('I hear French guys are amazing in bed', she adds, emphasizing that the nature of his allure is a feature of his 'foreignness'); in the same scene, she encourages Kim to 'lose' her virginity. Through this expository dialogue, the sexually active Amanda quite literally designates Kim's own apparent sexual 'purity'. The two women will continue to form a binary opposition of chaste and 'promiscuous' modes of womanhood for most of the film. Soon after this exchange, Kim realizes that Amanda was untruthful when she promised that her family would be present in the apartment. Moments later, Bryan calls Kim. During this conversation, which cuts between father and daughter, Bryan scolds Kim for failing to call him upon arrival as she had promised to do; she apologizes and admits that Amanda has lied: the apartment is completely unoccupied, and there is no adult supervision. As Kim continues to chat with Bryan, she – and the audience – looks through a window across to the opposite wing of the apartment. From her voyeuristic position, which echoes Hitchcock's famous set-up in *Rear Window* (1954), Kim spots Amanda dancing in one of the bedrooms. In mid-conversation, Kim suddenly cries out as she witnesses several men burst in, quickly overpower Amanda and carry her body out of sight. The film's viewer thus witnesses Amanda's abduction from a distance, as a framed monstrative spectacle, presented within the *mise-en-scène*. This voyeuristic perspective, however, does not last long. The invaders soon search the apartment for Kim. With her, the viewer is now sutured into the dangerous space, not only the space of the invaded apartment, but also the space of the global city full of unregulated immigrants and foreign criminals.

In their discussion of *Taken*, written in the context of discourses of homeland security in the US, geographers Klaus Dodds and Philip Kirby have argued that Morel's film portrays Paris as 'a bleak zone of myriad and lurking dangers' and that Europe, in general, appears as 'a darker, orientalised and othered geography' – 'a Hobbesian space in which violence must be used to confront other violence, and the rules of law, it appears, do not apply'.[47] Resonant of the 'global brothel' from the rhetoric of evangelical abolitionism, this space must be disciplined by the American father who happens to be a violent vigilante, articulated by the film as an agent of heteronormative and racial logic. Bryan orders Kim to go into the next room, hide under a bed and wait. Bryan, who remains on the line, announces: 'Now, the next part is very important. They are going to take you'. He demands that Kim accept the inevitable, to relinquish her agency and entrust herself completely to his agency and experience. In order to survive, Kim's body becomes compliant in two interrelated ways: obedient to Bryan's instructions, she assumes the shape and position of generic Hollywood victimhood; therefore, she becomes compliant with the instructions of the abductors, who can take her without any physical resistance. In one of the last scenes of the abduction sequence, the camera, hidden under the bed alongside Kim, follows the feet of two intruders as they enter and exit the bedroom. Kim and the viewer hope that perhaps the imminent danger has been averted. Kim communicates as much to her father on the phone. 'They are leaving', she whispers with relief.

Almost immediately, Kim is snatched by the legs and dragged out from the bed. Bryan's prediction becomes reality as the viewer loses sight of the girl. The camera cuts back to Bryan, focusing on his worried yet stoic face as he listens to the desperate cries and sounds of physical struggle, still within audible range of her phone.

The act of 'taking' Kim therefore happens off screen. This auditory representation of Kim's abduction is significant. On a formal level, it emphasizes the sounded action that is excluded from the visual register, an occlusion suggestive of its transgressive potential. As the consecrated object of paternal fantasy and protectionist anxiety, Kim is spared the spectacle of violation. This prevents the cinematic objectification of the child victim, signaling that Kim's body must remain 'immaculate' to justify and affirm the American vigilante justice that Bryan will mete out from France to Istanbul. Kim's white, middle-class body is not hers alone, but rather functions as a scaled-up body of the nation that must remain untouched and 'uncontaminated' by foreign, racialized villains. By contrast, Amanda, the fiercely independent and rebellious girl, is abducted on screen; her body becomes the object of a disciplinary spectacle which is constructed within a specifically scopophilic frame that demands to be looked at by Kim and the viewer, in a way that evokes the spectacle that was enforced on Raya and the captive audience of trafficked women in *The Whistleblower*. This spectacle is didactic – its explicitly scopophilic framing commands Kim and the viewer to look at Amanda's abduction as a double warning. In a practical and narrative sense, the scene foreshadows Kim's own abduction; in a larger sense, it demonstrates Amanda, who is soon found dead of a drug overdose in a brothel, as a counter-object of protectionism, a consequence of mobilized feminine sexuality.

The aural portrayal of the abduction allows for it to function as a not-yet-realized threat, a violation that has not been completed by the visual and is therefore held in suspense. This threat leads to a state of exception in which Bryan transcends domestic and international law to maintain Kim's sexual security, eradicate the foreign threat to the weakened American domicile and re-establish the nuclear family, all while displacing the root economic and political causes and consequences of the post-9/11 retrenchment of conservative family and gender politics. Indeed, Dodds and Kirby have interpreted the phone call framing of Kim's abduction as significant to the film's goal to pair domestic safety with homeland security, remarking on its resemblance to 'those snatched phone calls made by passengers on the ill-fated flight, United 93', one of the planes that was hijacked during the attacks on 11 September 2001. In order to understand its sexual politics, it is important to situate *Taken* as a post-9/11 film, as many critics have taken care to do. Drawing on Susan Faludi's work on post-9/11 culture, Daniel Abrahams has proposed *Taken* as part of the 'American reaction to 9/11 [. . . which] was understood as a violation of the American domicile' and which necessitated an attempt 'to reinforce a particular kind of gender ideal'.[48] As Faludi herself has put it, popular culture after 9/11 often revolved around anxiety regarding the safety of 'virginal girls' and involved frequent attempts to resurrect the 'neofifties nuclear family' with its 'redomesticated femininity and reconstituted Cold Warrior manhood'.[49] The 'abduction' of American innocence and its subsequent spectacular rescue, which *Taken* and its sequels perform flawlessly, if arrogantly, are fundamental elements of xenophobic reaction, whereby communal cohesion is produced through its rejection of the Other (perceived as a foreign, racialized 'invader'). In *Taken*, Kim's body acquires an almost ritual significance, acting as the sacred, 'virgin' ground on and over which this struggle takes place. As such, Kim is a cipher for a white, Western patriarchal imaginary, where sexual anxiety and nationalist fantasy overlap and even condition one another. This imbrication point calls for the reassertion of traditional gender norms in which women do not cross borders, whether these are the supposedly protective borders of the nuclear family or borders between countries. Even so, *Taken* shows a particular interest in the mobility of white, middle-class women, which, as other critics have noted, marks a serious departure from the statistical reality that those most likely to enter networks of sex traffic and trade are undocumented migrants and/or working-class women.

The abduction icon activates the issue of personal freedom, or lack thereof, through the often spectacularized seizing of the sex slave's ability to traverse space independently. In this respect, sex slavery films envision the violation of one of the basic human rights – the freedom of movement and residence described in Article 13 of *The Universal Declaration of Human Rights.* Further, on a certain level, sex slavery films eroticize the abolition of women's autonomy of movement by constructing an association between the demand for commercial sex and the forfeiture of the woman's freedom to move. Her unfreedom, her utter submission, is somehow configured as an integral factor in sex trade – not just a logistical necessity of illegal trafficking, but also a vaguely defining feature of commercial sex services. Simultaneously, the abduction scenario articulates the moralizing vision of sex trade as reliant on the coercion and physical confinement of women, thus suggesting that women sell sex only when they no longer have a choice to walk away. To a large degree, the scene of abduction represses the possibility of choice, instead promoting the puritanical vision of how women enter sex trade: always by force.

As I have suggested in Chapter 1, the eroticization of abduction of the female has been embedded in the medium of cinema from its beginnings.

***Figure 2.8*** The abduction of a girl in *El Satario* (Dir. Anon., *circa* 1907–15).

One of the earliest hard-core pornographic films ever made, the Argentinian *El Satario* (Dir. Anon., c. 1907–15; now available in the public domain) frames its erotic spectacle within a story of abduction. Within the nine minutes of its run-time, *El Satario* tells a story of six young women (they may be girls on the cusp of adulthood, or 'barely legal', to use the pornographic terminology), who are exploring the woods until one of them falls prey to a horny Satyr (the titular character). The first half of the film sets up a voyeuristic erotic spectacle, where the viewer, along with the Satyr, watches unsuspecting naked women as they frolic through the thicket, bathe in a stream, dance in meadows and eat a picnic of wild fruit, all while laughing and frequently caressing each other. Once they spot the stalking Satyr, the women begin to flee. The Satyr pursues and eventually pounces on one of the women, who trips and falls. Her companions quickly run away, leaving her in the Satyr's grip (Figure 2.8). This is where the hard-core sequence begins, as the Satyr manipulates the semi-conscious body of the woman, drags her into a clearing and enters into what at first appears as unconsented intercourse. A jump cut then transitions the viewer to a sequence of shots where the woman eagerly and energetically reciprocates the Satyr's caresses throughout numerous sexual positions. 'Meat shots', close-ups of genitals and what may be the first approximation of the 'money' shot committed to cinema make this sequence prototypical of pornographic optics. After the climax, both collapse from exhaustion and fall asleep. Soon, the other women return and rescue the abducted woman by waking the couple and chasing the Satyr away.

*El Satario* is paradigmatic in its use of the tropes of preying and abduction. By maintaining a binary in which men are predatory and women vulnerable, the film stages a spectacle of carefree female mobility (with the attendant erotic exploration) as an aberration that must be foreclosed with an act of physical control and sexual subjugation by a man. This scenario works to discipline female desires and illustrate their presumed dangers in terms of safety and integrity. Furthermore, the abduction scenario caters to the heteronormative phallocentric desire of seeing the independent female as malleable and corrigible, an object of other subjects' agential dominance illustrated in acts of possessing and repossessing her body. The jump cut that stitches the scene of abduction and rape to the subsequent scene of consensual sex works as a special effect of sorts that erases the woman's will altogether (her logical resistance to being abducted and raped), instead showing her succumb and even enjoy the sex act. Both body and mind of the woman are pliable as she undergoes complete objectification. Unlike pornography, sex slavery films are very careful about showing or ever suggesting the possibility of consent in sex scenes. While the body is abducted and raped (rape, indeed, is another dominant icon in sex slavery films), the sex slave's moral resistance takes on the dramatic meaning and drives the plot forward to the desired resolution: the rescue. In other words, women in sex slavery films are depicted as physically vulnerable, but morally and spiritually untainted. Their unwavering innocence is, after all, required to uphold the sex slavery narrative that codes sex work as always non-consensual and requiring the physical apprehension of the woman.

## Captivity: Dungeon and Mattress

Part of the abject horror invoked by the sex slavery films centers around the imagined spaces of captivity and physical confinement that are used to communicate enslavement. Orlando Patterson's foundational study on slavery, published in 1982 as *Slavery and Social Death*, has proposed a definition of slavery centered on the exclusion of the enslaved person from social life. Patterson talks about the 'sense of apartness' and 'not belonging' that characterize the 'social death' of the slave, who is 'violently uprooted from his milieu'.[50] A common icon in sex slavery films, the dungeon depicts the space where the sex slave is held captive. As such it serves as a visual metaphor of social death – a space of violent exclusion from social and familial ties, where, as Patterson has argued, the enslaved person becomes 'the ultimate human tool' – a totally 'imprintable' and 'disposable' entity.[51]

The dungeon as a clandestine space of social and bodily alienation stands in a peculiar position regarding the other spaces of social death that typify our times – for example, the refugee camp. Sex slavery films pitch the dungeon as the extreme space of social death, thus displacing the ubiquity of the refugee camp – that other space where social death is experienced by millions in broad daylight and with the official consent of the world community. As an extremely evocative icon, the dungeon distills our anxieties around the fate of social disenfranchisement, which is becoming the fate suffered by the steadily growing population of permanently displaced people. What the dungeon icon also accomplishes is the symbolic decoupling of this imagined extreme space of social death – concealed, dark and steeped in physical violence – from the more banal spaces where the political and economic forces of late capitalism deal social death to large numbers of people. Here, the refugee camp can be listed next to the prison, the homeless shelter, the sweatshop, or the wealthy household, for that matter, where live-in care workers provide uninsured and under-compensated affective and house labor around the clock.

The most iconic dungeon depicted in sex slavery films is a secluded structure that features bare cement walls, dirty floors, minimal light sources and very few creature comforts beyond the equally iconic soiled mattress. The dungeon in *The Whistleblower* is exemplary: a dark and dank space that speaks not only of sex slavery but also of the rape and sexual violence inflicted on women during the Balkan Wars. When Kathryn first discovers this space, it is empty since the women have been moved to a different location by the criminals who learned about Kathryn's investigative efforts. The viewer enters this space at night alongside Kathryn, who is seeing it for the first time. What follows is a suspenseful scene of cinematic monstration, the slow and strategic exposition of an engrossing sight. The camera in this scene constructs Kathryn's gaze as a mobile furtive gaze, which searches in the darkness, slowly bringing to light the scene of the crime. The view alternates between the shots of Kathryn's horror-stricken face and the shots of the room, uncovered gradually in small fragments as they become illuminated by the limited light emitted by Kathryn's flashlight. This construction of the look is designed to invoke a specific reaction in the viewer, a reaction that mimics Kathryn's. Trailing along her side, the viewer sees the floor strewn with used condoms, syringe needles and cigarette butts. There are metal buckets and bowls that must have served as improvised toilets and dirty mattresses as the only items of furniture brought into the dungeon. Chains with padlocks suggest physical restraint. When Kathryn moves one of the mattresses, she spots some writing scratched onto the surface of the cement floor, sums worked out by one of the captives to track the balance of her debt to the traffickers.

The graffiti motif links the sex slavery dungeon with the Holocaust spaces of ethnic genocide, where the victims of the Nazi regime inscribed their haunting messages on the walls, floors and ceilings of concentration camps and Gestapo prison cells in order to document their lives and their victimization in captivity.[52] The analogy drawn between the historical traces of captivity inscribed in the built environment by the Holocaust victims and the graffiti motif portrayed in sex slavery films, thus, articulates an equivalence between the two, leading to the rhetorical legitimation of the sex slavery narrative and its potential historical substantiation via an association with one of the most egregious incidents of mass captivity in the modern era. It is not surprising that the graffiti motif, which works to assign a certain level of gravity to the filmic representation of the sex dungeon, is especially present in the sex slavery films that are clearly pitched as social problem films, including *The Whistleblower* and Kreuzpaintner's *Trade*. The latter film amplifies the pathos of the sex slaves' graffiti by presenting the markings on the walls of the dungeon as children's drawings, with primitive stick figures and childlike flourishes that broadcast the interrupted innocence of the young sex slaves.

The amount of screen time and the dramatic visual emphasis given to the abandoned dungeon space in the diegesis of *The Whistleblower* makes it appear almost as a character within the film. The viewer sees the dungeon first without its inhabitants, the sex slaves, as not only a sort of silent witness and material participant in the women's suffering, but also an important harbinger of the later scene, when the viewer is finally admitted to see the sex slaves in their place of captivity. Ostensibly, Kondracki is showcasing the space of sex slavery before unveiling the sex slaves to build up suspense and to imbue the site of captivity with strong affect, which the viewer sees reflected on Kathryn's petrified face. But this strategy also distills the narrative of sex slavery down to a physical site of torture: the ground zero of human rights abuse. As a concentrated signifier, the sex slavery dungeon constructed in sex slavery films resides somewhere between the familiar historic images of captivity – such as the photographs of the cells from Guantanamo, Auschwitz, or S-21 – and the fictional spaces of captivity as a site of physical and sexual exploitation constructed in horror, slasher and torture porn films.

Interestingly, in the latter scene, when the viewer sees the dungeon again as it is now populated by women, the space loses some of its abject horror, even though all of the gory paraphernalia (including the chains, the soiled mattresses and the messages scratched into the cement floor) are featured in this space as well. It is the presence of the confined women who, although intimidated and traumatized, fill it with their sociality, which speaks of life that pushes against the 'ruin porn' aesthetic of the first scene.[53] When analyzed side by side, the two scenes of the dungeon in *The Whistleblower* – one of the empty haunted space of captivity and the other of a space occupied by a group of restrained women – bring into focus the subtle difference between captivity and confinement. The dungeon *qua* dungeon reifies the inegalitarian power relationship of the captive's total subordination to the captor as *fait accompli*. The latter scene depicts the dungeon as a site of confinement, where captivity is gradually enforced onto women and where specific relations of domination and submission are negotiated – the film, thus, spectacularizes the progressive erosion of women's autonomy. Indeed, in this latter scene, while some of the women still resist their subordination, even exchanging gestures of solidarity with one another, others are disciplined through rape. There are also women who have seemingly internalized the logic of the dungeon – they are shown as catatonic figures, slumped over in resignation.

If the scene from *The Whistleblower* where Kathryn inspects the abandoned dungeon – her searchlight resembling the bright beam of the projector cutting through a darkened auditorium, her glowing face imprinted with a strong emotional reaction that resembles the face of an impressionable spectator – gestures toward the meta-cinematic framing of the dungeon as a scene of cinematic spectacle, then Petrucci's *Hope Lost* makes this framing quite explicit. The most iconic form of captivity in the film occurs when the two sex slaves, Alina and Sofia, are held on a film set and forced to perform their own deaths on camera. The film set scenes of *Hope Lost* unabashedly expose cinema's own role in producing the symbolic space of captivity: cinema as a sex dungeon that captures female form and produces it as a commodity for public consumption within what Anna Agathangelou has called 'desire industries'.[54] Citing Alexandra Kollontai, the Marxist feminist thinker who has famously proclaimed that sex and desire are social and historical relations, Agathangelou has argued that we must analyze the processes of desire commodification, traditionally relegated to the private sphere, as a matter of economic relations of profit extraction, where women are 'hired and used by capital' to 'socially produce other subjects and their lifestyles' through providing 'sexual pleasures and other kinds of intimacies'.[55] Unlike the other sex slavery films that present the dungeon as a displaced space of social death, *Hope Lost* addresses how the camera technology functions to extract the surplus-value in the production of sexual pleasure and becomes the main technology of captivity utilized by today's desire industries, including cinema. On a related level, these film set scenes from *Hope Lost* comment on the gendered labor relations and exploitative labor conditions found throughout the film industry.

***Figure 2.9*** The slave mattress in *The Whistleblower* (Dir. Larysa Kondracki, 2010).

Aside from the grisly icon of the dungeon, the sex slavery film often depicts vehicles as mobile spaces of captivity. Cars, vans, trucks and buses used to transport the sex slaves – the abducted women and children – become charged spaces of forced mobility across borders. These films use the claustrophobic images of distressed victims crammed into vehicles to code the act of border-crossing as not only a criminal act but also an unconsented one – an act that degrades one's subjectivity, dehumanizes and links border-crossing with social death. In this respect, sex slavery films, with their deeply dystopic vision of border mobility, constitute an important addition to migrant and refugee cinemas.[56] Linking the act of border-crossing with the inegalitarian practice of enslavement contributes to the phobic discourse on migration and mobility employed by nation-states to control their populations, particularly women. Operating in the visual realm, sex slavery films thus contribute (in more or less deliberate fashion) to the state's rhetorical production of the category of 'illegal immigration' in order to distinguish undesired forms of human movement and to identify the undesired human subjects – 'those who are not wealthy, who are not nationals of affluent countries and/or who belong to racial groups deemed incompatible with "national attributes"'.[57]

To conclude this chapter, I turn to the mattress, one of the most indelible icons of the sex slavery film (Figure 2.9). My analysis of this icon grew out of a course titled 'Human Trafficking and Sex Slavery on Screen', which I designed and taught at a large public university in the United States. From the start of the course, students approached the films on the syllabus – which inform this book's filmography – as more or less realistic accounts of the widespread sex slavery epidemic, of which they had already been well informed by the pervasive 'War on Trafficking' discourse disseminated by the US government, the media and the many anti-trafficking campaigns, authored and carried out by national and international NGOs and present on the Internet. Although the graphic nature of the material made the students somewhat uncomfortable, the fact that they were able to consume the films well within what Laura M. Agustín has called 'the discourses of pity and helping' made the experience easily manageable.[58] It was only after reading a number of studies that question the exact nature and dimensions of sex slavery that the students became less comfortable with the abject images of the victimized women and with their own, already somewhat contentedly inhabited position of the agent who might bring about change to the unfortunate victims.

In the process of viewing over a dozen sex slavery films in our weekly screening sessions, my students and I noticed that the films more often than not chose to include the image of a soiled mattress, the imagined site of sex slavery: a bare mattress sitting directly on the floor, covered in stains, presumably of blood, sweat and semen. We called it the 'slave mattress'. Always a mere background detail in the *mise-en-scène*, this mattress called for our attention simply because of its recurring presence in the films under analysis and the arresting effect it had on us. We had to ask: What of the mattress?

Different students provided different readings of the mattress and its affective force. For some, it signified the illicit market in intimacy; as such it stood for pathological intimacy, the 'dirty' intimacy of the sex trade. For others, the slave mattress evoked the nightmare of extreme domestic confinement and brutal labor exploitation of those who must inhabit this constricted domestic sphere. The slave mattress disturbed some students in its oxymoronic juxtaposition of physical and psychological terror, taking place at the site of comfort, if a mattress is to furnish security and rest. Another interpretation focused on the metaphoric relationship between the slave mattress and the slave body, where the mattress stained with blood and semen speaks of the violated body of the sex slave, and as such communicates the material exhaustion of that body, its biological used-upness, with no potential for renewability. Another student saw the dirty mattress as representative of the desire for possession of one human being by another.

There were many other interpretations. We discovered that it was impossible to agree on the significance of the mattress. Yet, we concurred that the mattress often affected us more than the films' graphic scenes of abuse, bodily harm, even rape, directed against the body of the slave. The mattress elicited very strong subjective responses without saying anything specific about sexual exploitation. As such it was a source of discursive violence in the way in which it refused signification while insistently calling for our attention. Is it possible that the mattress functions as the Barthesian *punctum* in the cinematic narrative of trafficking?[59] If one reads Roland Barthes' concept of *punctum* as radical degradation of meaning and corruption of sanctioned symbolic value, the mattress takes on the role of a visceral void, which frustrates and confuses any attempt of meaning-making on the part of the viewer (while it paradoxically begs to be made sense of). The mattress becomes a source of discursive violence that possibly challenges the hermeneutic violence of fixed interpretation, the benevolent violence of the anti-trafficking discourse. In this odd balance of *punctum*, which hovers between the insinuation and refusal of story, I find home for a pedagogy of disempowerment.

In *Camera Lucida*, Barthes has theorized the photographic image in terms of *studium* and *punctum*. He has defined *studium* as the denotative and connotative meaning of an image, the cultural knowledge that explains the image. 'The *studium* is a kind of education (knowledge and civility, "politeness")', Barthes has argued.[60] *Punctum*, however, is the element within the image that punctures the politeness of *studium*'s education. It is a detail in the image that 'rises from the scene, shoots out of it like an arrow, and pierces'.[61] Barthes presents *punctum* as a traumatizing element within the image – 'that accident which pricks me (but also bruises me, is poignant to me)'.[62] The violence of Barthes' *punctum* questions and unsettles the 'politeness' of cultural knowledge. It is a mere detail but invested with the power to unsettle and overwhelm the reading of the entire image. On some level, then, *punctum* is a visual element that leads away from sanctioned knowledge, from communication, from representation, away from signification itself. Barthes has explained that, while 'the *studium* is always coded, the *punctum* is not'.[63] It is something that cannot be named. *Punctum* works much like Barthes' earlier iteration of the same concept – 'the third meaning', which emerged in his 1970 analysis of Eisenstein's film images:

> I read, I receive (and probably even first and foremost) a third meaning – evident, erratic, obstinate. I do not know what its signified is, at least I am unable to give it a name, but I can clearly see the traits, the signifying accidents of which this – consequently incomplete – sign is composed.[64]

The slave mattress functions precisely as such an 'incomplete sign', a sign that speaks of its own failure to signify in accordance with the *studium*'s official narrative. The slave mattress sends the viewer away from the disciplinary and corrective narrative of the 'War on Trafficking' by interrupting (puncturing) that narrative. Like Barthes' 'third meaning', the mattress 'belongs to the family of pun, buffoonery, useless expenditure. Indifferent to moral or aesthetic categories (the trivial, the futile, the false, the pastiche), it is on the side of the carnival'.[65] When students responded to the mattress, they responded to the break in the story of sex slavery that configures all sex work as slavery. And while initially they grasped for meaning that would help them to re-incorporate this break back into the story, they eventually gave in and agreed to treat the mattress as the moment of discursive impasse, but also a respite from the story, eventually also a joke. Perhaps there was no story of sex slavery after all. Along with this agreement came a shift in the overall mood in the classroom. The pity, disgust and horror with which students readily responded to the stories of trafficking and slavery were replaced with suspicion, consternation, doubt and even laughter. Did the mattress speak of the impossibility of representing sex slavery because there was nothing to represent, other than our own quaint fears? These latter feelings produced a distance, a form of skepticism and a recognition of the carnival in the mattress. We arrived at this new affective space with a degree of disempowerment since we could no longer act as the agents of knowledge if, as Barthes has argued, knowledge's power is a power of cohesion, with 'no duality, no indirection, no disturbance'.[66] The disturbance was ours to behold.

## Notes

1. Cody Delistraty, 'How Germany's Far Right is Co-Opting Art History', *Frieze*, 3 May 2012, www.frieze.com/article/how-germanys-far-right-co-opting-art-history (accessed 29 November 2023).
2. Bergstein, 'Freud, Saturn, and the Power of Hypnosis', p. 125.
3. See Eirikur Bergmann, 'The Eurabia Conspiracy Theory', in Andreas Önnerfors and André Krouwel (eds), *Europe: Continent of Conspiracies: Conspiracy Theories in and about Europe* (Abingdon and New York: Routledge, 2021), pp. 36–53.
4. The term 'Fortress Europe' was originally deployed in World War II to refer to Nazi-occupied Europe, but currently it refers to a set of border policies and discourses that have characterized EU member states' reactions, since 2014, to the influx of refugees and asylum-seekers fleeing humanitarian crises in the Middle East, North Africa and the Sahel region. The term was notably used by Amnesty International in a 2014 report which provided evidence of human rights violations at European borders. Here, 'Fortress Europe' has been defined as 'the sum total' of measures taken by EU member states to deter or deny refugees and asylum-seekers from crossing European borders. See Amnesty International, *The Human Cost of Fortress Europe* (London: Amnesty International, 2014), pp. 5–35. Elsewhere, scholar Inka Salovaara-Moring has provided a sustained historical and conceptual analysis of the term, which the author has regarded as a 'metaphor [that] has been used mostly to describe the tightening immigration policy of the EU', and that 'Europe has been seen as a wealthy fortress that is closing its gates against the poor, immigrants, ethnic minorities and the Third World in general'. See Salovaara-Moring, '"Fortress Europe": Ideological Metaphors of Media Geographies', in Andre Jansson and Jesper Falkheimer (eds), *Geographies*

*of Communication: The Spatial Turn in Media Studies* (Goteborg: Nordicom, 2006), p. 111 (pp. 105–23 inclusive).

5. Jean Baudrillard, *The Evil Demon of Images* (Sydney: The Power Institute of Fine Arts, 1988), p. 16.
6. Ibid. p. 23.
7. Ibid. p. 23.
8. On the new directions in theoretical thought on cinema's potential for indexicality as originally explored by André Bazin's theory of film ontology, see the special issue, edited by Mary Ann Doane and titled 'Indexicality: Trace and Sign', of *differences: A Journal of Feminist Cultural Studies*, 18:1, 2007. In an essay included in this special issue, 'Moving Away from the Index: Cinema and the Impression of Reality', Tom Gunning has provided a review of the index theory of cinema and a challenge to its early claims about cinema's evidentiary and realist nature based in the medium's photographic indexicality (pp. 29–52).
9. André Bazin, 'The Ontology of the Photographic Image', in *What is Cinema?* trans. Hugh Gray (Berkeley: University of California Press, 1967), pp. PAGES.
10. Patrick Maynard, 'The Secular Icon: Photography and the Functions of Images', *The Journal of Aesthetics and Art Criticism,* 42:2, Winter 1983, pp. 155–69.
11. 'Get Involved', International Justice Mission, www.ijm.org/get-involved/churches
12. Bernstein, 'The Sexual Politics of the "New Abolitionism"', p. 144.
13. Jasbir K. Puar, *Terrorist Assemblages: Homonationalism in Queer Times* (Durham: Duke University Press, 2007), p. 5.
14. Ibid. p. 140.
15. Amar, *The Security Archipelago*, pp. 21–22.
16. Ibid. p. 78.
17. Ibid. p. 78. Amar has provided an extensive critique of the multi-nodal phobic security discourse, which produces LGBTQ+ subjects as members of 'perverse cosmopolitanism' and the 'global brothel' culture. For this discussion, see 'Policing the Perversions of Globalization in Rio de Janeiro and Cairo: Emerging Parastatal Security Regimes Confront Queer Globalisms', in *The Security Archipelago*, pp. 65–98.
18. For discussions of this scene, see Janak Vetri Nathan, 'Nuovo Cinema Inferno: The Affect of Ambivalence in Giuseppe Tornatore's *La Sconosciuta*', in *From Terrone to Extracomunitario: New Manifestations of Racism*, ed. by Katarzyna Marciniak and Bruce Bennett (Leicester: Troubador Publishing, 2010), pp. 236–57; Francesco Pascuzzi, 'Motherhood and Mourning in Giuseppe Tornatore's *The Unknown Woman*', *Film International,* 30 April 2015 http://filmint.nu/motherhood-giuseppe-tornatores/
19. Kitchen timers show up in other sex slavery films, for example, in *Little Soldier*. In this film, one of Lily's regular clients, a necrophiliac, uses such a device to ensure that the tranquilizer he administers to her has enough time to take effect. Once the timer buzzes, the client has sex with her apparently lifeless body. The kitchen timers draw our attention to the strong connection that exists between

the realms of domestic work, reproductive work and sex work, as different yet related forms of feminized labor within the desire industry that continues to be defined by a gendered division of public versus private production of surplus-value.

20. Dimitris Eleftheriotis, *Cinematic Journeys: Film and Movement* (Edinburgh: Edinburgh University Press, 2010), pp. 18–25.
21. See the 2020 documentary *The Case You*, by Alison Kuhn, for a powerful critique of the sexual abuse that frequently occurs to women during film auditions.
22. For an insightful discussion of branding as a racializing biometric technology, see Simone Brown, 'Branding Blackness: Biometric Technology and the Surveillance of Blackness', in *Dark Matters: On the Surveillance of Blackness* (Durham: Duke University Press, 2015), pp. 89–129.
23. Agathangelou, *The Global Political Economy of Sex*, p. 124.
24. Mulvey, 'Visual Pleasure and Narrative Cinema', p. 11.
25. Ibid. p. 11.
26. Ibid. p. 12.
27. Ibid. p. 12.
28. Adrian Martin, 'Dance Girl Dance: Philippe Grandrieux's *La Vie Nouvelle* (*The New Life*, 2002)', *Kinoeye: New Perspectives on European Film* 4:3, 2004, www.kinoeye.org/04/03/martin03.php
29. Doris Bachmann-Medick, 'Alterity – A Category of Practice and Analysis, Preliminary Remarks', *On Culture*, 4, 2017, www.on-culture.org/journal/issue-4/bachmann-medick-alterity
30. Yana Hashamova, *Screening Trafficking: Prudent and Perilous* (Budapest and New York: Central European University Press, 2018), p. 133.
31. Ibid, p. 143.
32. Ibid, p. 133.
33. Michel Foucault, *Discipline and Punish: The Birth of the Prison* (New York: Vintage Books, 1995), p. 113.
34. Ibid. p. 113.
35. Hashamova, *Screening Traffic*, pp. 132–33.
36. Foucault, *Discipline and Punish*, p. 177.
37. Yasmin Nair, 'Somaly Mam, Nicholas Kristof, and the Real Sex Trafficking Story', 2 June 2014, https://yasminnair.com/somaly-mam-nicholas-kristof-and-the-real-sex-trafficking-story/#more-8665 (accessed March 20, 2024).
38. Tambay Obenson, 'How a Nollywood Netflix Drama Sheds Light on Nigeria's Human Trafficking Crisis', *IndieWire*, 7 October 2020, www.indiewire.com/features/general/oloture-nollywood-netflix-nigeria-1234590106/, (accessed on March 21, 2024).
39. Ibid.
40. Elisabeth Oxfeldt, 'White Guilt and Racial Imagery in Annette K. Olesen's *Little Soldier*', *Journal of Aesthetics and Culture*, 10:2, 2018, pp. 15–24. Oxfeldt's article has extensively analyzed the film's racial politics with particular reference to the relationship between Lily and Lotte.

41. Saidiya Hartman, *Scenes of Subjection: Terror, Slavery, and Self-Making in Nineteenth-Century America* (New York and Oxford: Oxford University Press, 1997), p. 19.
42. Frank B. Wilderson, *Afropessimism: An Introduction* (Minneapolis: Racket and Dispatched, 2017), p. 11.
43. Sara Ahmed, *Strange Encounters: Embodied Others in Post-Coloniality* (New York: Routledge, 2000), p. 34.
44. Ibid. p. 35
45. See, for example, Audra Simpson, 'From White into Red: Captivity Narratives as Alchemies of Race and Citizenship', *American Quarterly*, 60:1, June 2008, pp. 251–57.
46. Áine O'Healy, *Migrant Anxieties: Italian Cinema in a Transnational Frame* (Bloomington: Indiana University Press, 2019), p. 81.
47. Klaus Dodds and Philip Kirby, 'Resurrecting the Vigilante: Paternal Sovereignty, Exceptionality and Familial Security in *Taken* (2008) and *Taken 2* (2013)', *Critical Studies on Security*, 2:3, 2014, p. 254 (pp. 245–61 inclusive).
48. Daniel Abrahams, '*Taken* as a Genre', www.epicureancure.com/885/taken-as-a-genre (accessed 12 February 2024).
49. Faludi, *The Terror Dream*, pp. 9, 4.
50. Patterson, *Slavery and Social Death*, pp. 7, 38. For an interesting critique of Patterson's more recent scholarship on modern sex slavery, see O'Connell Davidson, *Modern Slavery*, pp. 191–92.
51. Ibid. p. 7.
52. Werner Jung, *Wände, die Sprechen: Walls That Talk: The Wall Inscriptions in the Cologne Gestapo Prison* (Köln: Emons, 2013).
53. On the culture of 'ruin porn', see Siobhan Lyons (ed.), *Ruin Porn and the Obsession with Decay* (Basingstoke: Palgrave Macmillan, 2018); Paul Mullins, 'The Politics and Archeology of "Ruin Porn"', *Archaeology and Material Culture*, 19 August 2012, www.paulmullins.wordpress.com/2012/08/19/the-politics-and-archaeology-of-ruin-porn/ (accessed 6 March 2024).
54. Agathangelou, *The Global Political Economy of Sex*, p. 5.
55. Ibid. pp. 13–14.
56. For a nuanced critique of the discourse of 'modern-day slavery' in the context of migration, see O'Connell Davidson, *Modern Slavery*. For a discussion of migrant consent and analysis of the distinction between 'people trafficking' and 'people smuggling', see Marie Segrave, Sanja Milivojevic and Sharon Pickering, *Sex Trafficking: International Context and Response* (London and New York: Routledge, 2011), pp. 42–44.
57. Davidson, *Modern Slavery*, p. 114.
58. Agustín, 'At Home in the Street, p. 69.
59. Roland Barthes, *Camera Lucida: Reflections of Photography* (New York: Hill and Wang, 1981).
60. Barthes, *Camera Lucida*, p. 28.
61. Ibid. p. 26.
62. Ibid. p. 27.

63. Ibid. p. 51.
64. Barthes, 'The Third Meaning', in *Image, Mustic, Text*, trans. Stephen Heath (Glasgow: Fontana Press, 1987), p. 53.
65. Ibid. p. 53.
66. Ibid. p. 41.

# CHAPTER THREE

# *Converging Slaves: The Case of Blaxploitation*

In 2012, Quentin Tarantino made his controversial film *Django Unchained*, the story of a renegade slave who rescues his beloved from slavery and in the process burns down the plantation. Much as he did in *Jackie Brown* (1997), Tarantino once again paid tribute to blaxploitation cinema, this time more emphatically and comprehensively. A genre created in the United States during the early 1970s, blaxploitation relied on the spectacle of sex and violence within race-centered narratives. In ways relevant to this study, the scenes of sexual exploitation featured in these commercially successful films must be analyzed as a spectacle with a specific historical subtext and therefore political potential; at the same time as they allude to the history of chattel slavery in the United States, its spectacularization is also a marketing strategy used by blaxploitation filmmakers to sell their films. However, it must be emphasized that blaxploitation, unlike other genres of exploitation cinema, offered strong themes of retribution and reclamation. On the one hand, these themes prevented the genre's entry into the mainstream; on the other hand, they radically and importantly reframed the figure of the slave, and, by extension the figure of the sex slave. The radical plot and formal elements of these films were used to envision often extravagant acts of black revenge that were central to securing popular appeal among the disenchanted black audiences. Arguably, the spectacle of revenge set blaxploitation cinema apart from the more temperate and more art-house-oriented, black-themed social problem films of the 1960s (such as Stanley Kramer's *Guess Who's Coming to Dinner*), which, as Christopher Sieving has persuasively argued, struggled at the box office and failed to attract black audiences because of their accommodating, non-threatening black characters, elitist aesthetics, inadequate budgets and predominantly white authorship.[1] I would add to this list the largely assimilationist politics of those films.

Steeped in the milieu of radical movements, including the civil rights and the Black Power movements, feminism, sexual revolution, the anti-war and free speech movements, blaxploitation cinema was specifically developed for black urban viewers, strategically deploying the black vernacular, black popular music (rhythm and blues, funk) and black action heroes and heroines, as well as utilizing the creative vision of a handful of black filmmakers who had been newly admitted to Hollywood's directing fraternity, as a result of the organized efforts mounted by the NAACP and the Equal Employment Opportunity Commission in the late 1960s.[2] Its unabashed exploitation style – characterized by 'deliberate camp aesthetics' as well as the 'empowerment themes and generic revisionism', combined with the coded references to the white-on-black oppression in the United States and the 'visceral representations of inverted race relations' – generated a product that quickly gained unprecedented mass appeal extending beyond the target audience and garnered a popular following which cut across established race, class and gender divides.[3]

While blaxploitation cinema received some serious backlash from contemporary critics for stereotyping African Americans, in addition to depicting too many criminal protagonists and their 'bad or questionable motives', it was also praised for depicting multi-dimensional black characters in both lead and supporting roles, characters who fought 'for the betterment of the black community', often resorting to violence as the necessary means to counter the destructive effects of white oppression.[4] Josiah Howard has astutely asserted that blaxploitation cinema earned its popularity thanks to its delivery of more realistic, more socially aware content and complex black characters, while it also, paradoxically, provided a much-needed 'escape' from the mounting pressures of the turbulent times.[5]

As Howard has carefully contextualized, blaxploitation cinema, with its hyperbolic screen violence, emerged in the 1970s out of the strained race relations in the United States, which were fueled by both the country's long history of racist violence and its mounting, more contemporary record of violence, including 'the ongoing war in Vietnam, the assassinations of Malcolm X, Martin Luther King Jr. and the Kennedys, combined with an ever-increasing number of inner-city race riots (most notably in Watts, Detroit and Newark)'.[6] The contemporary urban settings of many of the blaxploitation films attracted a younger, politically aware, black audience that was most impacted by poverty, rapid urban decline, white flight to the segregated suburbs, climbing inflation and the inundation of drug and sex traffic in black neighborhoods.

In the introduction to his study *Blaxploitation Films of the 1970s: Blackness and Genre*, Novotny Lawrence has mapped out the evolution of the African American representation on screen. In his discussions of blaxploitation cinema, Lawrence has commented on the emergence of the positive and overt representations of black sexuality in characters who are 'in control of their sexuality' and could 'dictate the circumstances of their erotic encounters', in contrast to all (or most) prior cinematic depictions of sterile, deviant, or pathological black sexuality.[7] Howard has further noted how the relaxation of film censorship laws immediately before the emergence of the blaxploitation phenomenon (that is, the replacement of the Production Code by the voluntary Motion Picture Association rating system in 1968) allowed for 'images that were specifically designed to excite, tempt and titillate in a way that filmmakers had never been allowed to before'.[8] Thus, by challenging the restrictions on the depiction of on-screen sex and violence, blaxploitation films opened up more roles for black women, which, as Howard has argued, typically 'featured females in the same violent, over-the-top narratives that African American men had popularized', offering the cinematic fare that was full of exploitation tactics, including explicit sex scenes, shocking language and fierce, visually arresting female action figures.[9] In blaxploitation films such as *Coffy* (Dir. Jack Hill, 1973), *Cleopatra Jones* (Dir. Jack Starrett, 1973), *Cleopatra Jones and the Casino of Gold* (Dir. Chuck Bail, 1975), *Foxy Brown* (Dir. Jack Hill, 1974), *Sheba Baby* (Dir. William Girdler, 1975), *Friday Foster* (Dir. Arthur Marks, 1975), *Sugar Hill* (Dir. Paul Maslansky, 1974), *Lady Cocoa* (Dir. Matt Cimber, 1975), *Velvet Smooth* (Dir. Michael Fink, 1976), *TNT Jackson* (Dir. Sirio H. Santiago, 1974) and *Emma Mae* (Dir. Jamaa Fanaka, 1976), black female performers created protagonists of great autonomy, carrying action-oriented storylines while exuding sexual charisma and educating audiences about the dynamics of female desire and women's right to sex work.

From these popularly acclaimed and publicly beloved black performances came cinema's first action heroine, one that, importantly, both preceded and inspired the appearance of the white action heroine in films such as *Alien* (1979) and *The Terminator* (1984). It is of great significance to the ensuing study to note that the black action heroine's sexual confidence, spectacularized and hyperbolized via the sexploitation formula, simultaneously engaged and countered the long history of sexual violence, reproductive exploitation and erotic colonialism that characterized the lives of black women in the United States, in ways that have been historically documented, within the institution of chattel slavery and outside of it, as the legacy of slavery continued to impact black lives long after slavery had been abolished.[10]

In *Women of Blaxploitation: How the Black Action Film Heroine Changed American Popular Culture*, Yvonne D. Sims has noted that 'the contradictory facets of the black action heroine in blaxploitation movies was that she was required to disrobe while simultaneously serving as the liberator of the evils confronting her family and community'.[11] Sims has argued that these two facets would appeal to different audiences: '[T]he physical attractive factor would appeal to teenage and young males and the spunk might appeal to young women'.[12] Unsurprisingly, contemporary critics of blaxploitation films zeroed in on the sensationalist framing of the black action heroine and were quick to dismiss her construction as vulgar, morally reprehensible and objectifying.[13] Yet, the feminist and queer scholarship on black action heroines consistently vindicates these early 1970s black female protagonists as empowering, agential and imbued with depth and sophistication by the actresses who played their roles – Pam Grier, Tamara Dobson, Jean Bell, Lola Falana, Marki Bey, Teresa Graves, Jerri Hayes and Johnnie Hill, among others.[14]

In order to understand how blaxploitation's sex spectacle could be considered as something more than a lurid and lucrative act of grindhouse exploitation, which it certainly also is, one may look at these scenes as counter-narratives of retributive agency, framed within the larger public discourse on African American women's bodies and sexuality within the context of US history, including the problematic representational history of the African American female subject. As such, Sims has suggested, blaxploitation heroines intervene and interrogate the literary and cinematic discourses that have been populated by figures of caricature, ranging from the asexual 'Mammy' to the promiscuous Exotic Other, embodied by racist clichés from Aunt Jemima to Sapphire and Jezebel. These figures were created as functions of white male fantasy and as props existing in the shadows of the dominant performance of white femininity, itself informed by Victorian ideals of respectability, self-control, sexual purity and moral fortitude.[15] At its height, blaxploitation cinema made several significant material and creative achievements: commercial success, an unanticipated power to attract diverse audiences, a radical and recurring retributive narrative element, a strong symbolic sense of black and female empowerment, and a cult status that continues to the present day. Importantly, as Sims has noted, the genre also facilitated a remarkable amount of creative control exacted by the star performers who played the featured action heroines.[16] Each of these factors must be considered in any exploration of the sexploitation formula's more damaging elements and their representational toll on the genre. Such an undertaking encounters a number of questions: How does blaxploitation cinema narrate and visualize sexual exploitation? How does the foregrounded category of race impact this portrayal? How does the history of chattel slavery, which to a more or less explicit degree is always bearing on blaxploitation narratives, shape this portrayal? And, finally, is the sexploitation spectacle, which is effectively demanded by the sexploitation formula, qualitatively or structurally different in the case of blaxploitation cinema than it is from the spectacle utilized in the sex slavery films in general, including those discussed in the other chapters of the ensuing study?

To begin my consideration, I return to Tarantino's *Django Unchained*, described by film scholar Mia Mask as the 'self-reflexive, Black westploitation mashup'.[17] While most of the film's critical appraisal focuses on the film's revisionist discourse on black masculinity and slavery, as well as on the ways in which Tarantino subverts the genre of the American western, mainly by recycling the more progressive discourses of the Italian and West German westerns (the spaghetti and sauerkraut westerns of the 1960s), I wish to investigate *Django Unchained* as a film focalized through a distinctive slave rescue narrative. This narrative is driven by a mission to rescue a female slave framed as a sexual commodity. This film, I argue, is non-conformist as it repudiates certain generic conventions of blaxploitation and disavows the spectatorial pleasures that such conventions were engineered to facilitate. Namely, the sexual exploitation of the female slave is clearly invoked on the level of form and content but never explicitly played out on screen. *Django Unchained* is stereotypical in summoning male agency to deliver the female (sex) slave from her bondage.[18] However, the film is atypical in its strategic containment of the prurient scenes of sexual exploitation, actively denying the visual and narrative pleasures that are signaled by the generic framing, but which are ultimately withheld and frustrated.

The film tells the fictional story of Django (Jamie Foxx), a slave freed by Dr King Schultz (Christoph Waltz), a German immigrant bounty hunter who travels across the antebellum South in search of fugitives from justice, collecting them dead or alive for income, as part of what he describes to Django as a trade much like slavery: 'a flesh for cash business'. Indeed, Schultz buys Django out of slavery at the very start of the film, hoping that Django can help him identify the Brittle brothers, now highly prized fugitives whom he may have met while enslaved at the Carrucan plantation. After Django successfully assists him, Schultz promises to help him find his beloved wife Broomhilda (Kerry Washington), a fellow slave who has been separated from Django and sold to another slave owner. Before they embark on their rescue operation, Django spends the winter as Schultz's apprentice, helping him round up criminals; he also scandalizes white Southerners by riding a horse, carrying a gun and bringing white men to justice. In these scenes, Jamie Foxx – an actor whose charisma has accrued through a series of critically acclaimed dramatic roles in films such as *Ali* (2001), *Ray* (2004) and *Collateral* (2004), which embody black defiance – reframes and permanently revises every John Wayne performance embedded in the American imaginary, in line with what Mia Mask has described as the film's 'pro-Black, abolitionist, anti-colonial stance'.[19]

The two men form a bond as they work together, which elicits Django to share with Schultz the story of his enslaved life and the tragic fate of his wife. They soon devise and execute the carefully planned rescue of Broomhilda, neatly combined with the fiery annihilation of her oppressor and his plantation – a fitting homage to blaxploitation's combustive economy, in what ulti-

***Figure 3.1*** Broomhilda in a hot box in *Django Unchained* (Dir. Quentin Tarantino, 2013).

mately becomes, as Joseph Vogel has persuasively argued, Tarantino's lesson in revisionist history, which 'represents a cultural desire in America to be rid of our atrocious history, to rewrite it in simpler, more heroic terms, rather than seriously confront its enduring legacy'.[20] Simplistic as it may be, Tarantino's revisionism is in line with blaxploitation's retributive logic and populist rhetoric. Additionally, I assert, the film offers a subtle but productive corrective of cinema's own legacy of the enslavement and commodification of the on-screen female figure, a practice that continues today: Broomhilda's (and Kerry Washington's) on-screen exploitation is foreclosed, only after the promise of such exploitation is pitched to the viewer. This gesture is very much in line with Tarantino's meta-cinematic practice, a method that can be observed across all of his films in their self-aware engagement with prior cinematic forms and traditions.[21] It is also characteristic of the director's complex work of camp parody used to queer normative gender roles, which are otherwise culturally maintained with the help of genre filmmaking.[22]

Using slave market records, Django and Schultz quickly establish Broomhilda's new location. Bills of sale show that she has been purchased by Calvin J. Candie (Leonardo DiCaprio), the grotesquely sadistic owner of Candyland, the fourth-largest cotton plantation in Mississippi. When the two protagonists arrive at Candyland, Broomhilda is being punished for yet another escape attempt, by being confined in the so-called 'hot box' (Figure 3.1) – an outdoor torture device historically used by slave owners in the South to discipline slaves through extreme heat exhaustion, sensory deprivation and crushing restriction of space. Although this scene introduces the viewer to Broomhilda in the diegetic present, her character is introduced much earlier in the film, through a series of highly subjective flashbacks and loving musings about her, presented from Django's point of view.

There is no smooth transition from these POV images, which project images of Django's loving memories of Broomhilda, which Vogel has skeptically characterized as the mirage of a 'distant damsel in distress', to the harsh image of the grounded, tortured body. In the latter image, the viewer is asked to internalize Broomhilda as she finally enters the diegesis in person, albeit in a state that denies her personhood.[23] In the scene under analysis, Candie's slave drivers stand in the plantation house's backyard, opening the hot box – a framed, shallow case dug into the ground – to let Broomhilda out after Schultz requests to see her. In an overhead shot, the lid of the box is flung open and Broomhilda's completely naked, sweat-drenched body is revealed, curled on its side, in a fetal position. A body in a box – a commodity in a 'flesh for cash' business, its object or cargo status visually underscored by the contours of the hot box that echo the shape of a shipping container. Its utility as a sex commodity is suggested through nudity.

Additionally, this image is a legible metaphor for the female figure perpetually enclosed within the boundaries of the screen, the Mulveyan female object fetishized and regimented by the cinematic gaze.[24] This meta-cinematic reading is suggested by the presence of the diegetic audience, which consists of the plantation owner, his family, slaves and guests, who all gather on the steps to watch Broomhilda's emergence from the ground. Thus, the film viewer follows the curious (and, in Django's case, horrified) looks of the characters who have congregated to watch the opening of the box. The viewer is sutured into this observational gaze. Tarantino structures this scene by heavily emphasizing the act of exposition, the unveiling of the female object as a cinematic attraction. Tom Gunning and André Gaudreault have defined such a strategy as monstration (see Chapter 1), the mode of cinematic spectacularization (the showing) that operates independently of the narrative (the telling), or sometimes even in counterpoint to it, by slowing the narrative down, or freezing it, with an intensified moment of sheer exhibition.[25] In its focus on the manipulation of the female form into and out of an enclosure, Tarantino's scene mimics Georges Méliès' *The Vanishing Lady* (1896) and early cinema's other trick films in which a male magician would show off his mastery over the obdurate female figure by transforming her into an ultimate prop that could be dis/appeared at will.

Drowning in punishing objectification, Broomhilda appears in this initial shot as what Giorgio Agamben has famously called 'bare life' – a human reduced to the abject existence of mere biological life. In Agamben's original

Italian phrasing, *la nuda vita* suggests a life disrobed, a life divested of political agency and access to juridical order, devoid of personal dimensions and social bonds.[26] It is, according to Agamben, a life 'set aside', excluded from the polis – a hijacked life that can be tortured or killed but not sacrificed, as it has no legal or divine value due to its exclusion.[27] Agamben has found contemporary examples of bare life in the figures of the refugee and the prisoner of the Nazi death camp. In *Necropolitics*, Achille Mbembe has added to Agamben's two examples of bare life the figure of the slave, whose existence on the plantation – shaped by absolute domination, natal alienation and social death – is reduced to 'a form of death-in-life', or a 'thing' submerged within a continuous 'spectacle of pain'.[28] Mbembe has extended Agamben's theory to colonial biopolitics and its violent mechanisms of extraction, including slavery.

In line with Mbembe's attention to colonial expansion and racialized practices of exploitation, Anca Parvulescu has refined Agamben's list of bare life figures by adding the life of a trafficked woman in the context of the contemporary sex industry. In her study on film representations of sex trafficking, *The Traffic in Women's Work*, she has argued that the trafficked life – for her, importantly racialized and gendered as female – is productive through a range of sexual, reproductive, regenerative and affective labor that is performed through a variety of roles, including nanny, wife, surrogate mother, egg donor, sex worker and domestic worker (and, I would add here, entertainer). Because it is productive, for Parvulescu, trafficked life is politicized, despite – or precisely because of – its exclusion and reduction to an abject existence. Its utility and eventual used-upness plays an essential role in biopolitics. She has argued that 'bare life is politicized life, but politicized in the very particular manner of its abandonment to, rather than protection from, violence and eventually, death'.[29] Parvulescu has thus complicated Agamben's theory as she deploys a Marxist feminist lens that asks us to consider the exploitation of women (bodily and affective) within the shadow economies (is cinema also a shadow economy, or an economy of shadows?) that extract 'women's work' without providing sufficient access to labor and reproductive rights or welfare protections. While Parvulescu has read the trafficked woman as a contemporary figure of bare life, she has also been careful to make a distinction between 'coerced and (relatively) noncoerced forms of traffic in women and the conditions that define them'.[30] The conditions of bondage, captivity and general unfreedom under which trafficked women often labor are produced by the shadow economies that exploit the vulnerability and precarity of female illegal migrants, who happen to constitute the largest and most mobile pool of the global workforce. Parvulescu's contribution to Agamben's thought on biopolitics is highly significant as it posits that bare life should be seen on a continuum, rather than concentrated within a few evocative figures. Her analysis connects the contemporary practices of sexual exploitation to historical ones without collapsing these categories or erasing their important differences. It also asks us to compare informal, clandestine practices of exploitation with institutionalized ones, while foregrounding the very different economic conditions that undergird these distinct forms of exploitation – and thus distinct forms of 'life disrobed'.

Deeply affective and shockingly simple, the 'hot box' image does a great deal of symbolic work within the only few seconds of its presence on screen. Mobilized by Tarantino's pastiche style of filmmaking, *Django Unchained* gestures toward a subset of films within the blaxploitation corpus, called 'slavesploitation', which featured, and ultimately capitalized on, the violence directed against slave characters, summoned to the screen to be exploited in graphic scenes of torture and abuse, in narratives typically set on a plantation in the Old South. This cinematic reference queues the viewer into a set of conventions that include images of extreme violence and sexual exploitation enacted onto the enslaved black bodies, followed by scenes of ecstatic and often cathartic vengeance directed at slave drivers and plantation owners. These conventions were established and exhaustively recycled in films such as *Slaves* (Dir. Herbert J. Biberman, 1969), *Black Agony: The Color of Truth* (a.k.a. *Quadroon*, Dirs Jack Weis and Herbert Janneke Jr 1971), *The Legend of Black Charley* (Dir. Martin Goldman, 1972), *Black Snake* (Dir. Russ Meyer, 1973), *Mandingo* (Dir. Richard Fleischer, 1975) and *Drum* (Dir. Steve Carver, 1976), to name the best-known titles in this prolific subgenre, which was produced in the US and elsewhere.[31]

The shot of Broomhilda's boxed-in, naked body is an effective synecdoche for the long history of violence perpetrated on black female bodies under slavery and within the medium of cinema. By invoking the shipping container, the shot also evokes contemporary anxieties that permeate the dominant discourse on sex slavery and sex trafficking; but it also importantly substitutes the black body for the over-played white body, which has long dominated the discourse in question. In doing so, the shot subtly demands that these conversations about sexual exploitation be critically reframed with regard to race. Tarantino's film invites this reading by intimating Broomhilda's status as a 'sex slave'. Right after arriving at Candyland, Schultz, as a ruse to gain access to her, casually asks Calvin Candie to use Broomhilda for quick sex before dinner, a courtesy that Candie is more than happy to extend to his guest, suggesting that he has a habit of exploiting his slaves for sex. Furthermore, before meeting Broomhilda, the viewer learns that Candie, a man who never misses a business opportunity, uses his most attractive female slaves in a brothel which he owns in town. This detail fuses farm labor exploitation with sex trade exploitation.

After teasing the viewer with the sexploitation set-up, however, Tarantino methodically withholds the erotic spectacle that typifies slavesploitation cinema. Instead, without a single scene of sex spectacle, Broomhilda is returned to her initial character parameters as a 'damsel in distress' who will be successfully rescued by her husband savior. While some critics regarded this plot resolution as reactionary and masculinist, largely because Broomhilda is never afforded agency to participate in her own liberation, I wish to argue for a reading that is more sensitive to what David Roche has described as Tarantino's consistent formal experimentation with genre conventions and their heavily racialized, 'and often racist', terms.[32] However, it needs to be noted that Tarantino's space of enunciation as a white male filmmaker who is addressing issues of race and sexual exploitation in a medium still governed by white male privilege resembles the fraught position of the many white filmmakers behind the 1970s blaxploitation cycle.

In its construction of the female slave figure, *Django Unchained* activates the terms of slavesploitation, only to undercut them by another, equally over-determined genre: the fairy tale, which, in turn, is undercut by a third generic convention. Earlier in the film, while Django and Schultz are resting at a campfire, Schultz compares Django's romance with Broomhilda to the love that bonds the mythical Germanic Princess Brunhilde, a daughter of Wotan, with Siegfried, the chivalrous hero who rescues her from her captivity, defying the most harrowing odds, simply because Brunhilde 'is worth it', as Schultz quips. He references the famous German fairy tale in an effort to hearten Django, convincing him that he too can rescue his beloved. But, on a meta-cinematic level, this reference plays an important role in Tarantino's experimental genre mash-up. Slavesploitation, populated by victimized female slave characters, is hybridized with a Nordic fairy tale about a divine princess. Both genres are highly racialized, in ways that define the gendered protagonists, and both feature male characters that come to the rescue. But this mash-up also implies (even if the film does not envision it) a heroic future for Django's Broomhilda, which follows the arc of Brunhilde, who in Germanic folklore is a fierce warrior as well as a princess. Indeed, in this story, Brunhilde eventually turns against her savior and slays him. By way of this reference, Tarantino thus invites viewers to anticipate such a development during the film's final scene, in which Django and Broomhilda leave the destroyed plantation and ride away on horseback. Indeed, as they move off screen, in the very last frame that includes her, we see Broomhilda pull a Remington rifle out of her saddle. The fairy tale tropes are invoked, but like the slavesploitation conventions, left undermined and unrealized. These omissions encourage a hyper-awareness of how gender and race shape genres and generic expectations (and *vice versa*). As in most of his films, Tarantino does not want his viewer to assume the expectations of one single genre. Instead, the filmmaker foregrounds the ways in which generic conventions narrativize differently gendered characters. In *Django Unchained*, the story of female captivity and sexual exploitation are given two alternative narrative framings, both of which are ultimately aborted.

This same strategy, which suspends generic expectations and habituated modes of spectatorship, plays out on the visual level. At first the viewer gets a glance of the classic sexploitation spectacle, a defining feature of slavesploitation film, when Broomhilda's naked body is presented in the hot box. This display is then followed by a shot where we briefly see her manhandled by a group of men, who toss her into a wheelbarrow and transport her to the house to be 'cleaned up'. Although extreme in their graphic portrayal of the woman's body and its brutal physical manipulation, these two shots occur rapidly, and the spectator's view is limited by visual obstructions in the foreground, frustrating any potential monstrative pleasure. Despite the many plot opportunities in the remainder of the film for Broomhilda's character to be spectacularized for erotic pleasure (for example, in the scene where she is sent to Schultz's bedroom to provide sex services, or in the latter scenes where her body could have been used as a site of exacting revenge on Django), the film spares her sexploitation display beyond the initial moment of objectification in the hot box. The final scene of the film returns her slave character to the aesthetic conventions of the fairy tale and the rescued 'damsel in distress' trope – with the gown, the horse and the knight included. This formulation is then suspended in the film's final shot when the couple rides away from the burning plantation and slowly disappears to the left of the screen. In the very last frame, after Django is partially off screen, we see Broomhilda pull a Remington rifle from her saddle, in a gesture that displaces the fairy-tale ending and invites the iconography of the film's third genre, the Western, whose heroine demonstrates her gunmanship in a pose that endows her with unexpected agency. This is Tarantino's nod to the celebrated action heroine of blaxploitation cinema.

The blaxploitation action heroine proper is foreshadowed by a key figure in the slavesploitation subgenre, the rebellious female slave, a figure arguably launched with Herbert Biberman's 1969 film *Slaves* – a tale of slave rebellion on a Mississippi plantation. Christopher Sieving has called the film a 'borderline sexploitation picture' and explained its genesis as a vehicle of re-entry into the film industry for the HUAC-blacklisted Biberman, who shared 'impeccable liberal credentials' with other blacklisted left-leaning liberals in Hollywood who advocated for African American causes and were otherwise engaged in civil rights activism.[33] Initially *Slaves* was conceived as a serious attempt at representing the institution of slavery in the United States. Its open

***Figure 3.2*** Dionne Warwick as Cassy in *Slaves* (Dir. Herbert Biberman, 1969).

and unapologetic depiction of slavery's most egregious abuses worked as 'a corrective to the sanitized and sentimentalized depictions of the antebellum period' and, as Biberman himself intended, it was also an exposé of contemporary racial tensions.[34] As Sieving has reported, while the film showed some serious artistic merit, having been positively received at the 1969 Cannes Film Festival, the critical reception within the United States was lukewarm to negative. The distributor, Continental, ultimately decided to market the film using a campaign that centered on the film's sexploitation dynamics. This marketing strategy proved highly effective. Exhibited in both white and black theaters, the film smashed house records across the United States and topped the lists of highest-grossing films in many cities.[35] The images that Sieving has identified as central to the sexploitation publicity campaign are drawn from the film's most controversial scene, which depicts non-consensual sex between the plantation owner and his favorite female house slave/mistress.

The plot of *Slaves* begins with Luke (Ossie Davis), a hard-working man enslaved on a plantation in Kentucky. His owner, in need of money to pay off debts, sells Luke to Nathan MacKay (Stephen Boyd), a particularly cruel plantation owner, thereby separating him from his family. Once the plot moves to MacKay's Mississippi plantation, the narrative focus shifts from Luke to Cassy (played by Dionne Warwick in her screen debut; Figure 3.2), a female slave who lives with MacKay and is expected to provide him with on-demand sex services. Unlike Luke's first owner, who is depicted as far more humane, MacKay runs his plantation with mean efficiency, calling his slaves 'the machines that reproduce themselves'. MacKay's characteristics – his pragmatic cynicism and razor-like focus on profitability, coupled with a violent temper and complete lack of moral code – make his plantation an especially dangerous environment for the enslaved workforce under his control. Eventually, Luke, Cassy and the other slaves organize a rebellion, which MacKay, having received word of their plans, crushes, in the course killing Luke and re-establishing order. However, Cassy and two other female slaves, including a newborn baby girl, whose brand-new life Luke wanted to emancipate, manage to escape. Overall, the film delivers a rather realistic portrayal of many aspects of life on a plantation and as such provides the much-needed visual testimony to both the brutal abuse and continuous violence that characterized the institution of slavery, as well as the culture of organized resistance that the slaves practiced. Biberman's film does not offer the retributive spectacle that is typical of blaxploitation cinema. However, it does include moments that anticipate what Joshua Gleich has called 'the hypersexualized empowerment of blaxploitation heroes' and, we might add, heroines.[36] Cassy's character, bolstered by Dionne Warwick's nuanced performance, presides over important moments in the film, moments that signal a narrative of resistance and revenge, which is still mostly repressed in *Slaves*, but becomes genre-defining in later blaxploitation films, including the slavesploitation cycle. Cassy's attempt to resist sexual exploitation, although relatively brief and contained to one scene, portends the physical defiance and ultimate emancipation of the black action heroine.

This scene, which according to Sieving was used in the film's promotional materials, is emphatically an act of sexual exploitation under institutional slavery, in ways that highlight the almost impenetrable enmeshment of coercion, blackmail, sexual violence (including rape), emotional terror, power play, labor extraction and extreme utilization of the human body that characterize the intimate relationship between MacKay and Cassy. Such a construction is in distinct accordance with historical accounts (including those offered in slave narratives) of the sexual exploitation of enslaved women, as well as, on a much smaller scale, of children and men.[37] The scene begins in the inner rooms of MacKay's plantation house, where Cassy is typically confined. MacKay enters the room as Cassy sits in front of a mirror and looks at her own reflection as she smears it with face cream. She looks dejected. Defacing her image, physically occluding it with a cream stain on the mirror, Cassy appears to struggle with her sense of self, enacting her sadness in a self-destructive gesture. MacKay witnesses Cassy's distress but, instead of offering consolation, he makes sexual advances, pulling and pushing Cassy's body around the bedroom. She musters verbal resistance, alternating between confronting MacKay and pleading to be left alone. He persists and forcibly kisses her neck. Although she begs him to stop, MacKay pushes her body onto a bed and orders her to take off her clothes. While on her back, with both arms pinned down, Cassy changes her strategy and begins performing as a servile slave, agreeing to MacKay's every word, mockingly responding 'yessa massa'. She then manages to delay MacKay's advances by suggesting that she needs a bath. She undresses and gets in the bathtub. As she washes her body slowly, she sings the famous spiritual 'Mary Don't You Weep', one of the earliest protest songs of the enslaved people and one that offers a coded message of rebellion. Ignorant of the song's meaning, MacKay stands back and voyeuristically consumes Cassy as a sex object. Once she gets out of the tub – her body completely naked and shown from the backside – a mood change is signaled by the soundtrack.

Cassy challenges MacKay to take her. Her body stance is powerful, prefiguring the action heroine's fighting stance. She advances and disrobes MacKay, while addressing him by his first name, Nathan. In speech, she continues to ironically perform the servile act, but physically she is imposing and unafraid, pressing on and challenging MacKay. The soundtrack of frenetic Afro beat, suggestive of mobilization or combat, scripts her antagonistic counterpose that appears to be a strategic response to MacKay's aggression. Once MacKay leans into her, lowering his head to kiss her, she spits into his face, then commands him to 'give it to' her. He tries again, and she spits into his face again, while continuing to challenge him to take her. Infuriated, MacKay throws Cassy on the bed. She still dares him to conquer her and threatens to kill him if he *does not* succeed. She continues to repeatedly spit into his face as he struggles to overcome her resistance. The shot ends *in medias res*, without spectacularizing the rape that might follow but which, as Cassy mounts a fierce defense, is not inevitable. Her rebellion is echoed in a later scene, where Cassy nearly kills the drunken MacKay. Armed with a knife, her hand is stopped in mid-air by Luke, who persuades Cassy to stop and instead join him in organized rebellion.

More audacious in its sexploitation approach than Tarantino's *Django Unchained*, *Slaves* stages an elaborate erotic spectacle, but it importantly refuses to showcase the moment of sexual violation itself, a paradigmatic feature of slavesploitation cinema and of the sex slave films discussed elsewhere in this book. If explicitly depicted, the rape of Cassy would categorically fetishize and commodify her as the sex slave figure. But that is not the case. Cassy's protracted and methodical resistance, coupled with her readiness and ability to kill MacKay, offers the promise of female empowerment that will become defining of the blaxploitation heroine in the films produced in the 1970s. Additionally, unlike the rest of the film's characters, who are dressed in period costumes, Cassy's character is costumed in a modernist Afrocentric wardrobe designed by Bob Rogers and inspired by the 1960s' Afrocentric fashion trends embraced by the intellectuals, activists and political leaders of the Civil Rights and Black Power Movements. Cassy's costumes thus become a coded way of portraying resistance, pride and power. The female slave's sexual victimization is clearly shown in the film, which Biberman intended to be a realistic recreation of the dire conditions of slavery. However, this victimization, while spectacularized to a great degree, is ultimately undercut by a strong message of retribution, which is the reason why many scholars consider *Slaves* to be the precursor to slavesploitation cinema, and why contemporary black audiences flocked to see the film.

In *Mandingo* (Dir. Richard Fleischer, 1975) – the most famous, arguably most controversial and certainly most scholarly appraised of the slavesploitation films – the message of retribution is more emphatic (the plantation owner is killed by a slave on screen), as is the extreme sexploitation aesthetic deployed in this mainstream studio production (made with a sizable budget). The film offers an informative case-study for my consideration of the sex slave figure: the plot largely takes place at a slave-breeding farm, dramatizing the very process of sexual exploitation for financial gain and situating the female slave as the *de facto* 'sex slave', as her role is defined by sexual and reproductive exploitation within the institution of chattel slavery. Based on the salacious and extremely popular novel written by Kyle Onstott in 1959, *Mandingo* is set in 1840s Alabama, on the Falconhurst plantation whose owners – Warren Maxwell (veteran English actor James Mason) and his son Hammond (Perry King) – specialize in breeding slaves for income instead of crop production.[38] The film adaptation of the novel, financed by Dino De Laurentiis, a successful producer of commercial cinema, focuses on the Maxwells' attempts to breed 'pure Mandingo' slaves ('Mandingo' is a malapropism for 'Mandinka', a West African ethnic group), who, so Maxwell Senior believes, are 'stronger and more submissive' than other slaves. The son, Hammond, supervises the farm's operations and exploits the female slaves for his own sexual needs. Anxious to preserve the family bloodline, Warren asks his son to marry a 'white woman' who will produce a legitimate heir and thus ensure the continuity of the Maxwell estate. Much of the film's melodramatic impetus revolves around Hammond's love for a slave named Ellen (played by Brenda Sykes, who also appeared in *Cleopatra Jones*, alongside Tamara Dobson) and his inability to forge a relationship with his wife, Blanche (Susan George), who eventually also turns her sexual interests to Mede (played by Ken Norton, an American professional boxer), a slave used by the Maxwells as a prize-fighter on the Mandingo fighting circuit. Ellen becomes pregnant with Hammond's child but miscarries after a vicious beating administered by Blanche in one of many jealous fits while her husband is away. Blanche also becomes pregnant, not by Hammond, but by Mede. Her mixed-race newborn is killed after birth, on the orders of the family doctor who decides to spare Hammond the 'disgrace' of facing an illegitimate heir. Enraged by the evidence of Blanche's infidelity, Hammond poisons his wife and brutally kills Mede. Agamemnon (Richard Ward), the plantation's head slave, witnesses Mede's murder and ends up shooting and killing the *paterfamilias* Warren at the conclusion of the film, which delivers a radical departure from the novel's more accommodating ending that preserves the lives of both Maxwells.

The critical reception of *Mandingo* was an exceptionally vehement rebuke of the film, which some critics regarded as even more offensive and exploitative than *Slaves*. Both the white and black press reached a consensus in pronouncing *Mandingo* racist, sadistic and pornographic. However, as with *Slaves*, American audiences, especially the urban African American audience, disregarded the critics' dismissal of the film and flocked to the theaters in record numbers. In his scrupulous archival study of the film's initial reception, Andrew DeVos has argued that white critics uniformly rejected the film in a gesture of outrage that 'bordered on a critical revolt', mainly on account of the film's explicit content.[39] As such, so DeVos has argued, the white critics' condemnation of the film was very much in line with the public uproar at the time about the explosion of sex and violence in the post-Hays cinema. The black critics' reviews were also overwhelmingly negative. DeVos' research suggests that the black critics saw the film as a symptom of systemic racism in the media industry – they found *Mandingo* to be in collusion with the racist film industry's goal to 'capitalize on black audience's desires to see themselves represented and empowered'.[40] Like their white counterparts, black critics found the film to be excessively graphic and exploitative. However, DeVos' research into the audience reception discloses impassioned reactions from the black viewers, including reports of standing ovations at the film's theatrical screenings. The majority of the interviewed black viewers found *Mandingo* to be realistic in its portrayal of the degradation of enslaved people and in its depiction of the white slaveholders' moral decay. Further, DeVos has argued that 'black filmgoers proved more receptive to the film's invitation to "expect the truth" and accepted the film's willingness to expose what decades of Hollywood films had suppressed: the ubiquitous sexual abuse of African slaves at the hands of their white masters'.[41] DeVos has also indicated that much of the film's success with black audiences rested on the film's refusal to shy away from visualizing a form of radical retribution in its conclusion.

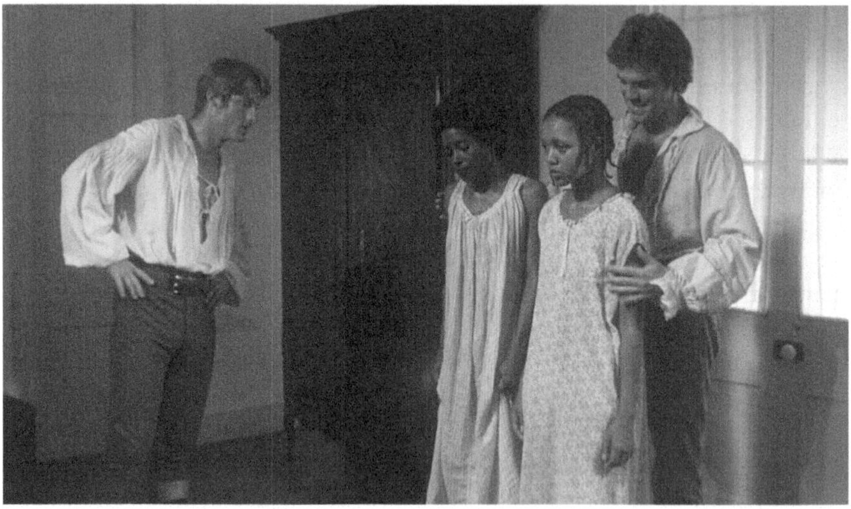

***Figure 3.3*** The sexual exploitation of slaves at the plantation in *Mandingo* (Dir. Richard Fleischer, 1975).

Slavesploitation films, indeed, demonstrated the sexual exploitation of the enslaved people in an unprecedented way, while crucially pairing this message with a vision of retribution. At the same time, the collusion of the film industry with the historic practice of sexual exploitation is also indisputable. In its commercial investment in spectacle – which often bordered on the pornographic – as the main mode of communicating its ostensibly radical message, the slavesploitation film capitalized on the very exploitation on which it sought to shed light (Figure 3.3). Further, it must be noted that all cinema, not just sexploitation cinema, is a technology of exhibition, and thus exploitation. It its exhibitionist momentum, cinema exploits. The word 'exploit', from which exploitation film subgenres take their name, has its roots in the Latin *explicāre*, which indicates unfolding, setting forth, displaying, unrolling, spreading out and bringing into play. Until the mid-nineteenth century, the word 'exploit' had a positive meaning. Before the birth of cinema, other media carried out the work of publicizing sex work: pornography, which etymologically stands for 'writing about prostitutes' (*pornē* is Greek for prostitute, and *graphein* means to write), began as a written text, but was quickly illustrated with visual text – the latter of which today dominates the pornographic discourse. Both cinema and pornography are important technologies that are employed in the marketing of sex as both service and commodity. The unfolding, or unrolling, that cinema and pornography carry out, are fundamental in selling sex. As the verb 'to prostitute' suggests, the act of public display is deeply constitutive of sex work. The word 'prostitute' derives from the Latin word *prostituere*, which connotes setting up front, setting before, or setting out. Thus, in the earliest definition of sex work as prostitution, the concept of public display is absolutely central on both a linguistic and practical level, and it is no surprise that most media would serve as platforms for such a display. In this sense, it may be argued that cinema has a fundamentally prostituting function in its ability to dynamically bring the human figure into the public light, unearthing, mining and publicizing our intimate lives, including our desiring lives.

In *Scenes of Subjection: Terror, Slavery, and Self-Making in Nineteenth-Century America*, Saidiya Hartman has cautioned against the dangers of spectacularizing anti-slave violence in narratives that routinely unfold the 'display of the slave's ravaged body', to the point at which indignation is replaced with indifference, and the images 'immure us to pain by virtue of their familiarity'.[42] Hartman has drawn our attention to the potential pornographic aspect of publicizing the suffering of the enslaved subject as spectacle, arguing that the line between witness and spectator is uncertain. It is this blurry line that Hartman has astutely isolated as the mechanism of visual media's exploitative capacity. Cinema has mastered techniques that dissolve this line, permitting the viewer's scopophilic voyeurism to masquerade as witnessing and, consequently, for acts of witnessing to degenerate into voyeurism. This potential for voyeuristic consumption reproduces what Hortense Spillers has recognized as one of the 'external meanings and uses' that tend to rewrite the captive body of the enslaved from the outside in four ways:

> 1) [T]he captive body becomes the source of an irresistible, destructive sensuality; 2) at the same time – in stunning contradiction – the captive body reduces to a thing, becoming *being* for the captor; 3) in this absence *from* a subject position, the captured sexualities provide a physical and biological expression of 'otherness'; 4) as a category of 'otherness', the captive body translates into a potential for pornotroping and embodies sheer physical powerlessness that slides into a more general 'powerlessness', resonating through various centers of human and social meaning.[43]

By mapping the dangers of representation regarding the enslaved body, Spillers has correctly diagnosed how cinema, in moments of spectacular monstration, can very easily provide a rhetorical space for the evacuation of an enslaved subjectivity, precipitating pornotroping and forcing a position of 'general powerlessness' that forecloses possibilities of resistance. This form of pornotroping the slave's violated body, I argue, is not only possible in slavesploitation spectacle, but *de rigueur* in the genre's construction of spectatorial pleasure, which stacks scenes of extreme objectification with scenes of retribution, where the latter are perceived to be exponentially justified if the former are sufficiently extreme. The powerlessness, however, that Spillers has warned about, is undermined in slavesploitation films by the characterization of the sex slave figure as deeply agential. As discussed above, in *Slaves* Cassy resists during and after the scene of violation and is constructed in make-up, costume and gestures as an Afrofuturist subject. Ellen, in *Mandingo*, plays a more conventional slave character, but she is hardly powerless. As she submits to Hammond's sexual and romantic advances, she begins to negotiate for her status, especially the status of her unborn child, whom she asks Hammond to emancipate. After a brutal assault by Hammond's wife, Blanche, causes Ellen to miscarry, Ellen shows off the jewelry that Hammond gave her to publicly humiliate Blanche and mark her own elevated status within the household. In the film's bloody finale, Ellen also takes the initiative to prevent the murder of Mede. Significantly, although *Mandingo* spectacularizes sex and violence to a far greater degree than *Slaves*, the film largely spares Ellen from a sexploitation spectacle. This is to say that Hammond's diegetic exploitation of Ellen does not take the aesthetic form of a sexploitation spectacle. Instead, the film depicts it as a subtler (and thus more insidious), non-spectacular method of coercion that is nonetheless violent. The scenes that depict Hammond's grooming of Ellen as his sex slave emphasize his 'tender' feelings for his slave and his desire for a more 'reciprocal' sex. In the scene of their first sexual encounter, Hammond asks Ellen to look up and back at him, to see him, before they engage in sex, which she hesitates to do at first. Hammond desires to possess Ellen as a subject and asks her for visual intimacy. This scene directly addresses the issue of the black subject's 'right to gaze' that bell hooks has famously theorized in her essay on the oppositional gaze.[44] Noting that the slave's 'right to gaze' was denied within the system of slavery, hooks has hypothesized that such systemic suppression of one's right to look shaped the development of the gaze – its directionality, its intention, its political potential – for the contemporary black subject. However, hooks has also argued that we must assume that this restriction invited a strong opposition and critique of power structures: 'I knew that the slaves had looked'.[45] The slave, according to hooks, looked to witness, to interrogate and to resist the oppressor. In the dramatized exchange of looks between Hammond and Ellen, *Mandingo* draws our attention to the politicized site of the gaze, including the erotic gaze. Ellen is ordered to gaze back during the act of forced sex. In the moment, she obliges Hammond, as she has no other viable choice. But she quickly extends this license to look, given to her by her oppressor, to advocate for herself and other slaves on the plantation. Thus, Ellen's visual agency illustrates hooks' theory that, 'even in the worst circumstances of domination, the ability to manipulate one's gaze in the face of structures of domination that would contain it, opens up the possibility of agency'.[46] On another level, *Mandingo*, in its unfiltered portrayal of the moral decrepitude of the white slaveholders, embeds the oppositional gaze as the dominant gaze of the camera in the film. This decidedly critical vision of the plantation was cited as one of the key factors responsible for the film's original success with black audiences, who commented on the realistic portrayal of the demoralizing brutality of white oppression.[47]

Desire in *Mandingo* is multi-directional, cutting across the lines of racial segregation, an aspect of the film that theorist and filmmaker Celine Parreñas Shimizu has noted in her appraisal of the film as an investigation of the Hegelian master-slave dialectic that foregrounds sexuality 'as the site of domination in slavery'.[48] Parreñas Shimizu has asserted that the film's explicit preoccupation with interracial sex within the framework of the plantation reflects the discussions and experiences of mixed-race partnerships in the 1970s. Through this analysis, there emerges a productive interpretation of the film's explicit sex scenes as an exploration of the contemporary interracial love, marriage and sex practices and how those practices are forever impacted by the legacy of sexual exploitation under the regime of slavery – what Hartman calls 'the afterlife of slavery'.[49] Diane Miller Sommerville has pointed out how *Mandingo* was, in fact, contributing an urgent progressive message, through its graphic scenes of interracial sex, to the public discourse that was taking place in the United States since the mid-1960s about the need for eradicating the racist anti-miscegenation laws. Miller Sommerville has argued that, despite the 1967 Supreme Court ruling that found Virginia's law against interracial marriage unconstitutional, the general public's attitudes, paired with the continued legal challenges to the Supreme Court's decision, made this matter far from settled. The brazen scenes of sex between the black man and the predatory white woman in the film, so Miller Sommerville has asserted, countered the long-standing phobic narratives about black men sexually assaulting white women – narratives often used to terrorize black communities and take the lives of black men.[50]

*Mandingo* is iconoclastic not simply because it offers a strong revisionist portrayal of slavery in the American South, harsher and more honest than the vision of slavery and white slavers characteristic of much-celebrated blockbuster hits of early Hollywood, such as *The Birth of a Nation* (Dir. D. W. Griffith, 1915) or *Gone with the Wind* (Dir. Victor Fleming, 1939), which normalized the master-slave relations through stories of care, collaboration and mutual respect. The iconoclasm of *Mandingo* becomes even clearer when it is compared to films that focus on the subject of sex slavery in the twentieth century, outside of the institution of chattel slavery. Along with other slavesploitation films, *Mandingo* offers a vision of the sex slave figure very different from the films that preceded it – the films discussed in Chapter 1 – and the films that came after – the sex slavery films of the 2000s, discussed in Chapters 2 and 4. The most revealing difference is, of course, the fact that the sex slave, in this case, is always an enslaved person of color. The latter fact undermines any hesitation, dramatization, or titillation around the issue of consent. In terms of race, *Mandingo*'s plot situates black and white women in constantly shifting positions of power within the patriarchal value system, but the black woman, Ellen, is consistently diegetically regarded as more valuable than her white master, Blanche, both as a worker and a romantic partner to Hammond. In early cinema's 'white slavery' films, discussed here in Chapter 1, white femininity is imbued with symbolic value – what Elizabeth Uzzell has called 'preciousness'.[51] This is also the case in the more recent cycle of sex slavery films. However, in *Mandingo* white femininity is methodically devalued and never becomes the site of consecrated group cohesion in a nationalist sense, nor the consecrated gender/race cohesion as the pride and trophy of white patriarchy.[52] *Mandingo*'s sex slaves are also of different genders and ages. We see women, men and children performing sex work for the benefit of the master. The sex slaves at the Falconhurst plantation are portrayed as sex laborers forced into a system of reproductive extraction. The film does not dramatize their abduction from innocence. The viewer knows how the slaves got to the plantation. Their work is clearly depicted as non-consensual, and the film makes it rather clear that the slaves are brutalized on a daily basis. These conditions are the function of a specific economic system, characterized by nineteenth-century global trade networks and colonial mechanisms of expansion.[53]

The coerced labor of enslaved people is guaranteed by the scale and operational efficiency of the system rather than pure physical terror. On this aspect of *Mandingo*, Robert Keser has commented: '[T]he film spends little time detailing the accoutrements of coercion – the clamps, clasps, leg irons – opting for the much subtler point that rebels are kept in line by the sheer pervasiveness of the system'.[54] Indeed, it is the banality of enforced sexual labor that is the most horrifying element of the film's narrative. By communicating this banality through repetitive scenes where the body of the enslaved woman is exploited, the film offers a grave indictment of white America's racial biopolitics. A race of people had been abducted by another group of people, but it was not until the 1970s that cinema openly addressed (and also 'exploited') the fact that sexual and reproductive labor were key to institutional slavery's economy of extraction, under which enslaved men, women and children were forced to work. As Miller Sommerville has suggested, *Mandingo* and other slavesploitation films can be seen as texts that provoked a public conversation about sexual exploitation as constitutive of the system of slavery. As such, these films played a key role in hastening the arrival of the concerted scholarly inquiry into this under-studied instrument of the economic extraction of enslaved bodies.[55] Similarly, after carefully distinguishing between good and bad slavesploitation films, Allyson Nadia Field has contended that some slavesploitation films – including *Mandingo*, *Drum*, *Blacula* (Dir. William Crain, 1972) and *Skin Game* (Dir. Paul Bogart, 1971) – explored slavery as 'a site of social critique'.[56]

Another feature that sets slavesploitation films apart from the other sex slavery films is the lack of the rescue figure. Instead, we see the slave characters plan, negotiate and carry out acts of liberation, or, more often than not, undertake small steps of resistance that may eventually lead to liberation. The forces of law and justice never swoop down on the plantation to stop the abject suffering of the enslaved, since these very systems in fact worked to perpetuate the system of enslavement. Rather, the films communicate a message difficult to accept: the colonial gains that funded the creation of the capitalist economy in the United States, now the richest country in the world, depended on the systemic sexual and reproductive enslavement of large numbers of people. The network of labor captivity could not be dismantled with a heroic rescue mission, delivered by agents of any system. In slavesploitation narratives, we therefore see enslaved people engaged in collective, bottom-up resistance and coalition-building meant to undermine the system on many different levels. The dramatic emphasis is on challenging the oppressors and carrying out radical acts of retributive justice – for example, the burning down of the plantation buildings in *Slaves*, the killing of the slaveholder in *Mandingo*, and both acts carried out in tandem in *Django Unchained.* While some of these acts, often hyperbolized in the service of spectacle, never occurred on antebellum plantations, blaxploitation cinema's retributive impulse responded to the pent-up frustration and anger among its contemporary black audiences who sought a message of reckoning, at a time when the advancements of the Civil Rights Movement had stalled following the wave of violence directed against leaders such as Martin Luther King Jr and Malcolm X throughout the previous decade. Blaxploitation cinema's violence coincided with the call for more immediate and more radical militant action, which emerged from the Black Power Movement, especially after the assassination of Malcolm X.

A similar affective dynamic – the pursuit of justified revenge by the victimized – would fuel another genre that rose to prominence in the 1970s: the rape-revenge film, which addressed sexual and gendered violence at a time when the second-wave feminist movement was beginning to be challenged by feminists, such as Gloria Steinem who wrote 'After Black Power: Women's Liberation'.[57] Cinematic enactments of retribution and revenge, common in 1970s cinema, were, therefore, a set of responses to mounting social tensions. They negotiated the racial and gender oppression on libidinal and affective levels for all viewers, not just those already invested in social justice movements, and they did so in the public sphere of the movie theater. When reviewing these filmic performances of revenge driven by racial or gender justice motivations, especially during times of political transformation, a pressing question comes to mind: Does a mediated spectacle of revenge serve as a politically radical act?

The unprecedented box office success of the films in question, combined with the reports of impassioned audience reactions during theatrical screenings, testify to these films' power to attract mass attention and stir up strong emotions. Whether such attention and emotions could in turn amount to a politically transformative impulse is famously theorized by Julia Kristeva in her essay 'Ellipsis on Dread and the Specular Seduction'.[58] Kristeva has proposed that the film industry functions as a commerce of affect. In her view, cinema is both a medium and an industry that capitalizes on providing a space for spectators to engage in 'sanitizing' their transgressive feelings by vicariously experiencing spectacular excess. Once such excess has been experienced within the diegetic world, not much of it remains to fuel a consciousness change. This is a dire diagnosis that suggests that the cinematic spectacle can only work to defuse political impetus. For Kristeva, spectacle in cinema is the very plane of meaning-making that enables the expression of strong affect – what she calls 'aggressivity' – via symbolic (visual) formulations in ways that narrative means alone can never accomplish. Thus, by emphasizing the spectacle as cinema's driving register of affective impact, Kristeva has aligned her theory of the medium with the theory of monstration proposed by Tom Gunning and André Gaudreault. By assigning the cathartic, rather than mobilizing, role to the act of cinematic exposition, Kristeva has explained why the spectacle continues to have such a seductive appeal for the viewer. Using psychoanalytic terms, Kristeva has argued that seduction by spectacle results in the discharge of transgressive energy and thus the pacification of transformational potential. It brings relief and release. At first glance, Kristeva's theory of cinema seems limiting, for it situates the medium as mechanism for a psychic inoculation of sorts – a space where transgressive sentiment is played out, spent and therefore defused. The viewer is too transfixed by the fascinating images to think and strategize politically. However, there is a way to read Kristeva's model of cinematic spectacle, steeped in affective work, as an instrument for generating a militant opposition to oppression, by providing a symbolic language (concrete images) of violent resistance. The spectacle of retribution offered by slavesploitation or rape-revenge films allowed for the viewers to envision, and indeed psychically experience, some form of justice, thus enriching the collective imaginary with the vision of a shifted power dynamic. Significantly, this psychic experience had a collective dimension within a theatrical setting. As such, the retributive images had a certain revolutionary dimension. It is not a coincidence that blaxploitation and rape-revenge films roused audiences across the United States, at a time when the Civil Rights Movement engaged civil-disobedience tactics, the Black Power Movement sanctioned the use of violence as a self-defense strategy and feminist formations such as the Redstockings, The Furies Collective, or Valerie Solanas' S.C.U.M. (Society for Cutting Up Men) movement galvanized women's liberation movement with radical approaches to emancipation.[59]

While slavesploitation films such as *Slaves* and *Mandingo* endow female sex slaves with agency and depict them as capable of mounting resistance, such films leave acts of vengeance and retribution to the male characters. This is not the case in the blaxploitation films that were set, at that time, in the contemporary United States. One film in particular visualizes an act of female retribution in the context of sexual exploitation, while also making careful reference to the history of sexual exploitation of the enslaved. In *Foxy Brown* (Dir. Jack Hill, 1974), Pam Grier plays the character of Foxy Brown – 'a protector of hearth, family, and community' – whose 'agonized raced and gendered body' is repeatedly placed in jeopardy as she combats racism, exploitation and crime.[60] The protagonist, Foxy Brown, is a young black woman who fights a network of drug and sex traffickers after her boyfriend, Michael (Terry Carter), a federal agent fighting a drug cartel, is murdered. The cartel is led by a female boss, Miss Katherine (Kathryn Loder). Foxy's own brother, Link (Antonio Fargas), turns out to be pushing drugs for Miss Katherine. Once he owes the cartel some money, Link betrays Michael by blowing his cover, hoping that Miss Katherine will forgive him his debt. The cartel's hit men invade Foxy's apartment and kill Michael. After Foxy discovers Michael's dead body, she decides to revenge her boyfriend. She infiltrates the cartel, posing as Misty Cotton, a sex worker, hoping to find and kill Miss Katherine and her henchmen. Foxy's revenge mission, the focus of the film, encounters many obstacles along the way, obstacles that compound her initial grief and anger, providing ample justification for her vengeance. Foxy overcomes each hurdle with her heroic mental and physical prowess. In fact, the character's courage, endurance and physical strength came to define the genre's quintessential black action heroine. The character's narrative prominence in Hill's film, combined with Grier's commanding performance, came into the public spotlight in an unprecedented way and offered an intersectional account of black and feminist empowerment in the 1970s.

Foxy's character is crucial to the ensuing analysis, as it is located at the convergence of the contemporary sex slave figure and the chattel slave figure, since the film concentrates both of these constructs within Foxy's highly spectacularized role. These figures converge in a scene at the ranch where

Foxy is shipped away and sequestered after she dares to help her fellow sex worker, Claudia (Juanita Brown), escape the cartel. As punishment, Miss Katherine orders Foxy to be tranquilized with heroin, 'broken in' with rape and forced into a sex slavery ring. The film, thus, draws an analogy – and simultaneously sets up a distinction – between the cartel's urban prostitution business, where sex workers perform coerced and underpaid work but are not held in captivity, and the remote rural base, where women are held captive, continuously drugged and exploited for unpaid sex service. The *mise-en-scène* throughout the ranch scene sequence invokes the sinister plantation setting of the slavesploitation film. Foxy's two handlers are coded as Southern men, with their costume and manner resonant of slave drivers. They use racial slurs to humiliate Foxy and reduce her to the abject state of a plantation slave. They proceed to bind, whip and rape her body, casually, in a series of shots that resemble the sexploitation aesthetics of *Mandingo*. The two white handlers are also depicted as despicable humans, thus politically situating *Foxy Brown* as a critique of white supremacy that is also found in the slavesploitation subgenre. Importantly, the act of rape itself is occluded from the spectacle; it happens off screen. Foxy's agony is still emphatically signaled through an extreme close-up of her terror-stricken face right before the men assault her. Further, following the rape, her nude body is depicted as a brutalized site of violence (her clothes in shreds, hair disheveled, skin bruised and stained), stripped of erotic appeal, and thus devoid of the typical 'pornotroping' common in sexploitation film, a tendency against which Hortense Spillers has cautioned. Joseph S. Valle has argued that this rape scene 'clearly evokes rape between white men and black women in the antebellum South'.[61]

What happens next folds Foxy's performance squarely into the conventions of the rape-revenge genre, where the raped woman rejects the position of victimhood and instead transforms her injury into fuel for merciless revenge, full of the baroque excess of severed penises and gouged-out eyes. One by one, Foxy dispatches her tormentors with speed and cold efficiency. Valle has observed that Foxy's revenge 'feels' gratifying and that the film ensures that her 'resourcefulness is admirable'.[62] The spectatorial pleasure of *Foxy Brown*, and all of blaxploitation cinema, I might argue, has much to do with the deployment of retributive violence dramatized as vigilante justice, which is specific to the victimized subject; in addition, as Foxy states at the beginning of film, vigilante justice is as 'American as apple pie'. This diegetic insight may elucidate part of the appeal of blaxploitation cinema to the broad American audience, across identity and specific history of violence. Writing about rape-revenge films, Judith Franco has theorized the feminist vigilante violence as 'orgasmic', and thus different in tenor from the cathartic violence of melodrama. The revenge narratives 'position the spectator to desire, rather

***Figure 3.4*** Pam Grier as the Black Power agent of vigilante justice in *Foxy Brown* (Dir. Jack Hill, 1974).

than fear' the eruption of violence. Franco has seen these films as texts that privilege the sadistic story of acceleration – speed and spectacle, affect and exhilaration – at the expense of victimization, which is considered the norm for female behavior under patriarchy, thus offering the female spectator the narcissistic-sadistic pleasure of identification with omnipotent thrill-killing heroines.[63]

As an action heroine who also functions as a site of empowerment, Foxy should be understood as a subject whose agency is a hyperbolic conglomeration of historic and contemporary resistance struggles. In her Afrocentric costume and hair style, Pam Grier as Foxy builds on the victimized yet rebellious slave characters in slavesploitation cinema (Figure 3.4). The figurative convergence of historical and contemporary resistance to sexual exploitation in *Foxy Brown* draws the viewer's attention to the historical continuity of the sexual subjugation of the black female body. The film also underlines the important quantitative and qualitative differences between the sexual exploitation and reproductive commodification suffered by the enslaved women within the system of chattel slavery, and contemporary sex workers whose emancipatory consciousness was informed by second-wave feminism, the Civil Rights and Black Power Movements, the Gay Liberation Front, and the Black and Gay Pride movements.

By creating the sexually emancipated black action heroine, so Sims has observed, blaxploitation cinema established a very specific tradition of feminist political performance where the body becomes 'a metaphor for a political instrument' and where the black heroine uses her 'sexuality as a vehicle for controlling her circumstances' without sacrificing intimacy and sensuality.[64] In her discussion of Pam Grier's eroticized performance, Sims has argued that Grier's Foxy departs from stereotypical forms of female representation by managing to be both an erotic object and an active subject within the very same body. According to Sims, this strategic contradiction is exemplified in the very first scene of *Foxy Brown*, which introduces Foxy as a sexual and romantic partner to her boyfriend as the two relax and play in bed. But it is Foxy, as Sims has observed, and not her boyfriend, who suddenly jumps out of bed, sticks a gun in her bra and runs to help her brother – literally busting out of the confines of sustained eroticization.[65]

The legacy of Grier's performances and, more broadly, the cultural and political empowerment manifested by the black action heroine, live on in present-day counter-narratives constructed by black female rap artists, including the veteran Inga DeCarlo Fung Marchand, a. k. a. Foxy Brown, Rihanna, Nicki Minaj, Beyoncé and Megan Thee Stallion, who frequently use the 'raunch' aesthetics to profit from the sexploitation spectacle, while also using it to push back against the enforcement of the Christian and white middle-class codes of politeness designed as strategies of female serfdom.[66] Creative appropriation of blaxploitation cinema also reaches across gender lines, as Janelle Monáe, a young nonbinary Afrofuturist musician, has demonstrated through the performance of their *alter ego*, Django Jane, who is badder than Tarantino's Django, sexier than Corbucci's Django and queerer than both. Critics and scholars have been quick to note how younger black artists steer their political activism away from 'the politics of respectability and dissemblance' in order to express 'pleasure, fluidity, transgression, queerness, and freedom'.[67]

## Notes

1. Christopher Sieving, *Soul Searching: Black-Themed Cinema from the March on Washington to the Rise of Blaxploitation* (Middletown: Wesleyan University Press, 2011), pp. 203–5.
2. Ibid. p. 204.
3. Mia Mask, *Black Rodeo: A History of the African American Western* (Urbana, Chicago and Springfield: University of Illinois Press, 2023), pp. 11–12.
4. Ibid. p. 215; Novotny Lawrence, *Blaxploitation Films of the 1970s: Blackness and Genre* (New York and London: Routledge, 2008), p. 19.
5. Josiah Howard, *Blaxploitation Cinema: The Essential Reference Guide* (Godalming: FAB Press, 2008), p. 10.
6. Ibid. p. 9.

7. Lawrence, *Blaxploitation Films*, p. 20.
8. Howard, *Blaxploitation Cinema*, p. 13.
9. Ibid. p. 15
10. For examples of a historical account and analysis of the sexual exploitation of enslaved women, see Alexandra J. Finley, *An Intimate Economy: Enslaved Women, Work, and America's Domestic Slave Trade* (Chapel Hill: The University of North Carolina Press, 2020); Garraway, *The Libertine Colony*; Rennie Simson, 'The Afro-American Female: The Historical Construction of Sexual Identity', in Ann Snitow, Sharon Thompson and Christine Stansel (eds), *The Powers of Desire: The Politics of Sexuality* (New York: Monthly Review Press, 1983), pp. 229–35.
11. Yvonne D. Sims, *Women of Blaxploitation: How the Black Action Film Heroine Changed American Popular Culture* (Jefferson and London: McFarland & Company, 2006), p. 45.
12. Ibid. p. 46.
13. For an account of such contemporary critiques, see George Alexander, 'Credits Due: The Rise of Black Women in Hollywood', *American Legacy Magazine: Woman*, 2002, p. 14; Chris Holmlund, 'Wham! Bam! Pam! Pam Grier as Hot Action Babe and Cool Action Mama', *Quarterly Review of Film and Video*, 22:9, 2005, pp. 107–8.
14. See, for example, Sims, *Women of Blaxploitation*; Yvonne Tasker, *Spectacular Bodies: Gender, Genre and the Action Cinema* (New York and London: Routledge, 1993); Holmlund, 'Wham! Bam! Pam!', pp. 97–112; Jennifer DeVere Brody, 'The Returns of Cleopatra Jones', in Shelton Waldrep (ed.), *The Seventies: The Age of Glitter in Popular Culture* (New York and London: Routledge, 2000), pp. 225–48.
15. Sims, *Women of Blaxploitation*, p. 33.
16. Ibid. p. 29.
17. Mask, *Black Rodeo*, p. 185.
18. In this assessment I agree with Joseph Vogel, who has argued that *Django Unchained* constructs black women 'as extensions of male pleasure and power'. Joseph Vogel, 'The Confessions of Quentin Tarantino: Whitewashing Slave Rebellion in *Django Unchained*', *The Journal of American Culture,* 41:1, 2018, p. 25 (pp. 17–27 inclusive).
19. Mask, *Black Rodeo.* p. 193.
20. Vogel, 'The Confessions of Quentin Tarantino', p. 27.
21. Peter and Will Brooker, 'Pulpmodernism: Tarantino's Affirmative Action', in Deborah Cartmell, I. Q. Hunter, Heidi Kaye and Imelda Whelehan (eds), *Pulping Fictions: Consuming Culture across the Literature/Media Divide* (London: Pluto Press, 1996), pp. 135–51.
22. In thinking through Tarantino's playful gender politics, I refer to Moe Meyer's theory of political camp and its use of queer parody. See Moe Meyer, 'Introduction: Reclaiming the Discourse of Camp', in Moe Meyer (ed.), *The Politics and Poetics of Camp* (London and New York: Routledge, 1994), pp. 1–22.
23. Vogel, 'The Confessions of Quentin Tarantino', p. 24.
24. Mulvey, 'Visual Pleasure and Narrative Cinema'.
25. Gaudreault, *Film and Attraction*, pp. 52–55.

26. Agamben, *Homo Sacer*, p. 8.
27. Ibid. p. 83.
28. Achille Mbembe, *Necropolitics*, trans. Steve Corcoran (Durham: Duke University Press, 2019), p. 75.
29. Parvulescu, *The Traffic in Women's Work*, p. 79.
30. Ibid. p. 92.
31. See the German film *Slavers* (Dir. Jürgen Goslar, 1977); the Italian films directed by Mario Pinzauti, *Mandinga* (1976) and *Passion Plantation* (1976); the Mexican film *Black Fire* (Dir. Raúl Fernández, 1979); and the Cuban film *The Last Supper* (Dir. Thomás Gutiérrez, 1976).
32. David Roche, *Quentin Tarantino, Poetics and Politics of Cinematic Metafiction* (Jackson: University Press of Mississippi, 2018), p. 40.
33. Sieving, *Soul Searching*, p. 125; p. 203.
34. Ibid. p. 151.
35. Ibid. pp. 151–52.
36. Joshua Gleich, 'Jim Brown: From Integration to Re-Segregation in *The Dirty Dozen* and *100 Rifles*', *Cinema Journal*, 51:1, 2011, p. 2 (pp. 1–25 inclusive)
37 See Thelma Jennings, 'Us Colored Women Had to Go through a Plenty: Sexual Exploitation of African-American Slave Women', *Journal of Women's History*, 1:3, January 1990, pp. 45–74; Brenda E. Stevenson, 'What's Love Got to Do with It? Concubinage and Enslaved Women and Girls in the Antebellum South', *Journal of African American History*, 98, 1, Winter 2013, pp. 99–125; Deborah Gray White, *Ar'n't I a Woman? Female Slaves in the Plantation South* (New York: W. W. Norton, 1999).
38. The existence of a slave-breeding industry is a highly controversial topic among the historians of slavery in the US context. While there is little evidence of the existence of specialized breeding farms, most historians have agreed that many slaveholders indeed invested in and promoted the reproduction of slaves as a relatively easy strategy to increase their property. For further discussion on the topic, see Daina Ramey Berry, *The Price for Their Pound of Flesh: The Value of the Enslaved, from Womb to Grave, in the Building of a Nation* (Boston: Beacon Press, 2017); Gregory D. Smithers, *Slave Breeding: Sex, Violence, and Memory in African American History* (Gainesville: University Press of Florida, 2012); Ned and Constance Sublette, *The American Slave Coast: A History of the Slave-Breeding Industry* (Chicago: Lawrence Hill Books, 2017).
39. Andrew DeVos, '"Expect the Truth": Exploiting History with *Mandingo*', *American Studies*, 52:2, 2013, p. 9 (pp. 5–21 inclusive).
40. Ibid. p. 12.
41. Ibid. p. 15.
42. Hartman, *Scenes of Subjection*, pp. 3–4.
43. Hortense Spillers, 'Mama's Baby, Papa's Maybe: An American Grammar Book', *Diacritics*, 17:2, Summer 1987, p. 67 (pp. 64–81 inclusive)
44. bell hooks, 'The Oppositional Gaze: Black Female Spectators', in *Black Looks: Race and Representation* (Boston: South End Press, 1992), pp. 115–31.

45. Ibid. p. 116.
46. Ibid. p. 116.
47. DeVos, 'Expect the Truth', p. 15.
48. Celine Parreñas Shimizu, 'Master-Slave Sex Acts: *Mandingo* and the Race/Sex Paradox', *Wide Angle*, 21:4, 1999, p. 48 (pp. 42–61).
49. Saidiya Hartman, *Lose Your Mother: A Journey along the Atlantic Slave Trade Route Terror* (New York: Farrar, Straus and Giroux, 2007), p. 6.
50. Diane Miller Sommerville, '"Now You Are Ready for *Mandingo*": Sex, Slavery, and Historical Realism', in Matthew Christopher Hulbert and John C. Inscoe (eds), *Writing History with Lightning: Cinematic Representations of Nineteenth-Century America* (Baton Rouge: Louisiana State University Press, 2019), p. 115 (pp. 112–24 inclusive). On the construction and dissemination of the harmful stereotype of the black rapist, see Diane Miller Sommerville, *Rape and Race in the Nineteenth-Century South* (Chapel Hill: University of North Carolina Press, 2004).
51. Elizabeth Uzzell, 'All the Precious White Women', *Medium,* 21 January 2018, at https://medium.com/@elizabeth.uzzell/all-the-precious-white-women-4f1109 1a493e (accessed 15 November 2023).
52. For a detailed account of the role of white women in perpetuating slavery in the United States, as market agents and slaveholders who were deeply implicated in the processes of brutal exploitation, including sexual exploitation, of the enslaved people, see Stephanie E. Jones-Rogers, *They Were Her Property: White Women as Slave Owners in the American South* (New Haven and London: Yale University Press, 2020).
53. For a reading of *Mandingo* as a critique of the capitalist system of extortion and oppression, see Robert Keser, '"The Greatest Film about Race Ever Filmed in Hollywood": Richard Fleischer's *Mandingo*', *Bright Lights Film Journal*, 7 November 2023 (an online repost of the original print article published in *The Film Journal* in 2006), https://brightlightsfilm.com/greatest-film-race-ever-filmed-hollywood-richard-fleischers-mandingo/ (accessed 15 November 2023).
54. Ibid.
55. Miller Sommerville, 'Now You Are Ready for *Mandingo*', p. 121. See note 29, p. 124, for a comprehensive list of historical scholarship on the issue of sexual exploitation and the role of sexual relations under the regime of chattel slavery in the American South.
56. Allyson Nadia Field, 'Stomping on Stepin Fetchit: Historicizing "Blackness" in African American Film Culture of the 1970s', in Novotny Lawrence and Gerald R. Butters, Jr (eds), *Beyond Blaxploitation* (Detroit: Wayne State University Press, 2016), p. 159 (pp. 157–79 inclusive). Field lists *The Arena* (Dir. Steve Carver, 1973) and *Passion Plantation* (Dir. Mario Pinzauti, 1976) as films that used slavery as a subject of titillation.
57. Gloria Steinem, 'After Black Power, Women's Liberation', *New York Magazine*, 7 May 2008 (an online repost of the original print article published in *New York Magazine*, 4 April 1969), at https://nymag.com/news/politics/46802/ (accessed 17 November 2023).

58. Julia Kristeva, 'Ellipsis on Dread and the Specular Seduction', trans. Dolores Burdick, *Wide Angle*, 3:3, 1979, pp. 42–47.
59. Joseph S. Valle, 'As Foxy as Can Be: The Melodramatic Mode in Blaxploitation Cinema', in Novotny Lawrence and Gerald R. Butters, Jr (eds), *Beyond Blaxploitation* (Detroit: Wayne State University Press, 2016), pp. 137–53.
60. Ibid, pp. 138–39.
61. Ibid, p. 147.
62. Ibid, p. 149.
63. Judith Franco, 'Gender, Genre and Female Pleasure in the Contemporary Revenge Narrative: *Baise moi* and *What It Feels Like for A Girl*', *Quarterly Review of Film and Video*, 21:1, 2004, p. 7 (pp. 1–10 inclusive).
64. Sims, *Women of Blaxploitation*, p. 81.
65. Ibid, p. 81.
66. On 'raunch aesthetics', see Jillian Hernandez, 'Carnal Teachings: Raunch Aesthetics as Queer Feminist Pedagogies in Yo! Majesty's Hip Hop Practice', *Women and Performance: A Journal of Feminist Theory*, 24:1, 2014, pp. 88–106.
67. For a recent black feminist critique of Evelyn Brooks Higginbotham's concept of 'politics of respectability' and Darlene Clark Hine's theory of 'dissemblance' in conjunction with contemporary black cultural production, see Marlo D. David, 'On Dirty Computers and Dissemblance', *Signs: Journal of Women in Culture and Society*, 45:3, 2020, p. 541 (pp. 541–46 inclusive).

# CHAPTER FOUR

# *White Slave: The Commodification and Securitization of Whiteness*

On 3 December 2023, Morgonn McMichael (@morgonnm) posted a video on Twitter (now known as X). Lasting only fourteen seconds, the cell phone video shows what appears to be a piece of candy, a Reese's Peanut Butter Cup, lodged in the door handle of a large white SUV (parked in the open garage of a residence). McMichael is only visible to the camera by her hand, which reaches into the frame to grab the Reese's Cup. The hand reveals that the chocolate is missing, yet the cardboard tray and empty paper cup have been painstakingly replaced into the wrapper. The appearance of an unopened candy bar is just a ruse. Above the video, McMichael wrote the following caption: 'Was almost trafficked today. . . LADIES! Always be aware of your surroundings! I was getting my nails done and saw this on my passenger door handle, empty and perfectly placed. Classic Kidnapping [sic] and trafficking tactic to distract you!!! So scary! I'm home safe now!'[1] McMichael's tweet received 6.7 million views, 1,200 retweets and 1,400 replies, which ranged from affirmation to ridicule. McMichael is a professional influencer who contributes content to Turning Point USA, a conservative NGO whose 'mission is to build the most organized, active, and powerful conservative grassroots activist network on high school and college campuses across the country'.[2] While beyond the scope of this discussion, but expressing a broader conservative phobic worldview, her pinned tweet is another video, one exhorting viewers to boycott Target (a well-known US chain of department stores) for stocking merchandise that celebrates the LGBTQ+ community.[3]

McMichael's ostensible near encounter with human traffickers, as well as its mediatization online, constitutes only one of the many examples of the plethora of fabricated scenarios that are being disseminated by predominantly white and conservative social media influencers who are part of the new wave of moral panic in the United States. Writing on this issue for *The Atlantic* in 2022, Kaitlyn Tiffany has traced and reviewed various strands of this vigilante movement; its major players include QAnon, a far-right American conspiracy movement, which in 2017 claimed that a group of high-profile Democrats were members of an international Satanic child sex-trafficking cabal and Operation Underground Railroad (OUR), a group founded by Tim

Ballard to rescue child-trafficking victims in international sting operations (which directly inspired the film *Sound of Freedom*). Tiffany has cited some of the trafficking conspiracies that gained most publicity and attention on social media, such as the 2020 Wayfair conspiracy, which claimed that the online home-goods retailer Wayfair was somehow involved in running child sex slave auctions. In its retail setting, the Wayfair conspiracy resembles the viral 2016 Pizzagate conspiracy theory (widely considered the predecessor to QAnon), which alleged that Democratic politicians were running a child sex slavery ring out of pizza restaurants in Washington DC. The retail setting also appears in the Target TikTok hoax, which reported an alleged sex-trafficking operation taking place in a Phoenix Target store, where children appeared to be lured by other children, away from the protection of their parents and into the arms of traffickers. Reporting on the Target rumor for *Rolling Stone* magazine, E. J. Dickson has commented on a wider trend of 'people posting videos warning about elaborate trafficking schemes at big-box stores'.[4] Dickson has mentioned TikTok videos that refer to traffickers who are stalking potential victims in Target's produce aisles and use zip ties to mark women's cars in the store parking lots. Emerging out of a confluence of tabloid spectacle, the surge of interest in true crime, the growing popular awareness of gendered violence and – importantly – the 'influencer economy', these paranoid videos signal not the death but the transmediation of cinema. Cinema's early preoccupation with monstration is now renewed and reactivated in TikTok videos and other new media that invest in populist exhibition culture.

Tiffany's critical analysis of the recent wave of panics that stoke the fantasy of imminent threat to the safety of white suburban women and children ties them to the recent anti-black and anti-immigrant fears and compares them to the white slavery panic of the early 1900s. She has argued: 'More recently, the panic has intersected with paranoia about immigration and the increase of migrants at the southern border, echoing arguments that a wall between the United States and Mexico would be a humanitarian effort to prevent child trafficking'.[5] Tiffany has also suggested that the trafficking panic's disproportionate concern for the safety of middle-class white American lives is a form of reactionary response to the Black Lives Matter movement. While both Tiffany and Dickson have rightly been careful not to dismiss the toll of sex trafficking on vulnerable populations, they both have noted that influencers who use social media to propagate conspiracy theories about organized kidnappings very much depart from the reality and demographic profile of sex trafficking. Spreading misinformation and stoking fear through their sensationalist narratives, influencers (most frequently white cisgender females) effectively displace the impoverished women of color and LGBTQ+ youth who statistically are the most likely victims of trafficking and coerced sex work, with the phantasm of imperiled suburban white women and children. Scholars of criminology and criminal justice who have studied the recent proliferation of sex-trafficking conspiracies on social media have commented on their volatility and impact on shaping public opinion as well as anti-trafficking resource distribution and policy.[6] In their study of the Wayfair conspiracy, Sarah Hupp Williamson, Sadie Creel and Emily Walker have observed the resemblance between recent social media panics and the white slavery panics of the late nineteenth and early twentieth centuries, each of which 'have centered white women as victims'.[7] The three scholars trace the role of Christian and patriotic discourses as key components in the modern sex-trafficking panics, where those two discourses are 'used to simplify the conspiracy and create an "us versus them" mindset, as seen with good versus evil or Democrats versus Trump'.[8]

Whether a symptom of white supremacy entrenching itself in the face of the many global challenges to its hegemony, or a continued mechanism to consolidate the Western nation-state around the purity and sanctity of the white woman's body, or simply a result of what Richard Dyer has defined as the 'representational power' of whiteness to pass itself off as the norm, the fascination with imperiled white femininity is at the heart of contemporary Western film and media cultures.[9] In an examination of how race, gender and class shape the performance of collective empathy and grief in the United States within the context of missing person news coverage, Jennifer Musial has engaged with African American news anchor Gwen Ifill's concept of 'Missing White Woman Syndrome'. Ifill, who coined the phrase in 2004 to describe the news media's racial bias in its coverage of missing persons, has famously defined the media's 'ideal' missing victim as a young attractive white woman of middle-to-upper-class background. Drawing on this, Musial has argued that Missing White Woman Syndrome is 'a deeply entrenched racialized and gendered narrative in the US', a narrative responsible for constructing white girls and women as 'idealized citizens that personify innocence and hope', whose disappearances 'tap into deeply-rooted fears of an aborted white future'.[10] Musial has aggregated the qualitative and quantitative research on the subject and confirmed the disproportionate hyper-visibility of the white woman in missing person reporting, despite the statistical preponderance of Black people among the missing persons. Her analysis of the qualitative studies underscores how missing white women are consistently represented in terms of their appearance ('beautiful' and 'attractive'), their family status ('loving' and 'loyal') and their morality ('good' and 'innocent').[11] Musial has argued that missing white women are imbued with symbolic value that correlates their disappearance with collective loss: 'The fact that they are missing takes on national importance: it is crucial to find this lost gem'.[12]

The endowment of white middle-class femininity with qualities of exceptionality, vulnerability and preciousness through scenarios of presumed abduction or a threat of abduction informs contemporary and past moral panics, as well as the tabloid spectacle of the missing white woman that has also permeated narrative cinema. Before I address how sex slavery films concentrate on imperiled white femininity, I wish to briefly address the commercial success of a pair of blockbuster thrillers that have capitalized on the Missing White Woman Syndrome: *Gone Girl* (Dir. David Fincher, 2014) and *The Girl on the Train* (Dir. Tate Taylor, 2016). Both films are very close adaptations of immensely successful crime novels that topped bestseller lists and sold millions of copies worldwide: *Gone Girl* (2012) by the American writer Gillian Flynn and *The Girl on the Train* (2015) by the British writer Paula Hawkins. Both novels are driven by the suspense created around the missing white woman, in both cases a conventionally attractive suburban housewife whose sudden disappearance mobilizes the community into a frenzied search. Significantly, the titles of both novels refer to adult women as 'girls', a rhetorical gesture that renders white femininity as the locus of innocence and vulnerability from the start. Additionally, both of the missing characters are pregnant, something Musial has recognized in her study as the maximizing factor in the protectionist anxieties stoked by the narratives of missing white women. Musial has linked the foregrounded prospect of the abducted white pregnancy (the imperiled white fetus) to the white supremacist fear of its own extinction, bringing the reproductive security of white domination into question.[13]

In *Gone Girl* and *The Girl on the Train*, respectively, the missing women, Amy Dunne (Rosamund Pike) and Megan Hipwell (Haley Bennett), are hardly paragons of virtue. Yet, in each case the plot dramatizes the woman's disappearance to such a degree that it becomes the sole constitutive factor within the diegetic world of the film. Importantly, this disappearance also dictates the viewer's investment in the film, which uses form and content to build up suspense around a potential rescue. In both stories, the urgency with which the search for the missing woman is conducted seems to depend on the woman's physical attraction, youth and whiteness, as well as her reproductive potential, rather than anything that they may have contributed to their families, communities and society at large, respectively. Yet, this is never explicitly stated. Rather, the narrative works because it captures a certain underlying truth behind the Western social contract: If gone missing, there are lives that will command a collective search, regardless of their individual value.

*Gone Girl* in particular highlights the societal obsession with imperiled white femininity. The fact that Amy stages her disappearance to punish her husband for cheating hardly attenuates her narcissistic and psychopathic motivations. Amy's husband, her best friend and other members of the suburban community where Amy lives, as well as the film viewer (and quite a few film critics who read Amy as a feminist character) fall for her ruse. Amy expects this and counts on the collective preoccupation with her symbolic worth. As she is concocting her plan, in voice-over she comments on how 'America loves pregnant women'. Then, after she goes missing, she is shown watching her case being reported on television by the 'protective and maternal' Ellen Abbott, a TV talk show host (a character based on the real-life TV personality Nancy Grace). Amy knows that her plan to frame her husband will be successful, because Abbott, as Amy observes in voice-over, gets 'rabid-dog vicious' once she zeroes in on the suspect, 'usually the husband'. In her analysis of the film, Amanda Ann Klein has focused on the issue of Amy's whiteness as the qualifying factor in the success of her staged disappearance. Amy's privilege is self-perpetuating: Her life is valuable when she is present (as the 'cool girl'), and even more valuable when she is absent (as the 'gone girl'). The value accrual in her absence becomes a way to frame the story of how her life became so valuable in the first place, as a site of desired, idealized personhood. Klein has argued that in *Gone Girl* David Fincher foregrounds the underlying assumption in the American social contract: The community will search for the missing person only if that person's vulnerability is established as female and white. Citing Alfred Hitchcock, Klein has observed how the white woman has become the privileged victim for Western audiences, on and off screen. Importantly, Klein has noted how this racialization – although emphasized in Fincher's adaptation (through the bleached blondness of Rosamund Pike, the showcasing of the white suburb setting and the lighting design that accentuates Amy's whiteness) – goes unnoticed in the source text because it works as the normative category: 'Whiteness in the novel *Gone Girl*, as in so much of American mass culture, is a neutral character trait, the default setting on a character, the box that remains unchecked'.[14]

Vulnerable whiteness presented as an entity in need of protection and conservation motivates most of the contemporary sex slavery films and all of the historic white slavery films. The previous chapters have traced the history of the sex slave alongside the history of cinema, outlining its roots in nineteenth-century Orientalist fantasies that captured colonial anxieties about race and gender. The afterlife of such fantasies manifested in the late nineteenth century (Europe) and the early twentieth century (United States) as the 'white slavery panics' that led to a variety of legislation advanced by colonizer countries to ensure racial homogeneity and white supremacy in the imperial metropole. Perhaps the most infamous example of such legislation is the 1910 Mann Act, a United States federal law that functionally enforced racial segregation under the auspices of protecting white women from sex trafficking. In cinema, this complex of fantasy and anxiety provided cover for the erotic titillation of respectable audiences, since films such as Johann Schwarzer's *The Slave Market* (1907) or August Blom's *The White Slave Trade* (1910), for example, purported to expose or otherwise raise awareness about sex trafficking, offering a didactic account of the danger and how it might be avoided. Since then, the cinematic figure of the sex slave has been situated at the discursive and symbolic confluence of labor, sexuality, migration and race. As argued in Chapter 3, blaxploitation cinema offers a notable exception to this trajectory, by reframing the racialization of the slave while simultaneously engaging in, and interrogating, the spectacle of sex slavery within the context of chattel slavery. The present chapter will examine the construction and maintenance of whiteness through (and as) white feminine innocence and vulnerability in commercial sex slave films, which include *Lilya 4-ever* (Dir. Lukas Moodysson, Sweden, 2002), *Girls to Buy* (Dir. Maria Sadowska, Poland, 2021) and *Taken* (Dir. Pierre Morel, France, 2008). Together, these films simultaneously depict and construct two schematic categories of whiteness: Second World whiteness and First World whiteness.[15] These forms of whiteness, which have a long and complex history but emerged more fully after the Cold War, are vital for a deeper understanding of the ideological structure of sex slavery films more generally. As this chapter will demonstrate, cinema does not just manufacture whiteness; it also reflects it, feeding into, as well as out of, a wider social, cultural and political context that is constantly being negotiated. Following this analysis, I will place these films in conversation with Nigerian director Kenneth Gyang's *Òlòtūré*. Gyang's film, distributed by Netflix, offers a rare counterexample that both challenges and confirms the racialization of whiteness exemplified by films such as *Taken* or *Lilya 4-ever*.

It is mainly within the figure of the sex slave, I argue, that sex slavery films construct vulnerable whiteness. To begin, I will examine Lukas Moodysson's *Lilya 4-ever* (2002) and Maria Sadowska's *Girls to Buy* (2021), two very different films about sex work and sex trafficking in post-socialist Eastern Europe, directed by a Swedish and a Polish director, respectively, two films which foreground the act of female mobility and the perceived feminization of European (and global) migration in divergent yet complementary ways. The pairing of these two cinematic texts is motivated by their construction of what I call Second World whiteness via the sexual objectification of the Eastern European woman as a commodity in the 'desire industries' driven by 'the political economy of raced sex'.[16] Second World whiteness is a form of racialization that emerged from the fall of the Soviet Union and the birth of the European Union to mark the post-communist subject as raced, and as such not perfectly aligned with the white Western liberal subject. Second World whiteness also points to the continued unease with regard to female migrant mobility and the complications that arise in the process of representing that mobility.[17] Many scholars have commented on this racialized articulation of whiteness as distinct from First World whiteness in the era of late capitalism, especially within the discourses of sex and reproductive labor. In what follows I will summarize the key contributions to this discussion that best inform my inquiry into the process of racializing the sex slave figure.

Anna M. Agathangelou, whose work on the racialized feminization of the desire industries deeply informs my own project, has defined Second World whiteness as a 'white but not quite' identity embodied by migrant sex and reproductive workers, including 'ethnics from Russia and Eastern Europe' who come from the transitional economies of the post-communist region, which is feminized and 'penetrated' within the global economy of the capitalist extraction of resources.[18] Áine O'Healy's account of Second World whiteness outlines the abject figure of the trafficked Eastern European woman in Italian cinema as 'a particularly potent terrain for explicit depictions of misogyny, xenophobia, sexual exploitation, and other traumatic abuses'.[19] O'Healy has stated:

> Although this Eastern European woman is apprehended diegetically as a white body, her presence is usually coded in ways that make her immediately distinguishable from other (white) on-screen characters through clues provided by clothing or posture, accented speech, or indeed lack of access to speech. [. . .] Though frequently presented as a sexualized body available for exchange on the sex market, the Eastern European woman is also occasionally configured as providing other forms of affective services, particularly in domestic settings, and is sometimes shown transiting from one to the other.[20]

In O'Healy's analysis, the racialized Eastern European woman is defined as the 'alien though ostensibly attractive figure' – a phrase that captures the ambivalence of this racialization and its utility in the reproductive 'crisis' of the quickly aging white Western European society that looks to Eastern Europe as the acceptably raced pool of reproductive labor.[21] This last argument is explored in detail by Anca Parvulescu in her pivotal 2014 work on cinema's role in European biopolitics, *The Traffic in Women's Work: East European Migration and the Making of Europe.* Parvulescu has argued that the racialization of the Eastern European woman in the political economy of migration as 'not quite white' needs to be carefully considered because it has received little attention, yet it is fundamental in establishing the Eastern European woman's value on the sex and reproductive labor markets.[22] Rather than collapsing this whiteness with Western whiteness, Parvulescu wants us to acknowledge the difference, while also paying close attention to the fact that the 'not quite white' Eastern European women should not be allowed 'to disavow the privileges that come with the possibility of passing' as white.[23] Indeed, this ability to pass, so Parvulescu has noted, directly determines Eastern European women's access to labor opportunities ahead of women of color. As is the case in other capitalist industries driven by the logic of white supremacy, the desire industries are structured in racialized terms. Whiteness is fetishized hierarchically in the global flesh commodities market, another aspect of what the Jamaican philosopher Charles Mills has recognized as modernity's racial order, which works at 'securing the privileges and advantages of the full white citizens and maintaining the subordination of nonwhites'.[24] According to Parvulescu, many Eastern European women work to reduce this hierarchical racial disadvantage by performing 'their hyperfemininity as a form of drag' and by playing up the fantasy of the Eastern European woman as a traditional 'good woman' – one who cooks, cleans and smiles, untouched by the feminist reform, thus attracting the more desirable Western men.[25]

Julietta Hua has discussed the complex forms of racialization and the race-informed notions of national belonging embedded in the visual imagery of sex trafficking generated within the US state and NGO anti-trafficking campaigns. Through a careful comparative analysis, Hua has been able to determine the differential representations of trafficked sexualities with regard to race. The imagery under analysis defines the trafficking victims as female immigrants (women and girls) mainly coming from South and Southeast Asia, Eastern Europe and the former Soviet Union. While Hua has not studied narrative cinema, her comments on how post-communist Second World women are racialized as white in the anti-trafficking discourse align with Parvulescu's findings and inform my investigation of the sex slave figure in contemporary sex slave films.

Hua has observed that, when US state and NGO agencies address the higher occurrence of sex trafficking in Asia, Eastern Europe and the former Soviet Union, there is a curious contrast between accounts of trafficked women from communist states and those trafficked from Asian countries. While these agencies tend to 'whiten' the women from communist states, whose cultures are qualified as 'neither traditional nor despotic', they typically emphasize the patriarchal traditions and enduring religious practices that they associate with Asian countries.[26] As Hua has observed, these agencies imagine post-communist Second World women as those whose poor social status is caused by the temporary economic crisis that occurred during the transition from communism to capitalism. These qualifications then cast 'two different stories of sex trafficking's regional origins through frames of civilizational development and linear progress toward modernity', something that Hua has seen reflected in the women's differential racialization.[27] In Hua's view, white women are featured in these narratives as subjects entitled to intervention by the state and security agencies, as sex trafficking causes only a temporary lapse in their otherwise guaranteed human rights' protections, while the non-white subjects are configured first and foremost as victims of their own cultures, where gender equality and human rights are scarce, thus priming the way to perpetual and pervasive sexual exploitation. Ultimately, Hua's study positions Second World whiteness in between the whiteness of the Global North/West and the 'Other' races of the Global South/East.

Both *Lilya 4-ever* and *Girls to Buy* romanticize and exoticize their white female protagonists who engage in different forms of sex trafficking and trade. When considered together, these films provide an accurate and relatively realistic depiction of the bifurcated nature of sex trade mobility in a unified Europe. In telling ways, both films racialize the female on the move and frame her within an economy of loss. As they do, the films perform what Ewa Mazierska and Laura Rascaroli in their important study of the European road movie have defined as the 'traditional pejorative link between femininity and mobility'.[28] Ultimately, my analysis of these two films showcases how the pre-Wall divisions between the First and the Second Worlds and the different degrees of involvement in the European (neo)colonial project appear to linger on in the united Europe, determining the possibilities of women on the move. These new inflections of the old divisions challenge the grand idea of post-war European community as one that has been successfully reconstituted in opposition to the violence precipitated by colonial, communist and Fascist ideologies.

In his 1998 book *Globalization: The Human Consequences*, Zygmunt Bauman has diagnosed the disconcerting bifurcation in the modes of global mobility when identifying the split between those who travel today as 'tourists', whose experience of mobility is desirable, and those who move with the stigma of being forever a 'vagabond', who move 'because they have no other bearable choice'.[29] As with any binary pair, so Bauman has explained, the two depend on each other: 'There are no tourists without vagabonds, and the tourists cannot be left free without tying down the vagabonds'. The economy of this relationship resembles that of the many exploitative contracts that characterize labor relations in the late capitalist economy. Within discourses of sex trafficking, Bauman's pair of concepts neatly maps onto a parallel dichotomy of sex slave versus sex worker. Arguably, Moodysson's and Sadowska's films, when viewed side by side, replicate the relationship and bring into focus the incommensurability of the vagabond as sex slave and the tourist as sex worker. Moodyson's Lilya (Oksana Akinshina) is the 'vagabond' – Bauman's abject metaphor for the migrant subject, and Sadowska's Emi (Paulina Gałązka) is the global 'tourist' – Bauman's figure that stands in for the member of the extra-territorial, supra-national corporate elites. Later in this chapter, I will return to *Taken* (see Chapter 2), which illustrates Bauman's theory of privileged 'tourist' mobility exceptionally well. When this privilege – which belongs to Kim, a young white American tourist – is dramatically threatened by the prospect of sex slavery, her father – a male personification of Bauman's 'tourist' – rushes to the rescue and single-handedly restores Kim's entitled position in a dazzling international security operation.

The protagonists in Moodysson's and Sadowska's films are polar opposites in terms of how they experience the celebrated freedom of movement (of labor, capital, resources and so on) that is the hallmark value of the European unification project. The two women traverse the same roads and cross the same 'open' borders within Europe, yet they do not meet, because, as Bauman would argue, the late capitalist 'tourists' and 'vagabonds' never meet in Fortress Europe. They might occupy the same spaces, often in very intimate proximity, but their economic and political status ensures their symbolic distance. This separation of space and trajectory is evident in the two films' visual construction of space. Lilya's Europe is decidedly claustrophobic, shot in urban spaces where dilapidated industrial and residential structures contain and obstruct her movement, and where the gray, foreboding skies steep the diegetic world in an atmosphere of despair. Emi's Europe, however, resembles the Europe found in the advertising brochures for Mediterranean cruises. The saturated light and the wide camera angles open up space and glamorize it. The exteriors and interiors of the hotels and yachts that populate Emi's itinerary are steeped in opulence and glitz. Shot in some of Europe's most popular jet-set resort towns, the film constructs its diegetic space as exotically seductive.

So what do *Girls to Buy* and *Lilya 4-ever* tell us about the journeys undertaken by women in the post-Wall Europe? One way to decode the politics of the two texts is by bringing into focus the treatment of the mobile female figure offered by the two filmmakers and the way in which that figure is discursively racialized and gendered. In a gesture reminiscent of classic blaxploitation cinema, where the spectacularized black female is endowed with agency that stands for Black Power, as in the fighting heroines in Jack Starrett's *Cleopatra Jones* (1973) and Jack Hill's *Coffy* (1973) and *Foxy Brown* (1974), Moodysson's film uses a spectacularized white female to speak of 'White Power'. In contrast to the blaxploitation genre where femininity is endowed, mature and fertile, here the White Power materializes as atrophied femininity in need of protection. *Lilya 4-ever* follows the sixteen-year-old Lilya – a Russian-speaking teenager in an unidentified post-Soviet country – on a perilous journey to Sweden, across national borders, a journey that ends in sexual coercion and exploitation, full of extreme physical violence.

An accomplished Swedish director, Moodysson bookends his film with Lilya's attempt to run away from her abusive employer – the sex trafficker who pimps out young women smuggled in from former Soviet republics to Swedish men in discreet transactions, carried out in the privacy of the client's residence. Her escape, however, is articulated as impossible. Hunted and desperate, Lilya in a suicidal act jumps from an overpass. Much of what is shown between these two bookends focuses on Lilya's impoverished life in an unnamed Baltic post-socialist state (those scenes of the film were shot in Tallinn and Paldiski, Estonia). At the start of the film, Lilya is abandoned by her single mother, who leaves to pursue a better life in the United States as a mail-order bride. After Lilya's aunt forces her to move out of her family home and into a small, decrepit room, she struggles to take care of herself. She spends most of her time with Volodya (Artyom Bogucharsky), her younger friend and confidant, whose abusive alcoholic father beats him for the slightest of infractions. At night, Lilya goes to nightclubs with her school friend Natasha who performs sexual favors on men she meets there in exchange for money. When Natasha's father finds her pocket money, she says that it belongs to Lilya who sells sex. As this rumor spreads, Lilya is ostracized at school. Later, she is raped by a group of neighborhood hoodlums who defile her on account of the rumor. Lilya and Volodya while away their largely unstructured lives by huffing glue in an abandoned communist military base, smoking cigarettes, playing basketball and dreaming of the West, Britney Spears and Michael Jordan.

Throughout this section, the film is full of aestheticized misery and what may be best described as poverty or ruin porn – there are shots where Lilya is shown sitting amidst piles of trash or where she is lying in mud, crying and being sniffed by a stray dog. This aesthetic changes slightly after Lilya is conned into leaving her forsaken home to go to Sweden in order to earn a living as agricultural worker. Once they embark on their journey, Lilya's new boyfriend Andrei (Pavel Ponomaryov) convinces her to hand him her passport and then swiftly traffics her to the Polish man Witek (Tomasz Neuman), who runs a prostitution racket in Malmö. Once she is transferred to her handler, Lilya's mobility becomes completely restricted. She is locked in a small, barely furnished apartment, which she is allowed to leave only when supervised by Witek. When she is not taxied around in the back of Witek's car from one client to the next, she is shown in scenes that depict her interactions with the clients as unconsented forced sex. When she resists, Witek beats her and threatens her with police intervention. Inspired by a daydream of Volodya, who appears to her as an angel, Lilya finally escapes her confinement, but the Swedish streets are hostile and there is no one to whom she can turn to for help. Significantly, Lilya's Sweden (shot in Trollhättan and Malmö) is also full of cheap housing projects, gray skies, dirty snow and dismal landscapes, as if Lilya's deprivation contaminated the capitalist paradise with her post-socialist misery. Frightened and confused, Lilya jumps to her death. The film ends with an ambiguous scene, where Lilya and Volodya as angels play basketball on a rooftop, finally free and happy. This is also the only scene in the film where warm sunlight pierces through the dreary gray skies. Overall, the film is melodramatic and very predictable, but also highly successful at articulating the cautionary tale of sex slavery. All the key elements are included: the naïve girl, the neglectful parents, the lack of economic prospects, the systemic violence, the promise of work in the West, the confiscated passport, the confinement and rape. Indeed, most scholars have emphasized that, since its release to almost unanimous critical acclaim, Moodysson's film has been used as a didactic tool in a number of well-publicized anti-sex-trafficking campaigns throughout the former Soviet states and in the West. It has also been screened to the members of several parliaments, as footage that ostensibly 'documents' the horrors of sex slavery, in support of passing security legislation that regulates sex work. In Swedish schools, it has been screened to students to demonstrate the link between gender equality and the perils of trafficking. When discussing the film's popularity among Sweden's and Europe's establishment and its various didactic applications, Anna Westerståhl Stenport has observed that Sweden, as the country that produced *Lilya 4-ever*, takes on the 'do-gooder' role of a state 'occupying the moral and political high ground', which articulates itself as 'carrying the torch of equality around the world'.[30]

Lars Kristensen has read *Lilya 4-ever* as 'a European (Nordic) narrative' in which Lilya is constructed as 'the non-European Other'. He has explained that Lilya 'fascinates us because we find her social decline unjust and horrific' and that her decrepit environment 'rouses the viewers' empathy and desire to rescue the film's victims'.[31] Kristensen has found this polarizing construction of the post-Soviet Europe to be Eurocentric, with Europe defined as the Western neoliberal supra-state and the post-communist states as Othered, thus not fully European, populated by impoverished citizens whose newly gained mobility poses a financial threat to the Western welfare systems.[32] Jennifer Suchland has considered the deficient status of Lilya's world to be established by the filmmaker through the process of representational abjection, whereupon Lilya's post-communist social reality is depicted as an 'eternal state of collapse'.[33] Suchland has contended that in Moodysson's film the post-Soviet states (and their populations) are no longer just the European 'Other' – they have been degraded to the status of the European abject that is voyeuristically consumed. Thus, according to Suchland, the decrepitude of the post-socialist abject is spectacularized in the film. This spectacularized abject adds a new dimension to the spectacle of the sexual violation that is typical in sex slavery films, and it is certainly featured extensively in *Lilya*

*4-ever*. There are sixteen shots that show Lilya in situations of rape or rape-like assault, each carried out by a different man. Suchland has borrowed the concept of the abject from Julia Kristeva, who has famously theorized it as an unassimilable non-subject, stuck between borders and boundaries.[34] Not only Lilya, but also her friends, family and all the inhabitants of the post-Soviet sphere are screened as belonging to the realm of the abject, where the liberal subject cannot emerge. Further, for Suchland, in Moodysson's film 'postsocialism and sex trafficking are mutually reinforcing tropes as sites of tragedy'.[35]

Arguably, then, Lilya is objectified in Moodysson's film in a double spectacle for the viewer's voyeuristic pleasure: Poverty and ruin porn combines with sex slavery porn to produce Lilya as an instrument of Swedish pedagogy. Both of these lenses contribute to Lilya's racialization as 'white but not quite'. This aspect of Lilya's character construction has been largely ignored by film critics and scholars. Only Westerståhl Stenport has commented on the 'conspicuous' whiteness of the film, observing that Lilya and Volodya are constructed as 'angelically white-complexioned' and noting Moodysson's general lack of explicit treatment of European race and ethnicity politics across his oeuvre.[36] I agree with Westerståhl Stenport that Moodysson's diegetic worlds are overwhelmingly white, and I believe that they need to be analyzed as such, even if Moodysson's white characters are invisibly raced because they pass themselves off as the norm in the all-white casts of his films.[37] But *Lilya 4-ever* is different from Moodysson's other films that feature Western white subjects. Here whiteness, due to the intense spectacularization of post-socialist abjection, gains a more pronounced and simultaneously fractured inflection. Second World whiteness is articulated as both dying whiteness and as a resource that promises white renewal across Europe.

Lilya is white enough to be considered a worthy victim in a sex slavery narrative that would attract the attention of white European philanthropists, security agencies and the general white European audience preoccupied with the shifting racial profile of Europe over the last two decades. According to this racist logic, Lilya's tragic story pitched as a protectionist narrative makes sense because she is white, and the film's heavy-handed symbolism accentuates her whiteness (Figure 4.1). When she is first introduced to the viewer, she is compared to the white bird flying above her as she tries to run to freedom. (This analogy is cemented by the film score, through the lyrics of 'Bomba', a song by the Russian-Ukrainian girl band Nu Virgos, which tells the story of a white bird flying over a gray city.) In the final sequence, she appears as an angel with a pair of large, snow-white wings. Her death is eulogized by Moodysson in a lyrical religious (and emphatically Christian) coda, as Lilya comes to embody the perishable autochthonous European whiteness that

***Figure 4.1*** Lilya racialized as abject whiteness in *Lilya 4-ever* (Dir. Lukas Moodysson, 2002).

is in need of protection. As a biopolitical resource, Lilya's whiteness is also like the whiteness of the millions of recent Ukrainian refugees; in their flight from Russian aggression, they have been warmly received by their Western European neighbors who simultaneously subject non-white refugees from the Middle East and Africa to routine border pushbacks and deportations. It is, indeed, in the biopolitical interest of the European supra-state, which, despite its splashy policy of multi-culturalism, continues to be governed by white supremacy (the fact glaringly visible in any of the executive sessions of the European Union's governing bodies). In this context, the Second World whiteness functions as a corrective and easily assimilable whiteness that can be used to forestall the demographic changes resulting from the growing mass migrations of people of color to Europe.

Even so, Lilya's Second World whiteness also sets her categorically apart from white Western women, which permits Lilya's desubjectification and instrumentalization as an object in an inegalitarian sex spectacle; the latter can unfold because the affordances of feminist emancipation and gender equality policies seem not to apply in Lilya's case. Combined with her abjection, Lilya's accentuated whiteness makes the film's sex spectacle eminently sellable as a rare regressive (and politically incorrect) eruption of explicit sexual violence featured in a mainstream production. While common in the pornographic register, such violence has been significantly censored out of commercial narrative cinema in the milieu shaped by the systemic critique of sexual abuse and gender violence, developments which have changed the acceptable thresholds of the spectacularization of sexual exploitation in mainstream media. The spectacle of Lilya's endless rape is only possible in today's cinema because it is framed within the security rhetoric of the sex slavery film. It is also because Lilya is white, but not quite. The parenthetical appearance of the violent sex spectacle within sex slavery films, which are often sold to audiences as activist media, meets an increased demand for sexually transgressive visual content. There is a distinctly reactionary impetus to the spectacle of Lilya's sexual degradation. Through her racial and phenotypical proximity, Lilya stands in for the emancipated and empowered white Western woman. The disempowerment and the corporeal domination to which Lilya is almost compulsively subjected on screen are the key images of the phallocratic disempowerment fantasy, whereby the white liberal feminist subject is recolonized, her power divested. Lilya's abject whiteness, her marked difference in the racial hierarchy, sets her apart as the Other that can be angrily defiled through such a disempowerment fantasy, without the danger of public outcry. In all of the rape scenes, Moodysson's camera captures the anger and satisfaction on the faces of the men who possess Lilya.

One of the most disturbing scenes in Moodysson's film that centers white paternalism and the reproductive colonization of the post-Soviet woman is the scene of role-played incest. One of Witek's wealthy clients, a blond man who lives in an enormous white house in the suburbs, buys Lilya for a specific sex service that entails her acting as the man's daughter. The man's house, whose Swedish interior design racializes the space as bourgeois white, is decorated with IKEA lamps and subtle Christmas decorations. As foreplay, the man makes Lilya, who is played by the very blond fifteen-year-old Akinshina, dress in his daughter's clothes and do homework at her desk. While obeying the man's initial instructions, Lilya grows increasingly disturbed by the role she is forced to play. She starts speaking in Russian and confronting the man for his desire to own her as his 'property'. The man angrily instructs her in English to 'shut up' and do her homework, while he proceeds to fondle his 'daughter' and speak to her tenderly. The scene ends with a quick shot of explicit sexual violence that would hardly be allowed in a mainstream film in 2024, especially considering the age of the child actor (Akinshina was fifteen at the time of the shoot). Lilya's face is pressed into the pillow, her back exposed to the camera, while the man rapes her. The soundtrack amplifies his angry grunting and her screaming in pain.

When Moodysson filmed this disturbing scene in the early 2000s, the birth rates of the autochthonous Swedish population were in decline, while at the same time immigration to Sweden from the Middle East and Africa was on the increase. In this sense, the scene can be regarded as an illustration of the operations that undergird the projection of the white male subject and his desired supremacy over the shifting demographics of the Swedish nation-state. One of these operations is the process of abjection, where the element that most threatens the white male subject must be defiled, including the defilement that takes place in the intimate sphere of sex and affect. Arguably, as an 'illegal' immigrant who can easily 'pass' for a Swedish citizen, and as a person with reproductive potential, Lilya is more threatening to the Swedish patriarchy: she can very easily blend in, become a daughter or mother of a Swede. Within this racist logic, Lilya's Second World whiteness threatens the nativist boundary in ways in which the racial difference of an immigrant of color paradoxically would not, as such difference is more visible and thus easy to police in the public and institutional spaces that are racialized as white. Furthermore, the assault that unfolds in the role-played incestual dyad of the Swedish father and his Swedish daughter, here impersonated by the intractable yet ultimately malleable sex slave, carries a didactic and punitive meaning, where the 'Swedish' female is returned from her liberal emancipation that rejects the reproductive burden, back to her father as his rightful property. The incestual rape then becomes an act of enforcement of the white patriarchal sexual and reproductive oppression, a corrective measure that punishes the Swedish woman for abdicating her reproductive and sexual duty. Ironically, the sex-slave-as-daughter discloses an uncomfortable affinity between the narrative of sex slavery and the European biopolitical agenda, both focused on the preservation of female whiteness as a reproductive, sexual, but also symbolic resource. *Lilya 4-ever* is a whitewashed tale of Europe's growing anxiety about the erosion of white supremacy engendered by the current mass movement of migrants of color to the continent. In this regard, Olof Hedling has found Moodysson's film to be a new iteration of the old anti-immigrant 'white slavery' story that cinema popularized in the early twentieth century, which I have addressed in Chapter 1.[38]

Configured as imperiled, female whiteness as a bio-resource in Europe, a supra-state concerned with the non-renewal of its white autochthonous population, enters the market as a commodity governed by the law of supply and demand within the context of the sex and reproductive labor markets. But, as Agathangelou has noted, the operations of racialization that emerge through the sex commerce of migrant women must be considered as constitutive of European white bourgeois identity and its own fantasy of itself as an agent of power and ownership. Looking at the sexualization and racialization of migrant labor within the context of the desire industries in Europe, Agathangelou has spoken of 'the production fantasies that circulate regarding accessing "white but not quite" and black women's bodies through the sale/purchase of that labor to enact a bourgeois "white" identity'.[39]

Viewing Sadowska's *Girls to Buy* together with *Lilya 4-ever*, one becomes aware of the complexities that characterize the new labor relations and migrant policies in Europe. Whether it is a grand myth of empowerment or a dark tale of clandestine exploitation, the cinematic fantasy of female mobility speaks of the new economy that problematizes the European unification and integration efforts. While mobility in 'borderless' Europe has been extended to an unprecedented number of its residents, the experience may not always conform to the ideal of mobility as a liberatory practice. In the process of on-screen visualization, the abstraction of the global flow predictably disintegrates and gives way to diverse fantasies that wrestle with local particularities. Sadowska's film retells the story of the so-called 'Dubai-gate', which took place in Poland in the early 2010s. It was first publicized in 2014 on the now discontinued blog 'TagTheSponsor', a vigilante site whose owner, a man, used to track the online activity of young women who trade sex for lavish lifestyles and international travel.[40] 'Dubai-gate' refers to the publicly exposed, much-debated and eventually prosecuted network of illegal sex trade that involved a large group of Polish women (including models, television celebrities, beauty pageant contestants, musicians and students) who engaged in international sex tourism. The trade was organized by female procurers who hired women to provide sex services to wealthy Arab clients, among whom were, allegedly, prominent businessmen, politicians, athletes and members of the Saudi royal family. While there were many stories about clients of other nationalities, including Polish businessmen and Russian oligarchs, those were quickly left out of the media hype, which assumed a predictably Orientalizing rhetoric that was solely preoccupied with the Arab clients. The profitable venture entailed the frequent travel of Polish women, not only to Dubai, but also to other glitzy locations that included London, St Tropez, Cannes, Ibiza, Beirut, Geneva, Monaco, Mykonos and Sardinia. Poland's public prosecutor investigated the network in 2013–14, which led to the trial and eventual sentencing of the female procurers, but not the women who provided the sex services. As in many post-communist countries, performing sex work does not constitute a crime under Polish law and is therefore not punishable.

In 2018, investigative journalist Piotr Krysiak republicized the case in his book, ostensibly framed as reportage, titled *Dziewczyny z Dubaju* (translated literally into English as *Girls from Dubai*).[41] This publication garnered wide press coverage and renewed public attention. The screen rights to Krysiak's story were subsequently purchased by Doda (a Polish celebrity music artist) and her husband Emil Stępień, who produced a feature film also titled *Dziewczyny z Dubaju*. For international distribution, the film was retitled *Girls to Buy*, a pun on 'Dubai'. Doda invited Maria Sadowska, a filmmaker with a portfolio of women-centered projects and sensitive to gender politics, to direct the film.[42] *Girls to Buy* premiered in Poland in November 2021 to great box office success and very mixed critical reception.

I read Sadowska's film as a narrative distinct from, yet in some respects cognate with, the over-determined and very popular narrative that emerged on social media in the wake of the court sentencing and the publication of Krysiak's exposé. That original narrative was, to a large degree, shaped by the contemporaneous public discourse generated around Poland's adamant refusal to accept the European Union's refugee quotas set in response to the Middle East refugee crisis unfolding along the southern and eastern borders of what by then had come to be called 'Fortress Europe'.[43] Predictably, this initial Dubai-gate narrative cast the Polish women selling sex to Arab men as victims. The social media commentary evolved with a heavy-handed rescue rhetoric full of racialized tropes of national pollution, Arab contagion, trade in 'live cargo', body horror, sex perversion and more. The cover of the 7–13 May 2018 issue of *Wprost* (a popular weekly news magazine) illustrates the tenor of the conversation (Figure 4.2). The headlines read: 'How Polish Women were Sold to Sheikhs: Behind-the-Scenes of the Live Cargo Trade: Female Celebrities, Actors, Politicians, Who are the Victims of the Sex Business in Dubai?'

Sadowska's film taps into this phobic story in order to capitalize on the controversy that turned a group of sex workers into a matter of state security and a symbolic threat to national identity. The film, then, pretty quickly restages Dubai-gate as a neoliberal romance that transposes the antiquated sentiments of national bonding and belonging into a spectacle of the global flow of capital, bodies and labor. In its imagery, this flow is somewhat different from the flow of refugees found in refugee cinema – Ai Weiwei's *Human Flow* (2017) being perhaps the most critically debated example of such cinema. Yet, like many visual representations of the refugee passage, *Girls to Buy* utilizes sea navigation as an operative term to draw spectatorial attention to the issues of movement and mobility across borders, both bodily and symbolic. In contrast to the long history of imperial expansion that featured the Western white male as master navigator, this film proposes a neocolonial vision in which Arab men (coded with a heavy hand as 'Gulf Arabs') navigate the seas, with Eastern European women who eagerly board their extravagant vessels providing sex services in exchange for money and global travel.

Although softening and displacing the phobic anti-refugee narrative of the ultra-right voices in Poland, and in Europe at large, by portraying Polish and Arab bodies in consensual sexual contact, the film's neoliberal fantasy has its own, not unrelated political problems. I argue that *Girls to Buy* is a project

***Figure 4.2*** A cover of *Wprost*. The headline translates, 'How Polish Women were Sold to Sheikhs'.

that co-opts, and ultimately exploits, feminism (and the issue of sex work rights) to peddle a spectacularized vision of the neocolonial Polish/European economic and cultural expansion racialized as white. Veiled in the spectacle of sex positivity, the film's *mise-en-scène* speaks of the kleptocratic flow of transnational capital and the ensuing military interventions that are at the root of the mass displacements of populations in the Middle East. The film's savvy entrepreneurial women who embrace the opportunity to engage in sex work with Arab men stand in for the neoliberal, pro-European Union, pro-global market forces that form much of today's political center-right government in Poland. The image of the Arab men constructed by the film, as well as the image of the romance between the Polish women and the Arab men, functions as a projection of an aspirational economic partnership with powerful stakeholders in the global economy. As it configures Poland (via the industrious Polish women) as a player in neo-imperial games, this fantasy of the imagined partnership is over-determined in its effort to distance itself from the ethnic and racial prejudice that characterizes the ultra-right, anti-refugee discourse of the Law and Justice Party that governed Poland between 2015 and 2023. In its affect, the film's excited, exoticizing xenophilia disguises the unpalatable xenophobia of the Polish nationalists.[44] As a text that activates both progressive and reactionary messages without committing to one or the other, the film appealed to viewers across the political spectrum and earned its producers an impressive return on their investment.[45]

Reviewers of *Girls to Buy* commented on Sadowska's progressive approach to the issue of sex work, which they described as shedding light on 'the systemic, socio-economic mechanisms' that shape this illegal business without 'condemning or celebrating' the women who make the decision to trade sex for money.[46] While some reviewers saw the spectacular representation of sex work in perceived exotic settings as undermining the film's avowed social critique, others thought that the film's employment of erotic spectacle was helpful in securing the viewers' moderate investment in the difficult subject-matter, on the grounds that doing so was faithful to the sex trade's actual reliance on spectacle.[47] In 'Dilemmas of the Sex Worker', for instance, Michał Piepiórka has argued that Sadowska's film works to normalize the status of the sex worker but ultimately fails, because the diegesis is filtered through an exploitative male gaze. This gaze, according to Piepiórka, objectifies doubly, as it frames the laboring female bodies of the sex workers as well as the laboring bodies of the actors playing them, especially within explicit sex scenes.[48] Ola Gersz, however, has admired the film's 'good acting, distinctive female characters, and the realistic sex scenes, which are rare in Polish cinema'.[49]

With symptomatic consistency, the Polish reviewers overlooked the racial dynamics of the film, which showcase the Arab clients' ease of mobility, the foregrounding of their capital, desire and power, the highlighted reciprocity of sexual desire between the Arab men and the Polish women, and the objectification of the male bodies (in addition to the objectification of the female bodies). Most reviewers simply remained silent on the Arabness of the clients. Since their presence constitutes much of the film's spectacle and cannot be ignored, the reviewers' silence is telling. But telling of what? Are the Polish reviewers afraid to put into words what they see on screen – the wealthy, physically attractive, sophisticated Arab men who eclipse the phobic phantasm of a 'sea of Arabs' (mis)figured as combative fanatics plotting to take over Europe by filing false asylum claims? Is *Girls to Buy* Arabophobic or, instead, Arabophilic, insofar as it constructs these men as eminently desirable but also desiring? Is their sexual desire, which Sadowska portrays as welcomed by the Polish women, consonant with what Edmund Ghareeb in 1977 identified as the stereotype of the oversexed Arab male?[50] Or is the reciprocal desire an image of the orientalizing 'romance' of Polish women with Arab men, as recently discussed by Agnieszka Kościańska and Michał Petryk in their historical study of Polish racism?[51] The reviewers' silence about the

Arab clients marks a twofold omission. First, the ensuing hyper-focus on the 'sponsorettes' rather than the 'sponsors', much like the vigilante focus behind the 'TagTheSponsor' project, renders *Girls to Buy* symptomatic of the neoliberal state's discourse that seeks to criminalize sex work and of the abolitionist feminist critique of sex work, which Juno Mac and Molly Smith have called the 'carceral-feminist perspective'.[52] Second, the Polish film critics' withholding of any critical assessment of the Arabness of the male characters speaks to the persistence of racist lensing in Polish culture and the critics' over-determined complicity in overlooking it, especially when it serves the neoliberal agenda.

Dubai-gate garnered much attention in Poland, for the political reasons already signaled. Aside from this local resonance, Dubai-gate also needs to be recognized as part of a larger international and very mainstream trend, wherein young women trade sex with wealthy and ultra-wealthy clients in exchange for material benefits and access to luxury commodities, including global travel, while simultaneously broadcasting the conditions and circumstances of their glamorous work online. In the last decade, this trend has been gaining cultural resonance on social media, where such women post, often in real time, updates about their luxurious adventures, illustrating their narratives with images shot and produced by professional photographers and championing clever ways of generating relatively easy income. Importantly, in their online accounts, the women never identify as 'sex workers'. In 2018, writing for *Cosmopolitan*, Jennifer Savin published a report titled 'The Secret Lives of Instagram "It" Girls', focusing on this phenomenon and its economic dimensions. Based on personal interviews and online research, Savin's article appeared before 'sex work' entered public discourse in the West as a new identity factor in labor rights debates and culture wars.[53] Savin has called the phenomenon she is studying 'the competitive paid-to-party scene' and described the pragmatic and nonchalant attitude adopted by the women when they talk to her about their engagement in transactional sex with the wealthy, as well as the strategic role of social media in these transactions.[54]

Sex work in exchange for petrodollars and cryptocurrency is not new, nor is its cinematic representation. What is new is the attendant media narrative generated by these women, as it embeds their libidinal transfers within information flows enabled by Big Technology, with minimal or no distribution lag. This easily accessible and visually captivating narrative challenges the predominantly clandestine register by which sex work is typically framed, especially in sex slavery films. The employment of Instagram as a platform for aspirational gazing showcases the elite sex trade as a form of status upgrade and projects it across the global visual commons with fiber-optic speed and trendsetting potential. The women's physical mobility is enhanced by the mobility of their stories in cyber-space – and *vice versa*. Their glamorous Instagram accounts function as storefronts that provide display space for facilitating the sex trade and pushing against the 'slut-shaming' rhetoric of the Internet morality police. But there is also a way to read the women's sex travelogues as a form of accruing and concentrating currency within the attention economy of social media, thus allowing them to earn capital from selling stories and producing lurid knowledge about their sex-trading experiences. In both pursuits – sex trade and storytelling – navigation guides the movement of the subject in/through space, challenging established accounts of female mobility. The resulting conjuncture of physical and cyber-mobility that enables the women to transgress geographical borders and narrative boundaries is bound to trigger, especially among the resurgent conservatives in Poland, phobic sentiments about women's place in the national imaginary and their role in symbolic boundary maintenance (as discussed by Mary Douglas and Julia Kristeva).[55] At the same time, the women's social media sex travelogues fold neatly into the neocolonial mediascape of the Global North/West and speak of the women's privilege.

Dubai-gate continues to echo in public conversation, as Poland continues to struggle with its official refugee protection and resettlement policy. The Polish government's adamant refusal to assist the Middle Eastern refugees arriving at the Poland-Belarus border while simultaneously opening the Poland-Ukraine border to over a million Ukrainian refugees in 2022 illustrates the government's race-informed motivations, drawing international and national outrage. While this urgent conversation undergoes intense mediatization, Sadowska's film enters the debate to visualize and deflect the anxieties stoked by the nationalist project of ethnic purity, as promoted by the recently deposed but still immensely popular right-wing Law and Justice Party led by Jarosław Kaczyński. In his frequent addresses to his constituency, Kaczyński spins tales of Muslim migrants carrying infectious diseases and 'all sorts of parasites and protozoa, which [. . .] while not dangerous in the organisms of these people, could be dangerous here'.[56] His vision of the Polish nation, framed within Poland's history of foreign-inflicted violence and subjugation, calls for policing the national borders against intruders from the East – as well as for policing the bodies of Polish women. In Kaczyński's rhetoric, the nation is mapped onto women's bodies through a host of restrictions on their rights. Most recently, the perceived threat of an Arab/Muslim invasion – not only physical, cultural and economic, but also affective and libidinal – has come to displace the long-standing trope of a Jewish threat (although the latter continues to play out, especially in debates over Jewish property restitution in Poland).[57]

Predictably, the Dubai-gate discourse in general (and, to a much smaller degree, Sadowska's film) stage the sex work performed by Polish women whose desires violate the ethnic prohibitions dictated by the neo-nationalist project, in the form of dangerous aberrations, thus pointing to a complex, if dubious, symbolic alignment between the mobility of Polish women engaged in sojourn sex work and the (im)mobility of Middle Eastern migrants and refugees on Polish territory. In the background of the national discussion about migrants and refugees are the increasing limitations placed around Polish women's rights, including reproductive rights, which the Law and Justice Party was methodically legislating and enforcing during the eight years of its government rule. This national conservative government also reduced the number of economically active women to the lowest percentage among the EU member states,[58] mainly by introducing 'a wide array of social benefits that encourage women to procreate, provide childcare, and perform housework', which are 'effectively taking them off the job market and potentially removing them from the public sphere, increasing the gender gap in economic ability, and depoliticizing their lives'.[59]

The aesthetic and plot configurations of *Girls to Buy* replicate another recent Polish film that centers on sex-across-borders: *365 Days* (Dirs Barbara Białowąs and Tomasz Mandes), the infamous 2020 Netflix sensation whose unapologetic political incorrectness was decried by celebrities (including the Welsh singer Duffy who wrote an open letter to the Netflix CEO Reed Hastings), LGBTQ+ activists and numerous outraged Netflix viewers who found the film's illiberal sex politics morally objectionable. *365 Days* tells the absurd story of a Sicilian mafia boss who abducts a Polish woman vacationing with her boyfriend in an Italian resort and keeps her captive in his lush villa, in an attempt to make her fall in love with him. He gives her 365 days to make up her mind. Of course, she does fall in love with her handsome captor who showers her with designer clothes, gourmet meals and sophisticated erotic play. *Girls to Buy* is similarly saturated with reactionary sexual spectacle (Figure 4.3); however, its narrative offers a more complicated vision of sex-across-borders in the global era, a vision that purports openness to women who trade sex and does not condemn them to the kind of captivity dramatized on screen by Białowąs and Mandes in their tongue-in-cheek spin on the sex slavery film. On the contrary, Sadowska visualizes a neoliberal story of white female mobility and, more narrowly, a story of navigation defined here as the ability of Polish women to smoothly traverse global space without the hassle of checkpoints and border patrols.

The super-yachts of the world's wealthiest provide a symbol of this kind of unobstructed mobility – a mobility that is facilitated by supra-national economic interests and networks, in Sadowska's film monetized by bags of

***Figure 4.3*** Reactionary sex spectacle in *Girls to Buy* (Dir. Maria Sadowska, 2021).

petrodollars. The super-yacht has recently become a highly visible subject of cultural, economic and environmental controversy, directly spurred by unprecedented instances of twenty-first-century private property redistribution directed against the Russian monied classes, whose super-yachts are being impounded by the local governments of NATO member states, and in some cases auctioned off, as a result of Western economic sanctions meant to inconvenience the Russian elite after their country's 2022 invasion of Ukraine.[60] The entrepreneurial Polish women, so the film excitedly suggests, get in on the action and become stakeholders in a global business venture. Furthermore, these ostensibly empowered, sex-positive female characters serve to allegorize Poland's economic ambitions that entail increasing openness to collaboration with Arab states, notwithstanding the deep-seated prejudice against Arab migrants and refugees within the country.[61]

On a material level, the Polish women in the film aspire to board the luxury yachts, which the sex workers from the West have already successfully boarded. While at Cannes, on one of their 'business trips', the Polish women get a glimpse of their Western counterparts conducting their business with the yacht-owning patrons. In one key scene, the main character, Emi (Paulina Gałązka), who starts as a woman trading sex but quickly ascends to become the brains of the operation, devises a strategy that would allow her and her associates to sell sex on the super-yachts. She eventually finds a way to do so. This competitive framing within the plot of *Girls to Buy* comments on the perceived status disparity between the Eastern European women from the former communist states and their Western neighbors in the integrated European community, while both are showcased in the film as contributors to and beneficiaries of the neoliberal economy.

This cinematized access of Polish women to the vessels of the super-rich shifts some of the convenient narratives that circulate in the media about the international sex trade, migrant work and movement across borders. Via the trope of luxury navigation, *Girls to Buy* debunks the well-worn morality tales of 'sex slavery', even as it remotely references both the nineteenth-century Orientalist tales of sex slavery and the transatlantic slave trade, thus drawing a connection between colonialism and neocolonialism that remains nonetheless critically undeveloped.[62] Although the film addresses some aspects of the illegal international sex trade, the framework of 'modern-day slavery' (or 'sex slavery') is not present until the very end, right before the credit sequence, where we see appended a few slides with statistics about sex trafficking understood as a massive criminal operation, where women are violently coerced into captivity. Eric Schaefer has discussed this kind of 'square-up' strategy as a way for exploitation cinema to get around censorship pressure by attributing an educational goal to an otherwise tawdry story.[63] In the case of *Girls to Buy*, this square-up comprises a half-hearted alignment of the film's neoliberal politics with the sort of mainstream rescue rhetoric used to narrate illegal international sex commerce, wherein women who engage in the sex trade become the ultimate victims of international organized crime networks.

As I have already suggested, yet another narrative confronted within *Girls to Buy* is the anti-refugee story. This narrative has been circulating in Poland since 2015 and figures Middle Eastern refugees mainly as economic migrants camouflaging as refugees in order to gain entry to European labor markets and secure access to the networks of social services offered within the European Union. This anti-refugee narrative reinforces normative gender roles by insisting that the only acceptable Middle Eastern refugees are women and children, since the perceived role of men is to stay in their country and struggle to change the conditions compelling emigration.[64] *Girls to Buy* ironizes these ideological lines by positioning Polish women as economic migrants, and Middle Eastern men as conspicuously wealthy, globe-trotting cosmopolitans whose high economic status enables them to cross borders unhindered, in search of entertainment that would be hard to procure in their home countries. The representational mapping (and visual style) that emerges in Sadowska's film thus stands in stark contrast to that of the much publicized 'necropolitics' of refugees navigating the Mediterranean Sea.[65] Much of the film's diegesis is set in the same geographic region and the same maritime waterways, yet Sadowska's illustration of the movement of bodies across national borders and class boundaries never materializes for them as a 'deathworld' – a new form of existence under neocolonial regimes, as conceptualized by Achille Mbembe, that subjects people to 'living conditions that confer upon them the status of the *living dead*'.[66] Instead, *Girls to Buy* offers a highly selective, Orientalizing spectacle with numerous displacements and symbolic substitutions. The most glaring of these is the producers' decision to use exclusively Italian actors to play the Arab characters in what amounts to a kind of brownface deployed to transform the Arab characters into safe, de-Othered objects of desire for Polish women, whose Second World whiteness is consequently re-articulated as First World whiteness. With this racial hierarchy set in place, the spectacle showcases the extravagant navigation of the super-rich, where Arab men are made to stand in for the growing international class of oligarchs, thus constructing a space in which the Global South/East is not only implicated in the kleptocratic operations of the Global North/West but becomes its face and body through a cinematic sleight of hand. In line with this dialectic, in scenes where the Arab characters suddenly become violent and are thus reduced, in an Arabophobic gesture, to fonts of angry and unhinged phallic desire (as in the scene of Emi's rape), the film also invites an alternate meaning for these evidently uncouth and retrogressive figures: They begin to function as a metaphor for the Polish ultra-masculinist, neo-nationalist phallocracy. The women's resistance to these aggressions in turn becomes an expression of 'liberal' feminist critique – a critique whose capacity for social change never materializes, as liberalism is always already operating well within the structural class and economic contradictions of the neoliberal capitalist regime. As these dynamics play out on screen, *Girls to Buy* illustrates the nexus of Global North power that Paul Amar has described in his 2013 study titled *The Security Archipelago: Human-Security States, Sexuality Politics, and the End of Neoliberalism* – that is, the convergence of the 'soft power' of liberal cultural diplomacy and the 'smart power' associated with enforcement and development interventions.[67] For Amar, the 'soft-and-smart power' paradigm is central to the Global North's human security doctrine, which dominates the transnational security discourse. The doctrine promotes North biases in regimenting the perceived chronic volatility of Southern nation-states.

In Sadowska's film, cinema returns to its early history, to the cinema of attractions of the first few decades of the medium's existence, and as such it operates as a naïve fantasmagoria with colonial undertones and racializing optics. Its glossy, opulent feel stands in stark contradiction to the bleak iconography of the sex slave film. More directly, *Girls to Buy* brings to mind the early burlesque nude films and the so-called 'scenics' of the 1910s and 1920s – film travelogues depicting tourist destinations and exotic landscapes otherwise inaccessible to most viewers at the time. In choosing Italian actors to play the Arab characters, the film engages in a brownface dynamic reminiscent of early cinema's saturation in the minstrel show and its blackface fetish. As André Gaudreault has argued, much of the early variety cinema privileged monstration, an aesthetic mode that performatively foregrounds the intense exhibition value and spectacular aspect of the image, in contrast to narration, which relies on editing to choreograph the images into a diegetic sequence.[68] Sadowska's film deploys monstration in its frequent sex and landscape scenes, fusing both in the process and thereby forging a libidinal link between the exploitation of bodies and the control of space. This demonstrates something that much of our political discourse occludes: the role of desire in our communal ways of inhabiting the world and structuring power in it. To think through this issue, I borrow the concept of libidinal economy from Frank B. Wilderson, who has used psychoanalytic theory to address racialized social relations. In his groundbreaking *Afropessimism: An Introduction*, Wilderson has described libidinal economy as 'the economy, or distribution and arrangement, of desire and identification, of energies, concerns, points of attention, anxieties, pleasures, appetites, revulsions, and phobias – the whole structure of psychic and emotional life – that are unconscious and invisible but that have a visible effect on the world, including the money economy'.[69] The racialized dynamics featured in *Girls to Buy* draws our attention to this kind of libidinal economy, emphasizing desire and identification by overlaying the money economy (the transnational capital flow) on the economy of sex commerce.

The sex positivity of the Polish women, who commodify their bodies with ease, is pitched by Sadowska as an act of resistance, but in fact it rather resembles Herbert Marcuse's concept of 'repressive desublimation', introduced in his analysis of modern ways of social repression, published as *One-Dimensional Man* in 1964.[70] According to Marcuse, in capitalism's 'affluent society', transgression becomes impossible as all pleasure (including the repressed kinds) becomes not only allowed but quickly commodified. The process of commodification secures societal control and leads to a 'one-dimensional', homogenous existence and the slow disappearance of the revolutionary instinct. *Girls to Buy* begins as a feminist manifesto of sorts, where the Polish women attempt to take agency over their economic lives by capitalizing on leisure, but this manifesto and the women's choices are quickly folded into a totalizing neoliberal hegemony. The reactionary spectacle that commodifies space and human bodies, which is undoubtedly responsible for the film's box office success, is also responsible for draining the film's progressive aspirations.

In Pierre Morel's *Taken*, First World female whiteness is also imperiled by the Arab consumerism fueled by Saudi petrodollars. Produced five years into the United States' Iraq War, the film tells the story of an American teenage girl, Kim, who, while vacationing in Paris, is abducted by Albanian sex traffickers, enslaved and prepared to be auctioned off to a Sheikh interested in purchasing a white virgin. Significantly, Kim's First World whiteness is coded as comfortably upper-middle-class, very different from the abject whiteness of Lilya or the aspirational whiteness of Emi. As discussed in Chapter 2, *Taken* is a rescue narrative mainly interested in showcasing the brain and brawn of the white American man, here personified by Bryan Mills. He is Kim's estranged father and retired special forces operative; he takes on the international organized sex trafficking network in a confrontation that Anna Szörényi and Penelope Eate have correctly interpreted as a spectacle of 'reclamation' of the US neocolonial supremacy through the Bond-like exploits of the white hyper-masculine protagonist. Szörényi and Eate have argued that in Morel's film, which begins by staging the crisis of US white masculinity, only to muster a grand overcoming of such a crisis, 'the redemption of patriarchal fatherhood is equated with the redemption of the protective masculine, warmaking nation: both projects undertaken in the name of the girl-child whose innocence is threatened not only by criminal foreigners but also by her own desire for independence'.[71] In this analysis, the imperiled female child becomes the accessory – 'justification for imperialist masculinity' – in weaving the nationalist narrative that has a strong anti-globalization and anti-immigration message.[72]

Within the diegetic world of *Taken*, Kim's virginal and monied First World whiteness allegorizes the innocence of the American nation-state and is a value that must be protected by all means necessary, including violence. This value carries an important meaning in the discourse that the Western imperial hegemony broadcasts about itself and its coming to power. The imperiled white innocence is used to displace the guilt of the (neo)colonial aggressor that arises from the violence implemented against the colonized people in the first place and helps to rearticulate the colonial aggressor's violence as self-defense. *Taken* and its two sequels create an alternate vision of the world, where only through global domination and subjugation – the *status quo* that in fact produces the conditions under which migrant sex work often becomes economically necessary and sexual exploitation may occur – will the white woman be safe. In alignment with what Amar has recognized as the Global North/West's security doctrine, this vision is saturated with anxiety about the erosion of white supremacy in its broadest and most diffuse sense. The image of the imperiled middle-class white woman – an innocent who must be protected by a violence that underwrites that imagined innocence in the first place – provides a personified focus that helps to mitigate the all-encompassing fear of the racialized Other. This figure becomes a useful orienting point in the messy task of dividing 'us' from 'them'. As such a construct, the character of Kim in *Taken* is the innocence that manufactures the rationale for racial and xenophobic violence (Figure 4.4).

***Figure 4.4*** First World whiteness embodied by Kim in *Taken* (Dir. Pierre Morel, 2008).

One of many cultural renditions of imperiled First World whiteness, *Taken*'s Kim provides the justification for Bryon Mill's (and figuratively the US's) violence abroad, especially at a time when the US (white) supremacy along with the country's credibility and economic domination have diminished within the multi-polar dynamics of the new global world order. In the context of the Iraq War, by 2008 (the year of *Taken*'s release), US violence in the Middle East was being questioned by the international community as well as by members of the US public. The phobic protectionism of First World female whiteness projected through the film resembles the recent social media panics that function as an ongoing mechanism in the process of reconsolidating white supremacy. In the current political climate within the US, anxiety about the foreign threat to America's white innocence now extends well beyond Islamic terrorist villains and includes such paranoid constructs as 'Mexican rapists', 'Wayfair sex traffickers' and Chinese 'fentanyl gangs'.

The cleansing and whitewashing that *Taken* so generously dispenses become all the more evident when Morel's film is compared to other sex slavery films. The most revealing distinction is found in what the film does *not* show in constructing the figure of the sex slave. Instead of the iconic scenes of defilement, Morel's film offers scenes where the white woman is consecrated and imbued with much symbolic potential. The care and attentiveness of her father, a former CIA super-agent, provides Kim with extraordinary value before she is ever entered as commodity into the sex-trafficking circuit. We learn that in the past Bryan may have botched one of his missions in Lebanon in order to attend Kim's birthday party, because 'he never misses' her birthday – a decision that informs the viewer of the utmost priority of Kim's life (and its central role in performing American exceptionalism abroad). Unlike Moodysson's Lilya, then, Kim is surrounded by an entourage of loving parents and supportive friends, while her life is accessorized by all the trappings of her affluent background. Her elevated status within the social hierarchy, today determined by one's consumer potential, is celebrated with a special gift that Kim enthusiastically receives from her stepfather: a racehorse. Kim's control of space – her privileged being in the world and the ease with which she travels and crosses international borders – situates her as a 'tourist' within Bauman's hierarchy of late capitalist mobility. Her family's wealth, her father's super-agent status and her US passport afford her the cosmopolitan transcendence of territoriality, a condition that Bauman has called the 'new exterritoriality of the elite'.[73] And that is precisely why the viewer is shocked when Albanian traffickers abduct Kim from her luxury vacation pad in Paris.

It is significant that, once Kim is enslaved, the film avoids any of the iconic violations that cinema uses to construct the sex slave figure: the spectacle of bodily abjection, which becomes a substitute for the hyper-visibility of the migrants, refugees and illegal workers within the panopticon of the security state. In contrast to the abject and highly spectacularized degradation of characters such as Lilya (*Lilya 4-ever*), Adriana (*Trade*), Holly (*Holly*), or Raya (*The Whistleblower*), which reduce them to objects within the economies of sex and cinematic trafficking, *Taken* never depicts overt sexual or physical violence against Kim. Her screen body is never explicitly abjected. It does not undergo the absolute reification that is emblematic of the genre and resonant of how the neoliberal security state configures 'insecure' human subjects. In fact, the traffickers handle Kim with care, and she soon arrives as a prize at an exclusive international sex slave auction, where the circumspect representatives of the uber-rich clients sit in semi-darkness, sip on champagne, consult prices in hushed Arabic and bid for female flesh. Kim is announced as the highlight of the event. The auctioneer informs the potential buyers of her 'certified pure' status and her language skills. She arrives in the spotlight dressed in a black hooded cape, dripping with crystals and shiny embroidery, wearing matching silver heels and commanding a high price of $500,000, only seconds after another woman has been sold for a mere $150,000. Once sold, Kim is quickly escorted to a yacht docked on the Seine, where she is presented in a diaphanous white veil and undergarments to her new owner, Sheikh Raman. Of course, Kim's father is there in time to protect Kim's 'certified purity'. Bryan forces his way onto the boat and dispatches Sheikh Raman's bodyguards with ease before bursting into the bedroom to kill Sheikh Raman, rescuing Kim from the threat of impending Arab 'contamination'.

In these scenes, Kim's value is established through racialization. Her First World whiteness is fetishized as desirable and exclusive, a luxury product; the film's dynamics are carefully choreographed to activate both old and new iterations of the Orientalist fantasy. The imagined threat, inherent in the fantasy, is then defused by Bryan's deployment of hyper-violence – his methodically murderous elimination of a boatload of Arab men – a vigilante mission justified by the films self-perpetuating logic. This paternalism foregrounds white female innocence as consecrated (at the auction, Kim's face is covered; on the yacht, she is dressed, bride-like, in white lingerie), which commands militant protection by violence. The violence is rationalized by the necessity of upholding her innocence. Once the protected innocence is coded as white, the ethnic/racial Other emerges at counterpoint as a threat to innocence, which in turn justifies the xenophobic violence. This dynamic is different from the situation that plays out in *Girls to Buy*, where the women who are racialized as 'white but not quite' enter into consensual sexual relations with the Arab men (albeit played by a cast of Italian actors). Ultimately, however, more than the female whiteness, it is the recuperated white masculinity that *Taken*'s rescue scenario pitches as salutary and indispensable. Szörényi and Eate have found this message to be central in their reading of Bryan Mills as 'a metaphor for the endangered global superiority of the USA' and his splashy rescue mission as compensatory theater.[74]

Within the context of the Global North/West, narratives such as *Lilya-4 ever*, *Girls to Buy* and *Taken* are used to discursively produce the foundation of personhood as white. They also work to cast the nation and the imperiled national subject as white. When the Black Lives Matter movement challenged these race-based foundations by proposing an inclusive revision to the modern definition of personhood, the white *status quo* recoiled and responded with defensive rhetoric – 'All Lives Matter' and 'Blue Lives Matter' slogans – thus minimizing the BLM movement's grievance that black lives have been systemically excluded from the established norm of 'human life'. The ensuing rhetorical sparring that took place in the eye of the public media brought into focus what Judith Butler has theorized in *Frames of War: When Is Life Grievable?* as our selective lensing of reality that leads to casting certain lives as valuable and others as disposable. Focused on how the photograph invites certain subjects into the field of vision while strategically leaving out others, Butler has chosen the metaphor of 'framing' to define her concept of inegalitarian representation that has a lasting impact on our lived material reality.[75] While this theory has some formidable precursors, including Zygmunt Bauman's vision of late capitalism's 'wasted lives', Butler's study on the rhetoric of framing is especially useful in my discussion of racialization performed in sex slavery films, because it is sensitive to the affective operations of meaning-making in which photography-based images engage.[76] Affect that resonates through photography is important for Butler as the underpinning of its power to persuade. Like the infamous photographic images from the Abu Ghraib prison that Butler has read as an example of dehumanizing framing, film images have – perhaps all the more intensely because they are *moving* images – a visceral and immediate impact on the viewer and insinuate a witnessing presence that certifies the imaged world as 'real'. Like photographs, film images can dignify or dehumanize the lives they portray, ratifying the suffering of some, while trivializing the injury of others. Butler's analysis of the sexual discourse of the Abu Ghraib archive discloses the photographs' rhetorical role in the colonizing gaze of the United States, thus drawing our attention to the fact that 'sexual politics are not discontinuous with racial, nationalist and imperialist politics, but deeply embedded in mutually reinforcing assemblages'.[77] Following this argument, I would like to propose that we read sex slavery films and their spectacle of dignified – because presented as 'precarious' and thus warranting protection – whiteness as an insistent, albeit over-determined discursive assemblage that reinforces the neoliberal security state and its white heteronormative presumption.[78]

Butler's theory of framed intelligibility of life (and the norms that accrue from such framing) offers an ethical postulate for change. Since for Butler 'human life' is a process of historical sedimentation (not subject to transcendental law) that builds up over time through the aggregation of singular 'iterative' acts of framing, to change the normative definition of 'human life', one simply needs to intervene in the repetition of the norm by revising the framing to interrupt the predictive instantiations of the norm. Within the new wave of sex slavery films, there are filmmakers who have begun such a subversive revision. The Nigerian film *Òlòtūré* directed by Kenneth Gyang (see Chapter 2) constitutes an important modification of the typical racialization tropes of the sex slave figure. Similar to the blaxploitation/slavesploitation corpus that casts the Black female action figure as central to the film's diegesis, *Òlòtūré* frames Nigerian female lives as precarious and in need of solidarity and protection. Gyang goes a step further in his revision of the sex slavery frame when he concludes his film with scenes that recast the female sex slaves as migrants who consciously avail themselves of the services of human smugglers, taking serious health, economic and existential risks, in their dangerous passage to find better life opportunities in today's imperial metropole. Gyang's reframing of the sex slavery narrative into a narrative of illegal international sex work migration sheds light on the fragility and insecurity of the populations of the Global South, whose lives have been disproportionately affected by perpetual war, climate change, resource extraction and labor exploitation (Figure 4.5). In replacing the Orientalist figure of the 'white slave' with the figure of a black sex worker accessing the illegal migration route and crossing borders to seek better prospects in Europe, *Òlòtūré* sets up new symbolic and cultural conditions for the representational

***Figure 4.5*** Nigerian sex workers and madam Alero (foreground, played by Omoni Oboli) who facilitates the workers' migrant passage to Europe. From *Òlòtūré* (Dir. Kenneth Gyang, 2019).

emergence of a more authentic figure of the precarious human life that is quickly becoming emblematic of global modernity.

In the following chapter, the book's epilogue, I will discuss Szabolcs Hajdu's *Bibliothèque Pascal* (2010), a film that preoccupies itself with the pressures of framing sex work as sex slavery. Using magic realism, the film critically confronts the 'epistemic violence' which, according to Molly Smith and Juno Mac, is inherent in the sex slavery narratives. Smith and Mac, scholars with extensive experience of sex work and sex work activism, have held the sex slavery narrative responsible for the persistence of the criminalization movement that seeks to regulate commercial sex and to 'rescue' women (self)employed in the sex industry, thus stalling their efforts to secure the sex workers' rights.[79]

## Notes

1. Morgonn McMichael (@morgonnm), Twitter, 3 December 2023, www.twitter.com/morgonnm/status/1731460640458625171?t=W0OrGhnAuchMstfE5gLHeA&s=19 (accessed 5 December 2023).
2. Turning Point USA, 'Morgonn McMichael', www.tpusa.com/morgonn-mcmichael (accessed 10 December 2023); Turning Point USA, 'About', www.tpusa.com/about (accessed 10 December 2023).
3. McMichael, Twitter, 15 May 2023, www.twitter.com/morgonnm/status/1658253880994705409 (accessed 10 December 2023). In recent years, Target has come under fire from conservative advocacy groups for its LGBTQ+ inclusive

merchandise. While a boycott was launched in 2023, conservative advocacy groups such as the American Family Association (AFA) have been boycotting the retailer for similar reasons since 2016. See *AFA Journal*, April 2020, www.afajournal.org/past-issues/2020/april/target-policy-claims-another-victim-boycott-continues (accessed 10 December 2023). See also American Family Association, 'Wildmon: Target Boycott Still the Right Thing', *AFA Journal*, January-February 2021, www.afajournal.org/past-issues/2021/january-february/wildmon-target-boycott-still-the-right-thing (accessed 11 December 2023); Matthew Impelli, 'Target Ends Year of Boycotts with Good News', *Newsweek*, 30 December 2023, www.newsweek.com/target-ends-year-boycotts-good-news-1855959 (accessed 1 January 2023). Around this time, Target sex-trafficking hoaxes began. See Lenore Skenazy, 'The Mom Who was Terrified of Becoming Sex-Trafficked at Target', *Reason*, 26 April 2021, www.reason.com/2021/04/26/mom-target-sex-trafficking-white-vans/ (accessed 11 December 2023).

4. E. J. Dickson, 'A Target Sex-Trafficking Hoax is Once Again Going Viral on TikTok', *Rolling Stone*, 9 September 2022, www.rollingstone.com/culture/culture-news/tiktok-target-sex-trafficking-hoax-marco-polo-1234589134 (accessed 11 December 2023).
5. Kaitlyn Tiffany, 'The Great (Fake) Child-Sex-Trafficking Epidemic', *The Atlantic*, January/February 2022, www.theatlantic.com/magazine/archive/2022/01/children-sex-trafficking-conspiracy-epidemic/620845 (accessed 20 December 2023).
6. Sarah Hupp Williamson, Sadie Creel and Emily Walker. '#Wayfairgate and the Growth of Sex Trafficking Panics across Social Media', *Critical Criminology*, 31, 2023, p. 618 (pp. 617–22 inclusive).
7. Ibid. p. 620.
8. Ibid. p. 629.
9. Richard Dyer, 'White', *Screen,* 29:4, 1988, p. 45 (pp. 44–64 inclusive).
10. Jennifer Musial, 'Pregnant and Disappeared: The Missing White Woman Syndrome in Magazines', in Karen Boyle and Susan Berridge (eds), *The Routledge Companion to Gender, Media, and Violence* (New York: Routledge, 2023), p. 271 (pp. 271–80 inclusive).
11. Ibid. p. 273.
12. Ibid. p. 274.
13. Ibid. p. 271.
14. Amanda Ann Klein, 'Unbearable Whiteness of Gone Girls', *LA Review of Books*, 21 October 2014, https://avidly.lareviewofbooks.org/2014/10/21/unbearable-whiteness-of-gone-girls/ (accessed 14 April 2024).
15. I have coined the phrase 'Second World whiteness' in alignment with Katarzyna Marciniak's concept of Second Worldness. Marciniak has argued for the continued relevance of the category of Second Worldness, as a culturally unique and politically distinct interstitial space, in discussions of globalization and in the post-colonial critique of Eurocentrism. See Katarzyna Marciniak, 'Second

World-Ness and Transnational Feminist Practices: Agnieszka Holland's *Kobieta Samotna* (*A Woman Alone*)', in Anikó Imre (ed.), *East European Cinemas* (New York: Routledge, 2005), p. 6 (pp. 3–20 inclusive).

16. Agathangalou, *The Global Political Economy of Sex*, p. 5.
17. Writing about whiteness as a structural factor in security discourses, Catherine Baker has pointed out how 'migration often exposes those who are racialized as unquestionably white in their nation of origin to being treated as not quite as white when they move'. Catherine Baker, 'The Contingencies of Whiteness: Gender/Racialized Global Dynamics of Security Narratives', *Security Dialogue,* 52 (Supplement), 2021, p. 124, (pp. 124–32 inclusive).
18. Ibid. p. 23.
19. O'Healy, *Migrant Anxieties*, p. 59.
20. Ibid. p. 53.
21. Ibid. p. 53.
22. Parvulescu, *The Traffic in Women's Work*, pp. 14–15.
23. Ibid. p. 14.
24. Charles Mills, *The Racial Contract* (Ithaca: Cornell University Press, 1999), pp. 13–14.
25. Ibid. pp. 39–41.
26. Hua, *Trafficking Women's Human Rights*, p. 82.
27. Ibid. p. 90.
28. Ewa Mazierska and Laura Rascaroli, *Crossing New Europe: Postmodern Travel and the European Road Movie* (New York: Wallflower Press, 2006), p. 186.
29. Zygmunt Bauman, *Globalization: The Human Consequences* (Cambridge: Polity Press, 1998), p. 93.
30. Anna Westerståhl Stenport, '*Lilya 4-ever*: Post-Soviet Neoliberal Angels and Nordic Intellectual Secularism', *Scandinavica*, 53:1, 2014, p. 50 (pp. 34–54 inclusive).
31. Lars Kristensen, 'Divergent Accounts of Equivalent Narratives: Russian-Swedish *Interdevochka* Meets Swedish-Russian *Lilya 4-ever*', *PORTAL: Journal of Interdisciplinary Studies*, 4:2, July 2007, p. 5 (pp. 1–22 inclusive).
32. Ibid. p. 20.
33. Jennifer Suchland, 'Double Framing in *Lilya 4-ever*: Sex Trafficking and Postsocialist Abjection', *European Journal of Cultural Studies*, 16:3, February 2013, p. 362 (pp. 362–76 inclusive).
34. For the theory of the abject, see Kristeva, *Powers of Horror*.
35. Suchland, 'Double Framing in *Lilya 4-ever*', p. 370.
36. Westerståhl Stenport, '*Lilya 4-ever*: Post-Soviet Neoliberal Angels and Nordic Intellectual Secularism', p. 48.
37. Richard Dyer has commented on this quality of white normative representation when arguing that 'whiteness secures white power by making it hard, especially for white people and their media, to "see" whiteness'. Dyer, 'White', p. 46.
38. Olof Hedling, 'Om Lilja 4-ever – en svensk film', in B. Jonsson, K. Nykvist and B. Sjoberg (eds), *Från Eden till Damavdelning* (Lund: Absalon, 2004), pp. 323–34.

39. Agathangelou, *The Global Political Economy of Sex*, p. 38.
40. TagTheSponsor.com is a website devoted to policing alleged sex work performed by Instagram influencers. The owners of the site call the women suspected of sex work 'sponsorettes'. The owners' stated purpose is to trace the women's travels and document their whereabouts to expose the influencers' sources of income from engaging in sex tourism and international prostitution services. See TagTheSponsor.com for the rationale and examples of their online 'investigative' activities.
41. In 2021, Krysiak published a follow-up book, *Boys from Dubai*, in which he presents a summary of his interviews with male and non-binary sex workers from Poland, Germany and Spain who are engaged in international sex tourism. Unlike *Girls from Dubai*, this subsequent account is more sensitive to non-normative gender identities, but, like the first book, it utilizes Orientalism in its narrative framing.
42. Before *Girls to Buy*, Sadowska had directed *Women's Day* (2012), a film about a single mother fighting for her labor rights in a corrupt corporation, and *The Art of Loving: The Story of Michalina Wislocka* (2017), a fictionalized account of the sexologist Michalina Wislocka's efforts to publish her famous sex manual in communist Poland, in order to educate women on birth planning and to liberalize sex practices, against the government's attempt to censor the book.
43. Harlan Koff, *Fortress Europe or a Europe of Fortresses? The Integration of Migrants in Western Europe* (Brussels: PIE Peter Lang, 2008), pp. 19–66.
44. For a discussion of xenophilia/xenophobia in sex slavery films, see Aga Skrodzka, 'Xenophilic Spectacle in Recent Films about Sex Slavery', *Transnational Cinemas*, 9:1, 2018, pp. 85–103.
45. Przemek Romanowski, 'To już pewne. *Dziewczyny z Dubaju* największym polskim przebojem 2021 r.', *Wirtualna Polska Film*, 7 December 2021, https://film.wp.pl/to-juz-pewne-dziewczyny-z-dubaju-najwiekszym-polskim-przebojem-2021-r-6712795340159712a
46. Jakub Majmurek, '365 dni w Dubaju', *Filmweb*, 5 December 2021, www.filmweb.pl/reviews/recenzja-filmu-Dziewczyny+z+Dubaju%C2%AE-24094 (accessed 30 March 2023).
47. Majmurek, '365 dni w Dubaju', [n. p.]; Michal Piepiórka, 'Dylematy seksworkerki', *Czas Kultury*, 20, https://czaskultury.pl/artykul/dylematy-sexworkerki/ (accessed 6 February 2023); Adriana Prodeus, 'Demontaż atrakcji: *Dziewczyny z Dubaju*', *Vogue Poland*, 28 November 2021, www.vogue.pl/a/demontaz-atrakcji-dziewczyny-z-dubaju. (accessed 7 February 2023).
48. Piepiórka, 'Dylematy sekswokerki', [n. p.].
49. Ola Gersz, 'Nie mogłam uwierzyć własnym oczom: Dziewczyny z Dubaju nie sa złym filmem', *Na Temat*, 29 November 2021, https://natemat.pl/385851,dziewczyny-z-dubaju-recenzja (accessed 7 February 2023).
50. Edmund Ghareeb, *Split Vision: The Portrayal of Arabs in the American Media* (Washington DC: The Institute of Middle Eastern and North African Affairs, 1977), p. 7.

51. Agnieszka Kościańska and Michał Petryk, *Odejdź: Rzecz o polskim rasizmie* (Warsaw: Wydawnictwo Krytyki Polityczenej, 2022), pp. 225–34.
52. Mac and Smith, *Revolting Prostitutes*, p. 58. Despite its name, 'TagTheSponsor' engages in tracking and shaming the female 'sponsorettes', while the 'sponsors' receive minimal investigative attention and none of the morality police bashing.
53. Since the publication of 'Why Sex Work is Real Work' in *Teen Vogue* (Spring 2019) by South African physician Dr Tlaleng Mofokeng – and the attendant media controversy – the conversation around sex work has evolved into a nuanced and destigmatizing public discourse. This new way of thinking about sex work includes a host of complex and often polemical issues, such as universal rights for sex workers, neoliberal forms of sex commodification, the exponential growth and impact of online commercial sex platforms, the legal limits of sex labor in the context of migration and exile, reproductive rights policy, the mainstreaming of sex work and more.
54. Jennifer Savin, 'The Secret Lives of Instagram "It" Girls', 'The Secret Lives of Instagram "It" Girls', *Cosmopolitan*, 13 December, www.cosmopolitan.com/uk/reports/a25422996/it-girls-of-instagram-secrets/ (accessed 1 April 2023).
55. The work of anthropologist Mary Douglas on symbolic boundary maintenance, published in 1966 as *Purity and Danger: An Analysis of Concepts of Pollution and Taboo*, influenced Julia Kristeva's theory of abjection of the female and the maternal in Western culture. In *Powers of Horror* (1980), Kristeva has offered a queer and feminist reading of the symbolic regimentation of queer and/or women's bodies in the phallocentric imaginary.
56. Jan Cienski, 'Migrants Carry "Parasites and Protozoa", Warns Polish Opposition Leader', *Politico*, 4 October 2015, www.politico.eu/article/migrants-asylum-poland-kaczynski-election/ (accessed 30 March 2023).
57. In August of 2021, Poland's president Andrzej Duda, a politician closely aligned with the conservative Law and Justice Party that then dominated the Polish Parliament, signed the bill to limit the ability of Jewish people to seek and recover property in Poland that had been seized from their families during the Holocaust. See Zosia Wanat, 'Poland's Restitution Law Sparks Row with Israel and the US', *Politico*, 13 August 2021, www.politico.eu/article/poland-parliament-restitution-law-property-compensation-nazi-communists (accessed 1 May 2024).
58. The number of economically active women in Poland has been dropping steadily since the national conservatives took power in 2015. Among the European Union member states, Poland has one of the highest rates of women staying off the job market in order to perform domestic labor and childcare. See the statistical data reported by the Central Statistical Office of Poland (2018).
59. Aga Skrodzka, '*Komunistki*: Visual Memory of Female Communist Agency', in A. Skrodzka, X. Lu and K. Marciniak (eds.), *The Oxford Handbook of Communist Visual Cultures* (New York: Oxford University Press), p. 674 (pp. 675–92 inclusive).

60. For relevant critiques of the super-yacht phenomenon, see Evan Osnos, 'The Haves and the Have-Yachts', *The New Yorker*, 18 July 2022, https://www.newyorker.com/magazine/2022/07/25/the-haves-and-the-have-yachts (accessed 20 August 2022); Joe Fassler, 'The Superyachts of Billionaires are Starting to Look a Lot Like Theft', *The New York Times*, 10 April 2023, www.nytimes.com/2023/04/10/opinion/superyachts-private-plane-climate-change.html (accessed April 15, 2023); and Ruben Östlund's 2022 feature film *Triangle of Sadness.*
61. Since the radical shift in fuel trade precipitated by the Russian war with Ukraine, Poland's Law and Justice government, previously distancing itself from the Arab world, has begun diplomatic courting of the United Arab Emirates, with a plan for cooperation in the fields of artificial intelligence, digital technology and energy. See Ayush Narayanan, 'UAE leaders meet Polish president in Abu Dhabi, Dubai', *Al Arabiya English*, 8 March 2023, https://english.alarabiya.net/News/gulf/2023/03/08/UAE-leaders-meet-Polish-President-in-Abu-Dhabi-Dubai (accessed 30 March 2023).
62. For a powerful example of a critique of such morality tales, see Nair, 'Somaly Mam, Nicholas Kristof, and the Real Sex Trafficking Story'. For a history of the Arab participation in the Islamic slave trade and the Atlantic trade, see Paul E. Lovejoy, *Transformations in Slavery: A History of Slavery in Africa* (Cambridge: Cambridge University Press, 2012).
63. Eric Schaefer, *'Bold! Daring! Shocking! True!' A History of Exploitation Films, 1919–1959* (Durham and London: Duke University Press), p. 71.
64. *Polityka*, 'Co Polacy myśla o uchodźcach?' *Polityka*, 5 October 2015, www.polityka.pl/tygodnikpolityka/kraj/1635669,1,co-polacy-mysla-o-uchodzcach.read. (accessed 30 March 2023).
65. For Lo Presti's study of map images that track refugee deaths along the Central Mediterranean Migration Route, see Laura Lo Presti, 'Terraqueous Necropolitics: Unfolding the Low-Operational, Forensic, and Evocative Mapping of Mediterranean Sea Crossings in the Age of Lethal Borders', *ACME: An International Journal for Critical Geographies*, 18:6, 2019, pp. 1347–67.
66. Mbembe, *Necropolitics*, p. 92. Original italics.
67. Amar, *The Security Archipelago*, pp. 22–23.
68. André Gaudreault, 'Narration and Monstration in Cinema', *Journal of Film and Video*, 39:2, 1987, pp. 29–36.
69. Wilderson, *Afropessimism*, p. 7.
70. Herbert Marcuse, *One-Dimensional Man: Studies in the Ideology of Advanced Industrial Society* (Boston: Beacon Press, 1991 [1964]), p. 59.
71. Anna Szörényi and Penelope Eate, 'Saving Virgins, Saving the US: Heteronormative Masculinities and the Securitisation of Trafficking Discourse in Mainstream Narrative Film', *Social Semiotics*, 24:5, 2014, p. 612 (pp. 608–22 inclusive).
72. Ibid. p. 615.
73. Bauman, *Globalization*, p. 23.

74. Szörényi and Eate, 'Saving Virgins, Saving the US', pp. 619–20.
75. Butler, *Frames of War.*
76. Zygmunt Bauman, *Wasted Lives: Modernity and Its Outcasts* (Cambridge: Polity Press, 2003).
77. Szörényi and Eate, 'Saving Virgins, Saving the US', p. 620.
78. Judith Butler first introduced their theory of 'precarious life' in *Precarious Life: The Powers of Mourning and Violence* (London: Verso, 2004). In *Frames of War*, precarious life is presented as constituted through performative iterations of discursive framing.
79. Mac and Smith, *Revolting Prostitutes*, p. 21.

# *Imagining away Sex Slavery, towards a Counter-Narrative*

> 'And they lived happily ever after', says the fairy tale. The fairy tale, which to this day is the first tutor of children because it was once the first tutor of mankind, secretly lives on in the story. The first true storyteller is, and will continue to be, the teller of fairy tales. Whenever good counsel was at a premium, the fairy tale had it, and where the need was greatest, its aid was nearest. This need was the need created by the myth. The fairy tale tells us of the earliest arrangements that mankind made to shake off the nightmare which the myth had placed upon its chest. – Walter Benjamin[1]

The words that open this epilogue come from Walter Benjamin's unforgettable 1936 essay 'The Storyteller: Reflections on the Works of Nikolai Leskov', written in exile from Hitler's Germany just years before the beginning of World War II. In this famous meditation on the waning role of the storyteller in a society transformed by industrialization and the first modern war, Benjamin has extolled the continued power of the fairy tale to give courage to mankind. In fairy tales, so Benjamin has argued, the narrator summons characters who are armed with 'cunning' and 'high spirits'. As children, we learn the 'liberating magic' from the fairy tale. The storyteller gives us strength to believe that 'the things we are afraid of can be seen through'.[2] It is exactly this liberating magic that is the domain of Mona Paparu (Orsolya Török-Illyés), the protagonist and narrator of Szabolcs Hajdu's 2010 film *Bibliothèque Pascal*, an unconventional film that foregrounds the act of storytelling. Mona is asked to recount her experience of sex trafficking, and when she produces a chronicle of her adventures as a sex worker, full of flair and whimsy, she is admonished by her listener and ordered to tell the terrifying story of sex slavery. By juxtaposing magic realism with realism, Hajdu's film replicates Benjamin's dialectical contrast between two forms of storytelling: the fairy tale – a story of human agency; and myth – a story where fate and tragedy control human life. It is as a storyteller that Mona confronts the 'myth' of sex slavery through the narration of her own experiences, often traumatic, as a migrant sex worker.

Hajdu's film both intervenes in and critiques the reality of female sex work mobility in post-communist Europe. He does so not with thriller tropes

(*Taken*), gritty realist aesthetics (*Trade*, *Trade of Innocents*), sex spectacle (*Girls to Buy*, *365 Days*), or by laying claim to 'true stories' (*The Whistleblower*, *Lilya 4-ever*), but by way of magic realism and its long and well-theorized tradition of political critique.[3] Constructing his narrative from the perspective of a Hungarian-Romanian woman saddled with the legacy of the political, economic and moral bankruptcy of the communist system, Hajdu's narrative is as hyper-conscious of its own fictitious status as it is simultaneously attuned to the social reality in which it unfolds. As she relates her experience of migration, Mona uses much creative license to paint an adult fairy tale, populated by fortune-tellers, puppeteers, carnival tricksters, cunning villains, lecherous beach bums, literature-obsessed brothel clients and characters who can enter each other's dreams. The film renders this oneiric story into an artful vision with the use of CGI, Švankmajer-like animation, a hyper-saturated color scheme and András Nagy's dazzling tracking shots. As fanciful as it becomes, the imaginary tale that Mona devises functions as a mechanism to reinsert herself into the normative fabric of her society, granting her agency and showcasing the political power of storytelling.[4] Among other notable 'Third Generation' filmmakers such as Ferenc Török, György Pálfi, Kornél Mundruczó and Benedek Fliegauf, Hajdu belongs to the post-1989 Hungarian New Cinema movement. Engaged in the experimental and auteur traditions, the movement is shaped by the radical experiences of mobility that emerged out of the transition from the communist past to the capitalist future. Those experiences are very much at the center of Mona's story in *Bibliothèque Pascal* as she leaves Romania for the United Kingdom, ultimately to return to Romania to pick up the pieces of her life and start anew. Flora Talasi has commented on the formative role of mobility in the lives of the 'transition generation':

> Born in the late 1970s, these filmmakers passed through the kindergartens and schools of the late-communist era – or at least came into contact with such typically Eastern European patterns of socialization. As teenagers they experienced the dissolution of the Eastern Bloc and the short period of political awakening at the beginning of the 1990s. It was a generation who saw a new world opening up around them, and for whom the experience of individual and cultural mobility became formative. As young adults, they found themselves in a free, but disillusioned and highly polarized society in Eastern Central Europe.[5]

In his film, Hajdu focuses on the challenges posed by the post-communist proliferation of cross-border mobility. Specifically, he confronts what Zygmunt Bauman has theorized as the 'vagabond' mobility of the dispossessed and the displaced in the era of globalization. The vagabonds who travel 'surreptitiously', Bauman has observed, are 'frowned upon' and, 'if unlucky, arrested and promptly deported'.[6] Hajdu's film promotes storytelling as a strategy that helps the migrant mitigate the discomforts and humiliations of the road to a better life. Symbolic agency offers dignity and a modicum of self-determination. *Bibliothèque Pascal* frames its narrative with an act of rhetorical resistance in which a woman storyteller describes her experience of being trafficked and exploited for sex labor abroad as a fanciful adventure. This fantastic element, I argue, points to continued unease with regard to female mobility as such, and the complications that arise in the process of representing that mobility. However, the film also articulates Mona's recourse to the fantastic as a successful strategy used to determine her life. Her extraordinary storytelling skills push against the regime of punitive institutional knowledge and ultimately allow her to reclaim her daughter.

The opening scene of *Bibliothèque Pascal* begins in a Romanian child welfare services office where an official is interviewing a mother (Mona) whose child is now under the state's care. The mother is petitioning to regain the custody of her child. The official, an older man, wants the mother to explain why she left her daughter Viorica in the care of an incompetent relative (who ends up exploiting the child's paranormal abilities for financial gain) and left the country. Specifically, the official wants to know what Mona was doing while living abroad. Mona tells her story which constitutes the narrative proper of the film and, in the end, wins back the custody of her child. It is not, however, because her fantastic story elicits sympathy from the official. Indeed, he clearly doubts every detail of Mona's colorful and self-empowering tale and ultimately forces her to change her account for the benefit of his official report. The story that Mona chooses to tell in the first place is not the story that the official wants to hear. The experience that she narrates is the experience that many Eastern European women have shared since 1989 when, in dire economic circumstances, they decide to leave their families behind and seek employment abroad as sex workers, nannies, maids and live-in nurses, hoping for the maximum income earned relatively quickly.[7] In most cases, much like the experience of most bonded laborers in other sectors of the global economy, the women soon discovered that their employment was exploitative at best (and coerced labor at worst), that worker's rights were non-existent and that the income they had hoped for barely paid the bills. The journey to a foreign country, often the first journey undertaken in the woman's life, may have ended in confinement and complete prohibition of mobility, both physical and economic. The official discourses (both the governmental discourse of state security and the philanthropic anti-trafficking discourse) insist on framing the migrant experience connected to sex-affective labor well within the vocabulary of criminality and modern-day slavery, completely removing agency from the women involved, often portraying them as victims of international organized crime syndicates. Laura Agustín, one of the growing number of scholars who question the medicalization and criminalization of sex work migration, has pointed out that official discourses remove all agency from 'the poorer women of the world' and frame the migrant sex workers, who often carefully plan out their migrant journeys, 'as though migrants were naïve women who only yesterday were carrying water on their heads in some remote countryside'.[8]

Mainstream cinema – numerous examples of which I have discussed throughout this volume – contributes to this sensationalizing and trivializing account of migrant sex work by producing semi-pornographic, eroticized spectacles filled with shackled, brutalized female bodies confined to the ubiquitous sperm- and blood-stained mattresses. In *Bibliothèque Pascal*, to the extent that she can control, Mona resists both the official discourse that pathologizes sex work migration, as well as the spectacularized version of that experience imagined in cinema, confabulating a story that portrays her as an agent more than a victim. Above all, however, the film portrays her as an effective storyteller. In the course of Mona's story, which is told in a distinctly picaresque tone, the viewer finds out how Mona becomes a mother as result of a one-night stand with a stranger on a beach, how subsequently the stranger is apprehended and killed by the police, how Mona raises her daughter as a single mother, eking out a living as a street puppeteer and how, eventually, her own estranged father precipitates her passage to an elite Liverpool brothel, the eponymous Bibliothèque Pascal, which caters to clients with literary sexual fantasies: different rooms of the brothel are devoted to different works of literature, including *Lolita* and *The Adventures of Pinocchio*. Mona delivers sexual services as Joan of Arc from George Bernard Shaw's play *Saint Joan*. Although she is confined to one room, the space of her confinement in no way resembles the dark and dirty dungeon staged in so many of the recent films that insist on addressing sex trafficking via the sex slavery narrative. As she narrates her experience of working abroad to the child welfare official (and, by extension, to the film viewer), Mona neither occludes nor dwells on the negative aspects of her migrant experience. In this, the film resembles Kenneth Gyang's sobering narrative about Nigerian migrant sex workers crossing international borders to reach more lucrative markets in *Òlòtūré*. *Bibliothèque Pascal*, too, stages a traumatic border-crossing, in which Mona is smuggled across the English Channel in a cargo container. Once there, Mona is sold from the trafficker to the brothel owner, who has her drugged and beaten into compliance. Throughout her ordeal, and in the scenes just mentioned, Mona is composed, observant and in control of her fate. She observes her new surroundings and never panics. When eventually she is brutalized, she questions her pimp and devises ways to protect herself.

As the narrator of her own story, she scrupulously protects her dignity in the midst of very undignified circumstances. When she prefers to take recourse to fantasy, the viewer gladly respects her choice. Thus, the film refuses to participate in what Agustín has referred to as the 'discourses of pity and helping' that are projected on workers in the sex industry.[9] Neither does the film resort to images that would open up the woman's experience to voyeuristic consumption and trivialization which, according to Ann Kaplan and Ban Wang, are real dangers involved in trauma representation.[10]

In the end, the viewer is only privy to the magic realist images that Mona evokes throughout her story, which constitute the film. This includes Mona's escape from the brothel, which is facilitated by a Balkan brass band 'projected' into reality by her own daughter's dream, which mobilizes the band all the way from the Romanian periphery to England. Both the viewer and the child welfare official may doubt this resolution, suspecting that Mona was victimized much more severely than she is willing to contemplate publicly. But the film cleverly denies the visual representation of what might have 'actually' happened; it also refuses to depict any images of the narrative that the official coerces Mona to verbalize for the sake of his official case protocol. The epistemic duel between the sex worker mother and the social worker resonates through the dialogue featured in one of the last scenes of the film:

> SOCIAL WORKER: Let's compose it together. Tell me what really happened to you. I'll help you sum it up, okay?
> [She begins crafting a new narrative. A typist in the corner transcribes it with interventions from the social worker.]
> MONA: I decided to go with him.
> SOCIAL WORKER: Why?
> MONA: Money reasons.
> SOCIAL WORKER: Was it your decision to go?
> MONA: Yes.
> SOCIAL WORKER: No. Let's write that he forced her to go . . . Good. That'll make a good start. [Moves toward the typist in the corner, away from Mona, literally behind her back] [To the typist:] But let's add: 'I came back determined to mend my ways, earn a respectable living, and create a healthy mental and physical environment for my child'.

However, the film does not volunteer a narrative of hyperbolic empowerment on par with Emi's story in *Girls to Buy* (Dir. Maria Sadowska). This might be because 'power feminism' is still rare in the vocabulary of Eastern European women, including those who are feminist-minded – but neither is it 'victim feminism', as Mona's tale suggests.[11] When the official convinces Mona to provide him with a more 'realistic' (that is, disempowered) version of her experience, so that he can issue a positive decision in Viorica's custody case, Mona reluctantly agrees to change her story. Significantly, in the process of this coerced retelling, she is reduced to tears and retraumatized. In this scene, the film subtly illustrates the rhetorical process through which the sex slave figure is manufactured by the security state. The film may suggest, then, that the enforced 'realistic' interpretation of Mona's experience is a result of the compulsory 'regime of truth', as Foucault would have it – the required 'sex slavery' narrative that consolidates the gendered and racialized myth of imperiled femininity and empowered patriarchy. This more 'plausible' version situates Mona as an absolute victim of sex trafficking, a woman of virtue who would never consider sex work as a viable means of supporting herself and her daughter, and even less so consider narrating her experience of engaging in sex work as a picaresque tale of bizarre adventures. Fortunately, the latter version does not materialize on screen (Hajdu does not grant it any diegetic space), leaving Mona's initial version, recorded in the cinematic register with vivid exuberance and sumptuous images, as the authoritative one. A work of a female storyteller who faces epistemic coercion, this is the brazen and beautiful counter-narrative to the sex slavery story.

## Notes

1. Walter Benjamin, *Illuminations: Essays and Reflections* (New York: Schocken Books, 1968), p. 102.
2. Ibid, p. 102.
3. For more on magic realism's capacity for political critique, see Aga Skrodzka (ed.), *Magic Realist Cinema in East Central Europe* (Edinburgh: Edinburgh University Press, 2012); Theo D'haen, 'Magical Realism and Postmodernism: Decentering Privileged Centers', in Lois Parkinson Zamora and Wendy B. Faris (eds), *Magical Realism: Theory, History, Community* (Durham: Duke University Press, 1995), pp. 191–208.
4. In her study on corporeality in Hajdu's film, Katalin Sándor has commented on Mona's 'particular mode of creativity and an ineffaceable capacity of storytelling, of narrating and continually re-telling, rethinking her "self"'. Katalin Sándor, 'Corporeality and Otherness in the Cinematic Heterotopias of Szabolcs Hajdu's *Bibliothèque Pascal* (2010)', *Ekphrasis*, 12:2, 2014, p. 88, (pp. 79–92 inclusive).
5. Flora Talasi, 'Benedek Fliegauf', *GoEast: Festival of Central and Eastern European Film*, www.filmfestival-goeast.de/index.php?article_id=394&clang=1 (accessed 18 March 2014).
6. Bauman, *Globalization*, p. 89.
7. See Cezara Crisan, 'Transnational Experiences of Eastern European Women and Feminist Practices after 1989', in Glenda Tibe Bonifacio (ed.), *Feminism and Migration: Cross-Cultural Engagements* (Dordrecht and New York: Springer 2012), pp. 165–84; Parvulescu, *The Traffic in Women's Work*.

8. Agustín, 'At Home in the Street', p. 68.
9. Ibid. p. 68.
10. Anne Kaplan and Ban Wang, 'Introduction: From Traumatic Paralysis to the Force Field of Modernity', in Anne Kaplan and Ban Wang (eds), *Trauma and Cinema: Cross-Cultural Explorations* (Hong Kong: Hong Kong University Press, 2004), pp. 11–12 (pp. 1–22 inclusive).
11. Naomi Wolf has used the dichotomy of 'power feminism' and 'victim feminism' in her work. See Naomi Wolf, *Fire with Fire* (New York: Random House, 1994). For a critique of this dichotomy, see Elizabeth M. Schneider, 'Feminism and the False Dichotomy of Victimization and Agency', *New York Law School Review*, 38, 1993, pp. 387–99.

# *Bibliography*


Abrahams, Daniel [n. d.] 'Taken as Genre', *The Epicurean Cure*, www.epicureancure.com/885/taken-as-a-genre

Achenbach, Michael, and Paolo Caneppele (1998) 'Saturn: The Erotic Beginnings of Austrian Cinematography', *Journal of Film Preservation*, 57, December, 13–14.

—— (1999) 'Born Under the Sign of Saturn: The Erotic Origins of Cinema in the Austro-Hungarian Empire', *Griffithiana: Journal of Film History*, 65, 126–39.

Adorno, Theodor, and Max Horkheimer (1972) *Dialectic of Enlightenment*, trans. Edmund Jephcott. New York: Continuum.

Agamben, Giorgio (1998) *Homo Sacer: Sovereign Power and Bare Life*, trans. Daniel Heller-Roazen. Palo Alto: Stanford University Press.

Agathangelou, Anna M. (2004) *The Global Politics Economy of Sex: Desire, Violence, and Insecurity in Mediterranean Nation States*. New York: Palgrave.

Agustín, Laura M. (2005) 'At Home in the Street: Questioning the Desire to Help and Save', in Elizabeth Bernstein and Laurie Schaffner (eds.), *Regulating Sex: The Politics of Intimacy and Identity*. New York: Routledge, 67–82.

——— (2007) *Sex at the Margins*. London: Zed.

Ahmed, Sara (2000) *Strange Encounters: Embodied Others in Post-Coloniality*. New York: Routledge.

Alexander, George (2002) 'Credits Due: The Rise of Black Women in Hollywood', *American Legacy Magazine: Woman*, 14.

Ali, Isra (2015) 'The Harem Fantasy in Nineteenth Century Orientalist Paintings', *Dialectical Anthropology*, 39, 1, 2015, 33–46.

Allen, Julie K. (2013) 'The White Slave Trade Gets Religion in *A Victim of the Mormons*', *Kosmorama*, 31 May, www.kosmorama.org/en/kosmorama/artikler/white-slave-trade-gets-religion-victim-mormons (accessed 15 August 2023).

Alloula, Malek (1986) *The Colonial Harem*, trans. Myrna Godzich and Vlad Godzich. Minneapolis: University of Minnesota Press.

Amar, Paul (2013) *The Security Archipelago: Human-Security States, Sexuality Politics, and the End of Neoliberalism*. Durham and London: Duke University Press, 2013.

American Family Association (2020) 'Target Policy Claims Another Victim, Boycott Continues', *AFA Journal*, April, www.afajournal.org/past-issues/2020/april/target-policy-claims-another-victim-boycott-continues (accessed 10 December 2023).

——— (2021) 'Wildmon: Target Boycott Still the Right Thing', *AFA Journal*, January–February, www.afajournal.org/past-issues/2021/january-february/wildmon-target-boycott-still-the-right-thing (accessed 11 December 2023).

Amnesty International (2014) *The Human Cost of Fortress Europe*. London: Amnesty International.

Applebaum, Anne (2022) 'America Needs a Better Plan to Fight Autocracy', *The Atlantic*, 15 March, www.theatlantic.com/ideas/archive/2022/03/russia-ukraine-senate-testimony-autocracy-kleptocrats/627061/ (accessed 17 May 2024).

Arendt, Hannah (2006) *On Revolution*. New York: Penguin Books.

Asendorf, Christoph (1993) *Batteries of Life: On the History of Things and Their Perception in Modernity*. Berkeley: University of California Press.

Bachmann-Medick, Doris (2017) 'Alterity – A Category of Practice and Analysis, Preliminary Remarks', *On Culture*, 4, Winter, www.on-culture.org/journal/issue-4/bachmann-medick-alterity/

Baker, Catherine (2021) 'The Contingencies of Whiteness: Gender/Racialized Global Dynamics of Security Narratives', *Security Dialogue*, 52 (Supplement), 2021, 124–32.

Bammer, Angelika (1995) 'Xenophobia, Xenophilia, and No Place to Rest', in Gisela Brinkler-Gabler (ed.), *Encountering the Other(s): Studies in Literature, History, and Culture*. Albany: SUNY Press, 45–62.

Barthes, Roland (1981) *Camera Lucia: Reflections on Photography*, trans. Richard Howard. New York: Hill and Wang.

——— (1987) *Image, Music, Text*, trans. Stephen Heath. Glasgow: Fontana Press.

Baudrillard, Jean (1988) *The Evil Demon of Images*. Sydney: The Power Institute of Fine Arts.

Bauman, Zygmunt (1998) *Globalization: The Human Consequences*. New York: Columbia University Press.

——— (2004) *Wasted Lives: Modernity and Its Outcasts*. Cambridge: Polity Press.

Bazin, André (1967) *What is Cinema?*, trans. Hugh Gray. Berkeley: University of California Press.

Beaulieu, Jill, and Mary Roberts (2002) *Orientalism's Interlocutors: Painting, Architecture, Photography*. Durham: Duke University Press.

Benjamin, Walter (1968) *Illuminations: Essays and Reflections*. New York: Schocken Books.

——— (1999) *The Arcades Project*, trans. Howard Eiland and Kevin McLaughlin. Cambridge, MA: Harvard University Press.

Bennett, Jane (2010) *Vibrant Matter: A Political Ecology of Things*. Durham: Duke University Press.

Bergmann, Eirikur (2021) 'The Eurabia Conspiracy Theory', in Andreas Önnerfors and André Krouwel (eds.), *Europe: Continent of Conspiracies: Conspiracy Theories in and about Europe*. Abingdon and New York: Routledge, 36–53.

Bergstein, Mary. 'Freud, Saturn, and the Power of Hypnosis', in Shawn Michelle Smith and Sharon Sliwinski (eds), *Photography and the Optical Unconscious*. Durham: Duke University Press, 104–33.

Bernstein, Elizabeth (2007) 'The Sexual Politics of the "New Abolitionism"', *differences: A Journal of Feminist Cultural Studies*, 18, 3, 2007, 144–51.

Berry, Daina Ramey (2017) *The Price for Their Pound of Flesh: The Value of the Enslaved, from Womb to Grave, in the Building of a Nation*. Boston: Beacon Press.

Bixenspan, David (2020) 'WWE Referee, Wrestler-Turned-Mayor Fundraiser for QAnon-Adjacent Charity', *Vice*, 29 September, www.vice.com/en/article/5dzx88/wwe-referee-wrestler-turned-mayor-fundraise-for-qanon-adjacent-charity (accessed 13 May 2024).

Boltanski, Luc (1999) *Distant Suffering: Morality, Media and Politics*. Cambridge: Cambridge University Press.

Borcila, Rozalinda (2014) 'The Political Aesthetics of Immigrant Protests', in Katarzyna Marciniak and Imogen Tyler (eds), *Immigrant Protest: Politics, Aesthetics, and Everyday Dissent*. Albany: SUNY Press, 45–62.

Bordino, Alex W. (2015) 'Modernity, Parallel Editing, and the Flâneuse: Examining the White Slave Narrative in Early and Contemporary American Cinema'. MA thesis, The City University of New York.

Brody, Jennifer DeVere (2000) 'The Returns of Cleopatra Jones', in Shelton Waldrep (ed.), *The Seventies: The Age of Glitter in Popular Culture.* New York; London: Routledge, 225–48.

Brooker, Peter, and Will Brooker (1996) 'Pulpmodernism: Tarantino's Affirmative Action', in Deborah Cartmell et al. (eds), *Pulping Fictions: Consuming Culture Across the Literature/Media Divide.* London: Pluto Press, 135–51.

Brown, Simone (2015) *Dark Matters: On the Surveillance of Blackness.* Durham: Duke University Press.

Brown, William, Dina Iordanova and Leshu Torchin (2010) *Moving People, Moving Images: Cinema and Trafficking in the New Europe.* London: Wallflower Press.

Butler, Judith (2004) *Precarious Life: The Powers of Mourning and Violence.* London: Verso.

——— (2009) *Frames of War: When is Life Grievable?* London: Verso.

Calinescu, Matei (1987) *Five Faces of Modernity: Modernism, Avant-Garde, Decadence, Kitsch, Postmodernism.* Durham: Duke University Press.

Central Statistical Office of Poland (2018), 'Labour force survey in Poland III quarter 2018', 31 January, https://stat.gov.pl/en/topics/labour-market/working-unemployed-economically-inactive-by-lfs/labour-force-survey-in-poland-iii-quarter-2018,2,31.html

Cienski, Jan (2015) 'Migrants Carry "Parasites and Protozoa", Warns Polish Opposition Leader', *Politics,* 4 October, www.politico.eu/article/migrants-asylum-poland-kaczynski-election/ (accessed 30 March 2023).

Corbin, Alain (1990) *Women for Hire: Prostitution and Sexuality in France after 1950*, trans. Alan Sheridan. Cambridge, MA: Harvard University Press.

Crary, Jonathan (1991) *Techniques of the Observer: On Vision and Modernity in the Nineteenth Century.* Cambridge, MA: Harvard University Press.

Creel, Sadie, Sarah Hupp Williamson and Emily Walker (2023) '#Wayfairgate and the Growth of Sex Trafficking Panics across Social Media', *Critical Criminology*, 31, 617–22.

Crisan, Cezara (2012) 'Transnational Experiences of Eastern European Women and Feminist Practices after 1989', in Glenda Tibe Bonifacio (ed.), *Feminism and Migration: Cross-Cultural Engagements.* Dordrecht; New York: Springer 2012, 165–84.

Cullen, Frank, Florence Hackman and Donald McNeilly (2007) *Vaudeville, Old and New: An Encyclopedia of Variety Performers in America*, 2 Volumes. New York: Routledge.

D'haen, Theo (1995) 'Magical Realism and Postmodernism: Decentering Privileged Centers', in Lois Parkinson Zamora and Wendy Faris (eds), *Magical Realism: Theory, History, Community.* Durham: Duke University Press, 191–208.

David, Marlo D. (2020) 'On Dirty Computers and Dissemblance', *Signs: Journal of Women in Culture and Society*, 45, 3, 541–46.

De Vries, Petra (2005) "'White Slaves' in a Colonial Nation: The Dutch Campaign against Traffic in Women in the Early Twentieth Century', *Social and Legal Studies*, 14, 1, 2005, 39–60.

Delistraty, Cody (2012) 'How Germany's Far Right is Co-Opting Art History', *Frieze*, 3 May, www.frieze.com/article/how-germanys-far-right-co-opting-art-history

DeVos, Andrew (2013) '"Expect the Truth": Exploiting History with *Mandingo*', *American Studies*, 52, 2, 2013, 5–21.

Dickson, E. J. (2022) 'A Target Sex-Trafficking Hoax is Once Again Going Viral on TikTok', *Rolling Stone*, 9 September, www.rollingstone.com/culture/culture-news/tiktok-target-sex-trafficking-hoax-marco-polo-1234589134 (accessed 11 December 2023).

Didi-Huberman, Georges (2003) *Invention of Hysteria: Charcot and the Photographic Iconography of the Salpêtrière*, trans. Alisa Hartz. Cambridge and London: MIT Press.

Dodds, Klaus, and Philip Kirby (2014) 'Resurrecting the Vigilante: Paternal Sovereignty, Exceptionality, and Familiar Security in *Taken* (2008) and *Taken 2* (2013)', *Critical Studies on Security*, 2, 3, 245–61.

Doezema, Jo (2010) *Sex Slaves and Discourse Masters*. London: Zed.

Douglas, Mary (2002 [1966]) *Purity and Danger: An Analysis of Concepts of Pollution and Taboo*. London and New York: Routledge.

Dyer, Richard (1988) 'White', *Screen*, 29, 4, Autumn, 44–64.

Eleftheriotis, Dimitris (2010) *Cinematic Journeys: Film and Movement*. Edinburgh: Edinburgh University Press.

Engberg, Marguerite (1993) 'The Erotic Melodrama in Danish Silent Films, 1910–1918', *Film History*, 5, 63–67.

Erdman, Dan (2021) *Let's Go Stag! A History of Pornographic Film from the Invention of Cinema to 1970*. New York: Bloomsbury Academic.

Esch, Michael G. (2021) 'Migrants from East-Central Europe in South America: Discourses and Structures between Mission, Pogrom, Escape, Human Trafficking, and "Whitening"', in Katja Castryck-Naumann (ed.), *Transregional Connections in the History of East-Central Europe*. Berlin and Boston: DeGruyter Oldenbourg, 259–90.

Faludi, Susan (2008) *The Terror Dream: Myth and Misogyny in an Insecure America*. New York: Picador.

Fassler, Joe (2023) 'The Superyachts of Billionaires are Starting to Look a Lot Like Theft', *The New York Times*, 10 April, https://www.nytimes.com/2023/04/10/opinion/superyachts-private-plane-climate-change.html (accessed 15 April 2023).

Felman, Shoshana (1992) 'Education and Crisis, or the Vicissitudes to Teaching', in Shoshana Felman and Dori Laub (eds), *Testimony: Crises of Witnessing in Literature, Psychoanalysis, and History*. New York: Routledge, 1–56.

Field, Allyson Nadia (2016) 'Stomping on Stepin Fetchit: Historicizing "Blackness" in African American Film Culture of the 1970s', in Novotny Lawrence and Gerald R. Butters, Jr (eds), *Beyond Blaxploitation*. Detroit: Wayne State University Press, 157–79.

Finley, Alexandra J. (2020) *An Intimate Economy: Enslaved Women, Work, and America's Domestic Slave Trade*. Chapel Hill: University of North Carolina Press.

Fischer, Lucy (1983) 'The Lady Vanishes: Women, Magic, and the Movies', in John L. Fell (ed.), *Film before Griffith*. Berkeley and Los Angeles: University of California Press, 339–54.

Foucault, Michel (1977) *Discipline and Punish: The Birth of the Prison*, trans. A. Sheridan. London: Alan Lane.

——— (1990) *The Use of Pleasure: History of Sexuality, Volume 2*, trans. Robert Hurley. New York: Vintage.

Franco, Judith (2004) 'Gender, Genre and Female Pleasure in the Contemporary Revenge Narrative: *Baise moi* and *What It Feels Like for A Girl*', *Quarterly Review of Film and Video*, 21, 1, 1–10.

Fronc, Jennifer (2017) *Monitoring the Movies: The Fight over Film Censorship in Early Twentieth-Century Urban America*. Austin: University of Texas Press.

Galusca, Roxana (2012) 'Slave Hunters, Brothel Busters, and Feminist Interventions: Investigative Journalists as Anti-Sex-Trafficking Humanitarians', *Feminist Formations*, 24, 2, 1–24.

Garraway, Doris (2005) *The Libertine Colony: Creolization in the Early French Caribbean*. Durham: Duke University Press.

Gaudreault, André (1987) 'Narration and Monstration in Cinema', *Journal of Film and Video*, 39, 2, 29–36.

——— (2011) *Film and Attraction: From Kinematography to Cinema*, trans. Timothy Barnard. Urbana, Chicago and Springfield: University of Illinois Press.

Gersz, Ola (2021) 'Nie mogłam uwierzyć własnym oczom: Dziewczyny z Dubaju nie sa złym filmem', *Na Temat*, 29 November, https://natemat.pl/385851,dziewczyny-z-dubaju-recenzja (accessed 7 February 2023).

Ghareeb, Edmund (1977) *Split Vision: The Portrayal of Arabs in the American Media*. Washington DC: The Institute of Middle Eastern and North African Affairs.

Gleich, Joshua (2011) 'Jim Brown: From Integration to Resegregation in *The Dirty Dozen* and *100 Rifles*', *Cinema Journal*, 5,1, 211, 1–25.

Gordon-Chipembere, Natasha, ed. (2011) *Representation and Black Womanhood: The Legacy of Sarah Baartman*. New York: Palgrave Macmillan.

Grieveson, Lee (2004) *Policing Cinema: Movies and Censorship in Early Twentieth-Century America*. Berkeley: University of California Press.

Gunning, Tom (1990) 'The Cinema of Attractions: Early Film, Its Spectator and the Avant-Garde', in Thomas Elsaesser and Adam Baker (eds), *Early Cinema: Space, Frame, Narrative*. London: BFI Publishing, 56–62.

——— 'The World as Object Lesson: Cinema Audiences, Visual Culture and the St. Louis World's Fair, 1904', *Film History*, 6, 4, 422–44.

——— (1995) 'Tracing the Individual Body: Detectives, Photography, and Early Cinema', in Vanessa Schwartz and Leo Charney (eds), *Cinema and the Invention of Modern Life*. Berkeley and Los Angeles: University of California Press, 15–45.

——— (1986) 'The Cinema of Attraction: Early Film, Its Spectator, and the Avant-Garde', *Wide Angle*, 8, 63–70.

——— (1997) 'From Kaleidoscope to the X-Ray: Urban Spectatorship, Poe, Benjamin, and *Traffic in Souls* (1913)', *White Angle*, 19, 4, 25–61.

——— (2004) 'Flickers: On Cinema's Power for Evil', in Murray Pomerance (ed.), *Bad: Infamy, Darkness, Evil, and Slime on Screen*. Albany: Albany State University Press, 21–37.

—— (2007) 'Moving Away from the Index: Cinema and the Impression of Reality', *differences: A Journal of Feminist Cultural Studies*, 18, 1, 29–52.

Haag, Matthew (2019) 'Thousands of Immigrant Children Said They were Sexually Abused in U.S. Detention Centers, Report Says', *New York Times*, 27 February, www.nytimes.com/2019/02/27/us/immigrant-children-sexual-abuse.html (accessed 14 May 2024).

Hains, Rebecca (2009) 'Power Feminism, Mediated: Girl Power and the Commercial Politics of Change', *Women's Studies in Communication*, 32, 90–113.

Halsted-Stauter, Keely (2015) *The Devil's Chains: Prostitution and Social Control in Partitioned Poland*. Ithaca and London: Cornell University Press.

Hansen, Miriam (1999) 'The Mass Production of the Senses: Classical Cinema as Vernacular Modernism', *Modernism/Modernity*, 6, 2, 59–77.

Hartman, Saidiya (1997) *Scenes of Subjection: Terror, Slavery, and Self-Making in Nineteenth-Century America*. New York and Oxford: Oxford University Press.

——— (2007) *Lose Your Mother: A Journey along the Atlantic Slave Trade Route Terror*. New York: Farrar, Straus and Giroux.

Hashamova, Yana (2018) *Screening Trafficking: Prudent and Perilous*. Budapest and New York: Central European University Press.

Haynes, Dina Francesca (2014) 'The Celebrization of Human Trafficking', *The ANNALS of the American Academy of Political and Social Science*, 653, 25–45.

Hedling, Olof (2004) 'Om Lilja 4-ever – en svensk film', in B. Jonsson, K. Nykvist and B. Sjoberg (eds), *Från Eden till Damavdelning*. Lund: Absalon, 323–24.

Hernandez, Jillian (2014) 'Carnal Teachings: Raunch Aesthetics as Queer Feminist Pedagogies in Yo! Majesty's Hip Hop Practice', *Women and Performance: A Journal of Feminist Theory*, 24, 1, 88–106.

Hitchens, Christopher (2005) *Brave New World and Brave New World Revisited.* New York: Harper Perennial.

Hoffner ex-Prvulovic, Ana (2019) 'Non-Aligned Extinctions: Slavery, Neo-Orientalism, and Queerness', *e-flux journal*, 97, February, www.e-flux.com/journal/97/252398/non-aligned-extinctions-slavery-neo-orientalism-and-queerness/ (accessed 15 June 2023).

Holmlund, Chris (2005) 'Wham! Bam! Pam! Pam Grier as Hot Action Babe and Cool Action Mama', *Quarterly Review of Film and Video*, 22, 9, 97–112.

hooks, bell (1992) *Black Looks: Race and Representation.* Boston: South End Press.

Howard, Josiah (2008) *Blaxploitation Cinema: The Essential Reference Guide.* Godalming: FAB Press.

Hua, Julietta (2011) *Trafficking Women's Human Rights.* Minneapolis and London: University of Minnesota Press.

Huynh, Anjali (2023) 'Trump Promotes *Sound of Freedom*, a Conservative Hit About Child Predators', *New York Times*, 19 July, www.nytimes.com/2023/07/19/us/politics/trump-sound-of-freedom.html (accessed 13 May 2024).

Impelli, Matthew (2023) 'Target Ends Year of Boycotts with Good News', *Newsweek*, 30 December, www.newsweek.com/target-ends-year-boycotts-good-news-1855959 (accessed 1 January 2023).

Imre, Anikó (2005) 'Whiteness in Post-Socialist Eastern Europe: The Time of the Gypsies, the End of Race', in Alfred J. Lopez (ed.), *Postcolonial Whiteness: Critical Reader on Race and Empire.* Albany: State University of New York Press, 79–102.

International Justice Mission [n. d.] 'Get Involved', *International Justice Mission*, www.ijm.org/get-involved/churches

Irwin, Mary Ann (1996) '"White Slavery" as Metaphor: Anatomy of a Moral Panic', *Ex Post Facto: The History Journal*, 5, 1–22.

Jennings, Thelma (1990) 'Us Colored Women Had to Go through a Plenty: Sexual Exploitation of African-American Slave Women', *Journal of Women's History*, 1, 3, January, 5–74.

Jones-Rogers, Stephanie E. (2020) *They Were Her Property: White Women as Slave Owners in the American South.* New Haven and London: Yale University Press.

Jung, Werner (2013) *Wände, die Sprechen: Walls That Talk, The Wall Inscriptions in the Cologne Gestapo Prison.* Köln: Emons.

Kabbani, Rana (2008) *Imperial Fictions: Europe's Myths of Orient.* London: Al Saqi Books.

Kaldor, Mary (2003) 'The Idea of Global Civil Society', *International Affairs*, 79, 583–93.

Kaplan, Anna, and Ban Wang (2004) *Trauma and Cinema: Cross Cultural Explorations.* Hong Kong: Hong Kong University Press.

Kaplan, E. Ann (1997) *Looking for the Other: Feminism, Film, and the Imperial Gaze.* New York: Routledge.

Keire, Mara L. (2001) 'The Vice Trust: A Reinterpretation of the White Slavery Scare in the United States, 1907–1917', *Journal of Social History*, 35:1, 5–41.

——— (2010) *For Business and Pleasure: Red-Light Districts and the Regulation of Vice in the United States, 1890–1933.* Baltimore: Johns Hopkins University Press.

Keser, Robert (2023) '"The Greatest Film about Race Ever Filmed in Hollywood": Richard Fleischer's Mandingo', *Bright Lights Film Journal*, 7 November, www.brightlightsfilm.com/greatest-film-race-ever-filmed-hollywood-richard-fleischers-mandingo/ (accessed 15 November 2023). Originally published in *The Film Journal* (2006).

Klee, Miles (2024) 'God's Children: New Lawsuit against Tim Ballard Also Targets *Sound of Freedom* and Angel Studios', *Rolling Stone*, 23 February, www.rollingstone.com/culture/culture-news/sound-of-freedom-tim-ballard-angel-studios-lawsuit-1234974841/ (accessed 13 May 2024).

Klein, Amanda Ann (2014) 'Unbearable Whiteness of Gone Girls', *LA Review of Books*, 21 October, https://avidly.lareviewofbooks.org/2014/10/21/unbearable-whiteness-of-gone-girls/ (accessed 14 April 2024).

Koff, Harlan (2008) *Fortress Europe or a Europe of Fortresses? The Integration of Migrants in Western Europe*. Brussels: PIE Peter Lang.

Kościańska, Agnieska, and Michal Petryk (2022) *Odejdź: Rzecz o polskim rasizmie*. Warsaw: Wydawnictwo Krytyki Polityczenej.

Kristensen, Lars (2007) 'Divergent Accounts of Equivalent Narratives: Russian-Swedish *Interdevochka* Meets Swedish-Russian *Lilya 4-ever*', *PORTAL: Journal of Interdisciplinary Studies*, 4, 2, July, 1–22.

Kristeva, Julia (1979) 'Ellipsis on Dread and the Specular Seduction', trans. Dolores Burdick, *Wide Angle*, 3:3, 42–47.

——— (1982) *Powers of Horror: An Essay on Abjection*, trans. Leon S. Roudiez. New York: Columbia University Press.

Krysiak, Piotr (2018) *Dziewczyny z Dubaju*. Warszawa: Deadline.

——— (2021) *Chlopaki z Dubaju*. Warszawa: Deadline.

Lawrence, Novotny (2008) *Blaxploitation Films of the 1970s: Blackness and Genre*. New York and London: Routledge.

Lee, Lorelei (2021) 'The Roots of "Modern Day Slavery": The Page Act and the Mann Act', *Columbia Human Rights Law Review*, 52, 3, Spring, https://hrlr.law.columbia.edu/hrlr/the-roots-of-modern-day-slavery-the-page-act-and-the-mann-act/

Lewis, Reina (1996) *Gendering Orientalism: Race, Feminism and Representation*. Abingdon and New York: Routledge.

Littler, Jo (2008) '"I Feel Your Pain": Cosmopolitan Charity and the Public Fashioning of the Celebrity Soul', *Social Semiotics*, 18, 237–51.

Lo Presti, Laura (2019) 'Terraqueous Necropolitics: Unfolding the Low-Operational, Forensic, and Evocative Mapping of Mediterranean Sea Crossings in the Age of Lethal Borders', *ACME: An International Journal for Critical Geographies*, 18, 6, 2019, 1347–67.

Lovejoy, Paul E. (2011) *Transformations in Slavery: A History of Slaves in Africa*. Cambridge: Cambridge University Press.

Georg Lukács (1971 [1923]) History and Class Consciousness, trans. Rodney Livingstone. Cambridge, MA: MIT Press.

Lyons, Siobhan, ed. (2018) *Ruin Porn and the Obsession with Decay*. Basingstoke: Palgrave Macmillan.

Mac, Juno, and Molly Smith (2018) *Revolting Prostitutes: The Fight for Sex Worker's Rights*. London: Verso.

Macmaster, Neil, and Toni Lewis (2005) 'Orientalism: From Unveiling to Hyperveiling', in Haideh Moghissi (ed.), *Women and Islam: Images and Realities, Volume I*. London and New York: Routledge, 147–62.

Majmurek, Jakub (2021) '365 dni w Dubaju', *Filmweb*, 5 December, www.filmweb.pl/reviews/recenzja-filmu-Dziewczyny+z+Dubaju%C2%AE-24094 (accessed 30 March 2023).

Marciniak, Katarzyna (2005) 'Second World-Ness and Transnational Feminist Practices: Agnieszka Holland's *Kobieta Samotna* (*A Woman Alone*)', in Anikó Imre (ed.), *East European Cinemas*. New York: Routledge, 3–20.

——— (2017) 'Aporias of Foreignness: Transnational Encounters Through Cinema', in Gavin Rae and Emma Ingala (eds.), *Subjectivity and the Political: Contemporary Perspectives.* New York: Routledge, 91–109.

Marciniak, Katarzyna, and Bruce Bennett, eds. (2016) 'Introduction', in *Teaching Transnational Cinema: Politics and Pedagogy*. New York, Routledge, 1–35.

Marcuse, Herbert (1991 [1964]) *One-Dimensional Man: Studies in the Ideology of Advanced Industrial Society*. Boston: Beacon Press.

Martin, Adrian (2004) 'Dance Girl Dance: Philippe Grandrieux's *La Vie Nouvelle* (*The New Life,* 2002)', *Kinoeye: New Perspectives on European Film*, 4, 3, www.kinoeye.org/04/03/martin03.php

Marx, Karl (1973) *Grundrisse: Foundations of the Critique of Political Economy.* London: Alan Lane.

Mask, Mia (2023) *Black Rodeo: A History of the African American Western.* Urbana, Chicago and Springfield: University of Illinois Press.

Maynard, Patrick (1983) 'The Secular Icon: Photography and the Functions of Images', *The Journal of Aesthetics and Art Criticism,* 42, 2, Winter, 155–69.

Mazierska, Ewa, and Laura Rascaroli (2006) *Crossing New Europe: Postmodern Travel and the European Road Movie.* London: Wallflower Press.

Mbembe, Achille (2019) *Necropolitics*, trans. Steve Corcoran. Durham: Duke University Press.

McMichael, Morgonn (2023) [*Twitter*], 3 December, www.twitter.com/morgonnm/status/1731460640458625171?t=W0OrGhnAuchMstfE5gLHeA&s=19 (accessed 5 December 2023).

Meyer, Moe (1994) *The Politics and Poetics of Camp.* London and New York: Routledge.

Mills, Charles (1999) *The Racial Contract.* Ithaca: Cornell University Press.

Minh-ha, Trinh T. (1993) 'The Totalizing Quest of Meaning', in Michael Renov (ed.), *Theorizing Documentary*. New York: Routledge, 90–108.

Miriam, Kathy (2005) 'Stopping the Traffic in Women: Power, Agency and Abolition in Feminist Debates Over Sex-Trafficking', *Journal of Social Philosophy*, 36, 1–17.

Miroff, Nick (2020) '"Kids in Cages": It's True That Obama Built the Cages at the Border. But Trump's "Zero Tolerance" Immigration Policy Had No Precedent', *The Washington Post*, 23 October 2020, www.washingtonpost.com/immigration/kids-in-cages-debate-trump-obama/2020/10/23/8ff96f3c-1532-11eb-82af-864652063d61_story.html (accessed 15 May 2024).

Mofokeng, Tlaleng (2019) 'Why Sex Work is Real Work', *Teen Vogue*, 26 April, https://www.teenvogue.com/story/why-sex-work-is-real-work (accessed 6 March 2024).

*Motherwell Times* (1911) 'New Century Theater', 19 May, p. 7.

Mullins, Paul (2012) 'The Politics and Archaeology of "Ruin Porn"', *Archaeology and Material Culture*, 19 August, www.paulmullins.wordpress.com/2012/08/19/the-politics-and-archaeology-of-ruin-porn/ (accessed 6 March 2024).

Mulvey, Laura (1975) 'Visual Pleasure and Narrative Cinema', *Screen*, 16, 3, 6–18.

Murray, Conor (2023) '*Sound of Freedom* Inspiration Tim Ballard and Film Producer Face Allegations of Sexual Impropriety', *Forbes*, 20 September, www.forbes.com/sites/conormurray/2023/09/20/sound-of-freedom-inspiration-tim-ballard-and-film-producer-face-allegations-of-sexual-impropriety/?sh=67bdf830d0f1 (accessed 13 May 2024).

Musial, Jennifer (2023) 'Pregnant and Disappeared: The Missing White Woman Syndrome in Magazines', in Karen Boyle and Susan Berridge (eds), *The Routledge Companion to Gender, Media, and Violence.* New York: Routledge, 271–80.

Nair, Yasmin (2014) 'Somaly Mam, Nicholas Kristof, and the Real Sex Trafficking Story', 2 June, https://yasminnair.com/somaly-mam-nicholas-kristof-and-the-real-sex-trafficking-story/#more-8665 (accessed 21 March 2024).

Narayanan, Ayush (2023), 'UAE leaders meet Polish president in Abu Dhabi, Dubai', *Al Arabiya English*, 8 March, https://english.alarabiya.net/News/ gulf/2023/03/08/UAE-leaders-meet-Polish-President-in-Abu-Dhabi- Dubai (accessed 30 March 2023).

Nathan, Janak Vetri (2010) 'Nuovo Cinema Inferno: The Affect of Ambivalence in Giuseppe Tornatore's *La Sconosciuta*', in Katarzyna Marciniak and Bruce Bennett (eds), *From Terrone to Extracomunitario: New Manifestations of Racism*. Leicester: Troubador Publishing, 236–57.

*Nelson Leader* (1911) 'The New Electric', 7 April, p. 7.

O'Connell Davidson, Julia (2015) *Modern Slavery: The Margins of Freedom*. Basingstoke: Palgrave Macmillan.

O'Connor, Clint (2011) '"Bibliothèque Pascal": The Weird, the Dark, the Literary at the Cleveland International Film Festival', *Cleveland*, 30 March, www.cleveland.com/moviebuff/2011/03/bibliotheque_pascal_the_weird.html

O'Healy, Áine (2019) *Migrant Anxieties: Italian Cinema in a Transnational Frame*. Bloomington: Indiana University Press.

Obensen, Tambay (2020) 'How a Nollywood Netflix Drama Sheds Light on Nigeria's Human Trafficking Crisis', *IndieWire*, 7 October, www.indiewire.com/features/general/oloture-nollywood-netflix-nigeria-1234590106/, (accessed 21 March 2024).

Olmstead, Molly (2023) 'The Damning Details of the Lawsuit Against *Sound of Freedom*'s Hero', *Slate*, 16 October, https://slate.com/news-and-politics/2023/10/tim-ballard-lawsuit-sound-freedom-lds-couples-ruse-trafficking.html (accessed 13 May 2024).

Osnos, Evan (2022) 'The Haves and the Have-Yachts', *The New Yorker*, 10 April, https://www.newyorker.com/magazine/2022/07/25/the-haves-and-the-have-yachts (accessed 20 August 2022).

Oxfelt, Elisabeth (2018) 'White Guilt and Racial Imagery in Annette K. Olesen's *Little Soldier*', *Journal of Aesthetics and Culture*, 10, 2, 15–24.

Parvulescu, Anca (2014) *The Traffic in Women's Work: East European Migration and the Making of Europe*. Chicago and London: University of Chicago Press.

Pascuzzi, Francesco (2015) 'Motherhood and Mourning in Giuseppe Tornatore's *The Unknown Woman*', *Film International*, 30 April, http://filmint.nu/motherhood-giuseppe-tornatores/

Patterson, Orlando (1982) *Slavery and Social Death: A Comparative Study*. Cambridge, MA, and London: Harvard University Press.

Payne, Leah (2023) '*Sound of Freedom* and the Media Fueling Belief in America's "Special Role" in Human History', *Public Religion Research Institute*, 27 September, www.prri.org/spotlight/sound-of-freedom-and-the-media-fueling-belief-in-americas-special-role-in-human-history/ (accessed 14 May 2024).

Piepiórka, Michał, 'Dylematy seksworkerki', *Czas Kultury*, 20, https://czaskultury.pl/artykul/dylematy-sexworkerki/ (accessed 6 February 2023).

*Polityka* (2015) 'Co Polacy myśla o uchodźcach?', *Polityka*, 5 October, www.polityka.pl/tygodnikpolityka/kraj/1635669,1,co-polacy-mysla-o-uchodzcach.read (accessed 30 March 2023).

Prodeus, Adriana (2021) 'Demontaż atrakcji: Dziewczyny z Dubaju', *Vogue Poland*, 28 November, www.vogue.pl/a/demontaz-atrakcji-dziewczyny-z-dubaju (accessed 7 February 2023).

Puar, Jasbir K. (2007) *Terrorist Assemblages: Homonationalism in Queer Times*. Durham: Duke University Press.

Riemer, Willy (2004) 'The Cultural Status of Early Austrian Cinema and Film', *Modern Austrian Literature*, 37, 3–4, 1–12.

Roche, David (2018) *Quentin Tarantino, Poetics and Politics of Metafiction*. Jackson: University Press of Mississippi.

Romanowski, Przemek (2021) 'To już pewne: *Dziewczyny z Dubaju* największym polskim przebojem 2021 r.', *Wirtualna Polska Film*, 7 December, https://film.wp.pl/to-juz-pewne-dziewczyny-z-dubaju-najwiekszym-polskim-przebojem-2021-r-6712795340159712a (accessed 5 February 2023).

Said, Edward (1978) *Orientalism*. New York: Vintage Books.

Salovaara-Moring, Inka (2006) '"Fortress Europe": Ideological Metaphors of Media Geographies', in Andre Jansson and Jesper Falkheimer (eds), *Geographies of Communication: The Spatial Turn in Media Studies*. Goteborg: Nordicom, 105–23.

Samota, Neena, and Debbie Ariyo (2023) *Modern Slavery and Human Trafficking: The Victim Journey*. Bristol: Policy Press, 130–45.

Sándor, Katalin (2010) 'Corporeality and Otherness in the Cinematic Heterotopias of Szabolcs Hajdu's *Bibliothèque Pascal* (2010)', *Ekphrasis*, 12, 2, 79–92.

Savin, Jennifer (2018) 'The Secret Lives of Instagram "It" Girls', *Cosmopolitan*, 13 December, www.cosmopolitan.com/uk/reports/a25422996/it-girls-of-instagram-secrets/ (accessed 1 April 2023).

Schneider, Elizabeth M. (1993) 'Feminism and the False Dichotomy of Victimization and Agency', *New York Law School Review*, 38, 387–99.

Scribner, Herb, and Will Sommer (2023) '*Sound of Freedom* is a Box Office Hit Whose Star Embraces QAnon', *The Washington Post*, 7 July, www.washingtonpost.com/arts-entertainment/2023/07/07/sound-of-freedom-qanon-theories-jim-caviezel (accessed 13 May 2024).

Segrave, Marie, Sanja Milivojevic and Sharon Pickering (2011) *Sex Trafficking: International Context and Response*. London and New York: Routledge.

Schaefer, Eric (1999) *'Bold! Daring! Shocking! True!' A History of Exploitation Films, 1919–1959*. Durham and London: Duke University Press.

*Sheffield Daily Telegraph* (1911) 'The Pictures Hall', 11 April, p. 11.

Shimizu, Celine Parreñas (1999) 'Master-Slave Sex Acts: *Mandingo* and the Race/Sex Paradox', *Wide Angle*, 21, 4, 42–61.

Shohat, Ella, and Robert Stam (2014) *Unthinking Eurocentrism: Multiculturalism and the Media*. London and New York: Routledge.

Shohat, Ella (1990) 'Imaging Terra Incognita: The Disciplinary Gaze of Empire', *Public Culture*, 3, 2, 41–70.

Sieving, Christopher (2011) *Soul Searching: Black-Themed Cinema from the March on Washington to the Rise of Blaxploitation*. Middleton: Wesleyan University Press.

Simpson, Audra (2008) 'From White into Red: Captivity Narratives as Alchemies of Race and Citizenship', *American Quarterly*, 60, 1, 251–57.

Sims, Yvonne D. (2006) *Women of Blaxploitation: How the Black Action Film Heroine Changed American Popular Culture*. Jefferson and London: McFarland and Company.

Simson, Rennie (1983) 'The Afro-American Female: The Historical Construction of Sexual Identity', in Ann Snitow, Sharon Thompson and Christine Stansel (eds), *The Powers of Desire: The Politics of Sexuality*. New York: Monthly Review Press, 229–35.

Skenazy, Lenore (2021) 'The Mom Who was Terrified of Becoming Sex-Trafficked at Target', *Reason*, 26 April, www.reason.com/2021/04/26/mom-target-sex-trafficking-white-vans/ (accessed 11 December 2023).

Skrodzka, Aga (2016) 'Disempowering Knowledge: How to Teach Not to Help', in Katarzyna Marciniak and Bruce Bennett (eds), *Teaching Transnational Cinema: Politics and Pedagogy*. New York: Routledge, 236–54.

Skrodzka, Aga (2018) 'Xenophilic Spectacle in Recent Films About Sex Slavery', *Transnational Cinemas*, 9, 1, 85–103.

——— (2020) '*Komunistki*: Visual Memory of Female Communist Agency', in Aga Skrodzka, Xiaoning Lu and Katarzyna Marciniak (eds), *The Oxford Handbook of Communist Visual Cultures*. New York: Oxford University Press, 675–92.

——— 'Dubai-Gate and the Libidinal Operations of Nation-Making in *Girls from Dubai*', *Journal of Contemporary Iraq and the Arab World*, Special Issue: 'Interventions in Film Studies', 18, 1, 47–58.

Skrodzka, Aga (2012) *Magic Realist Cinema in East Central Europe*. Edinburgh: Edinburgh University Press.

Smithers, Gregory D. (2012) *Slave Breeding: Sex, Violence, and Memory in African American History*. Gainesville: University Press of Florida.

Sommerville, Diane Miller (2004) *Rape and Race in the Nineteenth-Century South*. Chapel Hill: University of North Carolina Press.

——— '"Now You Are Ready for *Mandingo*": Sex, Slavery, and Historical Realism', in Matthew Christopher Hulbert and John C. Inscoe (eds), *Writing History with Lightning: Cinematic Representations of Nineteenth-Century America*. Baton Rouge: Louisiana State University Press, 112–24.

Spillers, Hortense (1987) 'Mama's Baby, Papa's Maybe: An American Grammar Book', *Diacritics*, 17, 2, Summer, 64–81.

Spivak, Gayatri Chakravorty (2012) *An Aesthetic Education in the Era of Globalization*. Cambridge, MA: Harvard University Press.

Stam, Robert (2000) *Film Theory: An Introduction*. Oxford: Blackwell Publishing.

Stamp, Shelley (1999) 'Moral Coercion, or The National Board of Censorship Ponders the Vice Films', in Matthew Bernstein (ed.), *Controlling Hollywood: Censorship and Regulation in the Studio Era*. London: The Athlone Press, 41–59.

——— (2000) *Movie-Struck Girls: Women and Motion-Picture Culture after the Nickelodeon*. Princeton: Princeton University Press.

Steinem, Gloria (2008 [1969]) 'After Black Power, Women's Liberation', *New York Magazine*, 7 May [4 April], www.nymag.com/news/politics/46802/ (accessed 17 November 2023).

Stenport, Anna Westerståhl (2014) '*Lilya 4-ever*: Post-Soviet Neoliberal Angels and Nordic Intellectual Secularism', *Scandinavica*, 53, 1, 34–54.

Stevenson, Brenda E. (2013) 'What's Love Got to Do with It? Concubinage and Enslaved Women and Girls in the Antebellum South', *Journal of African American History*, 98, 1, Winter, 99–125.

Sublette, Constance, and Ned Sublette (2017) *The American Slave Coast: A History of the Slave-Breeding Industry*. Chicago: Lawrence Hill Books.

Suchland, Jennifer (2013) 'Double Framing in *Lilya 4-Ever*: Sex Trafficking and Postsocialist Abjection', *European Journal of Cultural Studies*, 16, 3, February, 362–76.

Szörényi, Anna, and Penelope Eate (2014) 'Saving Virgins, Saving the US: Heternormative Masculinities and the Securitisation of Trafficking Discourse in Mainstream Narrative Film', *Social Semiotics*, 24, 5, 608–22.

Talasi, F. (2014), 'Benedek Fliegauf', *GoEast: Festival of Central and Eastern European Film*, www.filmfestival-goeast.de/index.php?article_id=394&clang=1 (accessed 18 March 2014).

Tasker, Yvonne (1993) *Spectacular Bodies: Gender, Genre and the Action Cinema*. New York and London: Routledge.

Telesca, Jennifer (2013) 'Preface: What is Visual Citizenship', *Humanity: An International Journal of Human Rights, Humanitarianism, and Development*, 4, 3, 339–43.

*The Bioscope* (1911) 'We are Informed That the Nordisk . . . ', 6 April, p. 33.

Tiffany, Kaitlyn (2022) 'The Great (Fake) Child-Sex-Trafficking Epidemic', *The Atlantic*, January/February, www.theatlantic.com/magazine/archive/2022/01/children-sex-trafficking-conspiracy-epidemic/620845 (accessed 20 December 2023).

Todorov, Tzvetan (1995) *The Morals of History*. Minneapolis: University of Minnesota Press.

Turning Point USA [n. d.] 'About', *Turning Point USA*, www.tpusa.com/about (accessed 10 December 2023).

Turning Point USA [n. d.] 'Morgonn McMichael', *Turning Point USA*, www.tpusa.com/morgonn-mcmichael (accessed 10 December 2023).

Uzzell, Elizabeth (2018) 'All the Precious White Women', *Medium*, 21 January, www.medium.com/@elizabeth.uzzell/all-the-precious-white-women-4f11091a493e (accessed 15 November 2023).

Valle, Joseph S. (2016) 'As Foxy as Can Be: The Melodramatic Mode in Blaxploitation Cinema', in Novotny Lawrence and Gerald R. Butters (eds), *Beyond Blaxploitation*. Detroit: Wayne State University Press, 137–53.

Vogel, Joseph (2018) 'The Confessions of Quentin Tarantino: Whitewashing Slave Rebellion in *Django Unchained*', *The Journal of American Culture*, 41, 1, 17–27.

Wanat, Zosia (2021) 'Poland's Restitution Law Sparks Row with Israel and the US', *Politico*, 13 August, www.politico.eu/article/poland-parliament-restitution-law-property-compensation-nazi-communists (accessed 1 May 2024).

Ward Mahar, Karen (2006) *Women Filmmakers in Early Hollywood*. Baltimore: Johns Hopkins University Press.

Whissel, Kristin (2008) *Picturing American Modernity: Traffic, Technology, and the Silent Cinema*. Durham: Duke University Press.

White, Deborah Gray (1999) *Ar'n't I a Woman? Female Slaves in the Plantation South*. New York: W. W. Norton.

Wilderson, Frank B. (2017) *Afropessimism: An Introduction*. Minneapolis: Racket and Dispatched.

Wolf, Naomi (1994) *Fire with Fire: The New Female Power and How to Use It*. New York: Fawcett Columbine.

# *Index*

Note: Index is ordered letter-by-letter. *Italic* page numbers indicate illustrations.

EU Authorised Representative:
Easy Access System Europe Mustamäe tee 50, 10621 Tallinn, Estonia
gpsr.requests@easproject.com

Printed and bound by CPI Group (UK) Ltd, Croydon, CR0 4YY
08/09/2026
02213211-0003